Governing the World's Money

A volume in the series

Cornell Studies in Political Economy

Edited by Peter J. Katzenstein

A full list of titles in the series appears at the end of the book.

Governing the World's Money

Edited by
DAVID M. ANDREWS,
C. RANDALL HENNING,
& LOUIS W. PAULY

Cornell University Press

Ithaca and London

First published 2002 by Cornell University Press

Printed in the United States of America

Library of Congress Cataloging-in-Publication Data

Governing the world's money / edited by David M. Andrews, C. Randall
Henning, and Louis W. Pauly.
    p. cm. — (Cornell studies in political economy)
  Includes bibliographical references and index.
  ISBN 0-8014-4019-X (cloth : alk. paper)
  1. International finance. I. Andrews, David M. II. Henning, C.
Randall. III. Pauly, Louis W. IV. Series.
HG3881 .G6185 2002
332' .042—dc21

                                             2002003802

Cloth printing   10 9 8 7 6 5 4 3 2 1

For Benjamin Jerry Cohen,
scholar, mentor, friend

CONTENTS

PREFACE

International monetary and financial relations have produced heated political debates for generations. Among scholars, economists showed the first interest in related research. In recent years, however, such debates spawned a new field of scholarship combining economics with political science, international relations, and cognate disciplines in the social sciences.

The subject matter was compelling: failed efforts to restore a functioning gold standard during the interwar period, planning for the post–World War II exchange-rate system, the collapse of that system in the early 1970s, explosive growth in cross-border financial markets, and unprecedented turbulence in the wake of that growth. Understanding the causes and implications of such developments required combining the tools of economic, political, and social analysis. This book is dedicated to a pioneer in that effort.

Benjamin Jerry Cohen began his career as an economist. He continues it as a political economist of the first rank. When he wrote *The Future of Sterling as an International Currency* in 1971 and *The Question of Imperialism* in 1973, the modern study of international political economy was but a fledgling academic pursuit.[1] But these books demonstrated how one could rigorously combine economic and political insights to understand subjects that were, and remain today, as controversial as they are important.

Although his empirical interests range widely across such issues as trade, money, finance, and investment, Cohen's boldest contributions emphasize the challenge of international monetary management in a world now often evoked by the amorphous term "globalization." But those contributions are anything but amorphous. In a seminal 1974 essay, Cohen was among the first to explore systematically the in-

---

[1] *The Future of Sterling as an International Currency* (London: Macmillan, 1971); *The Question of Imperialism: The Political Economy of Dominance and Imperialism* (New York: Basic Books, 1973).

teraction between the "high politics" of foreign affairs and the "low politics" of economic management.[2] In 1977, shortly after the Jamaica Agreement formally ratified the shift from pegged to floating exchange rates, Cohen published *Organizing the World's Money*, a much-cited volume that examines the role of states in the design and management of the monetary system. Shortly thereafter, his attention turned to the plight of developing countries caught up in recurrent debt crises and its implications for U.S. foreign policy;[3] at the same time, he pushed forward the study of regional monetary integration and the global dilemmas thereby created.[4] And in 1998, his critically acclaimed book *The Geography of Money* took a major step toward expanding the already interdisciplinary scope of a now vibrant field.

Cohen's past and continuing research enrich a field devoted to understanding the complex interplay between states and markets in the continuing struggle to create stable structures of international political authority. In making these contributions, Cohen has long acknowledged his intellectual debt to Peter Kenen. Early in his career, Cohen's work was also shaped by professional dialogues with Robert Gilpin and the late Susan Strange. While sometimes differing sharply on key questions in the field, the dialogues among Cohen, Gilpin, and Strange helped to construct a durable bridge between the study of international economics and the study of international politics. Kenen and Gilpin have both contributed chapters to this book, and the impact of Susan Strange will be evident to all who knew her. The volume's other authors are leading scholars in their respective areas of expertise, known for their interdisciplinary inquiry. Their collaborative effort has resulted in an original work focusing on the monetary and financial dimension of the international political economy.

The contributors presented early versions of their papers at a special conference coinciding with the 2000 annual meeting of the International Studies Association in Los Angeles. A second conference followed in September of that year in Washington, D.C., during the annual meeting of the American Political Science Association. An extraordinary degree of cooperation and camaraderie prevailed throughout that time and during the subsequent period of anonymous peer review and final chapter revision, for which the editors are grateful.

We wish to thank as well several individuals whose outstanding contributions to this project might otherwise go unacknowledged. Among this distinguished group, we mention first Joanne Gowa, Judith Goldstein, and Barry Eichengreen. Jonathan Aronson provided outstanding commentary at the first conference; Joanne Gowa did the same at the second; and Beth Simmons went beyond the call of duty in providing the contributors with detailed advice at both meetings. Two anonymous ref-

[2] "The Revolution in Atlantic Economic Relations: A Bargain Comes Unstuck," in W. F. Hanrieder, ed., *The United States and Western Europe: Political, Economic and Strategic Perspectives* (Cambridge, Mass.: Winthrop Publishers, 1974).

[3] *In Whose Interest? International Banking and American Foreign Policy* (New Haven: Yale University Press, 1986).

[4] Several of these contributions are included in *Crossing Frontiers: Explorations in International Political Economy* (Boulder, Colo.: Westview, 1991).

erees influenced the final process of converting conference papers into polished chapters; the introductory chapter in particular benefited from their engagement. Roger Haydon of Cornell University Press took a strong interest in the project from the beginning, and we all benefited from his advice and high standards. Judith Barker Sandbrook, Michael Harvey, Tina Lagopoulos, Marketa Evans, and Diane Granato assisted in the final production.

Financial support for the project came from the Center for International Studies of the University of Toronto and from the European Union Center of California. Louis Pauly's contribution depended on generous assistance from the Social Sciences and Humanities Research Council of Canada.

DAVID M. ANDREWS
C. RANDALL HENNING
LOUIS W. PAULY

CONTRIBUTORS

David M. Andrews is Associate Professor of Politics and International Relations at Scripps College, The Claremont Colleges, and Director of the European Union Center of California.

Philip G. Cerny is Professor of Government at the University of Manchester.

Robert Gilpin is Eisenhower Professor of Public and International Affairs Emeritus at Princeton University.

Eric Helleiner is Canada Research Chair in Political Economy at Trent University.

C. Randall Henning is Associate Professor in the School of International Service at American University and Visiting Fellow at the Institute for International Economics in Washington, D.C.

Miles Kahler is Rohr Professor of Pacific International Relations in the Graduate School of International Relations and Pacific Studies at the University of California, San Diego.

Peter B. Kenen is Walker Professor of Economics and International Finance at Princeton University.

Kathleen R. McNamara is Assistant Professor of Politics and International Affairs at Princeton University.

John S. Odell is Professor of International Relations in the School of International Relations at the University of Southern California.

Pier Carlo Padoan is Executive Director at the International Monetary Fund.

Louis W. Pauly is Professor of Political Science and Director of the Centre for International Studies at the University of Toronto.

Thomas D. Willett is Horton Professor of Economics at Claremont McKenna College and Claremont Graduate University and Director of the Claremont Institute of Economic Policy Studies.

Governing the World's Money

CHAPTER ONE

Monetary Institutions, Financial Integration, and Political Authority

David M. Andrews, C. Randall Henning, and Louis W. Pauly

"Money alone sets all the world in motion."[1] The values behind this ancient Roman maxim may be debatable, but the judgment is astute. Many civilizations before and after Rome experienced disaster when monetary order broke down, and the real world of economic production was no longer "in motion." This book speaks to efforts by modern societies and governments to avoid such disasters. Its subject is monetary and financial governance in the global economy emerging at the dawn of the twenty-first century.

The nature of this new economy remains in dispute. Even close observers differ over whether a truly integrated world economy is an imminent prospect or a distant possibility. Many see current circumstances as a deepening of the interdependence much of the world experienced after the Second World War. Others, however, sense a more profound change in recent years. In increasingly passionate debates over the meaning of "globalization," champions as well as opponents of borderless markets have cited global finance as a harbinger of the future.

Whatever their normative inclinations, few careful students of the subject doubt that the effective management and the authoritative legitimation of border-spanning financial claims constitute fundamental policy challenges. Few also doubt the need for deeper engagement between theory and practice in the monetary and fi-

---

We are especially grateful to Peter B. Kenen and Thomas D. Willett, among other contributors to this volume, for comments on this chapter. We alone are responsible for any remaining errors or omissions.

[1] Publilius Syrus, *Maxim* 656, 1st century B.C. The translation is from J. Bartlett, *Familiar Quotations* (Boston: Little, Brown, 1968), 126. Professor Timothy Barnes from the Classics Department of the University of Toronto advises, however, that this widely accepted rendering is too free. The text, passed down from medieval sources to the 1880 edition of the *Oxford Latin Dictionary*, is "pecunia—regimen est rerum omnium." A word is missing in the text, probably "unum" or "una," which would leave the literal translation, "money is the one controller of all things."

nancial arena. Thus, the task of understanding what Robert Solomon calls "money on the move" now lies at the heart of the scholarly field conventionally labeled international political economy.[2]

These issues—how to manage international monetary relations effectively and how to resolve the authority or legitimacy issues arising from these plans—provide the overarching thematic framework for this volume. This introductory chapter discusses these challenges inherent in managing international monetary relations. We then explore different local and regional responses to these challenges, ranging from nineteenth century state-building efforts to contemporary efforts—largely but not exclusively in Europe—aimed at reconfiguring institutions of monetary governance along regional lines. Finally, we turn to the emerging global dimensions of the authoritative governance problem. Perennial management issues, the shift towards regionalism, and the implications of contemporary monetary and financial developments for global governance comprise the sub-themes of this chapter and of the book as a whole. In the chapters that follow, leading scholars well known for bridging the economic and political dimensions of these interrelated themes offer original contributions that push critically important debates forward and indicate pathways for future research.

Monetary Governance: Agreements and Controversies

"The central problem of international economic cooperation . . . is how to keep the manifold benefits of extensive international economic intercourse free of crippling restrictions while at the same time preserving a maximum degree of freedom for each nation to pursue its legitimate economic interests."[3] In this noteworthy formulation, Richard Cooper drew attention to a policy predicament inherent in the deepening of transnational economic ties: the increasing disjunction between political and economic spheres of action. Many, perhaps even most, of the assorted projects and problems associated with the ubiquitous term "globalization" spring from this disjunction. Whether in cases of deep integration such as the European Union (EU), regional commercial agreements such as the North American Free Trade Agreement (NAFTA), or multilateral institutions that address particular problems of global economic collaboration such as the World Trade Organization (WTO), the same underlying dilemma is manifest: zones of economic activity are increasingly distinct from the territorial boundaries of political governance.[4] Collectively and individually, the chapters of this book explore this conundrum.

The core dilemma is clear enough: the logics of economics and politics often diverge. During the first several decades after the Second World War, policymakers and scholars tended to focus their attention on the trade and investment dimen-

    [2] R. Solomon, *Money on the Move* (Princeton: Princeton University Press, 1999).

    [3] R. N. Cooper, *The Economics of Interdependence: Economic Policy in the Atlantic Community* (New York: McGraw-Hill, 1968), 5.

    [4] J. G. Ruggie, "Territoriality and Beyond," *International Organization* 47, no. 1 (1993): 139–74.

sions of this quandary. But in the three decades since Cooper challenged the academy to think about the larger problem, its monetary and financial aspects have become ever more evident.

Consider in this regard the European commitment to Economic and Monetary Union (EMU). As of 2001, twelve European states had voluntarily subordinated formal authority over their national monetary affairs to a supranational institution, the European Central Bank, which in turn functions within the context of a network of independent national central banks (the European System of Central Banks). The resulting "euro area" does not correspond to any political system as traditionally understood; the participants are instead but a subset of the overall membership of the European Union. Thus while the finance ministers of states participating in EMU meet in the "Eurogroup" to consider issues facing the monetary union, they can act authoritatively only as the Economic and Finance Ministers (Ecofin) Council, a body which includes representatives from EU countries that have not adopted the euro.

But the problem of governance within EMU is emblematic of a more general phenomenon and a correspondingly widespread problem. Whether in the case of a formal monetary union, the unilateral relinquishment of national control over monetary policy (for example, through the establishment of currency boards, or through effective dollarization), or even multilateral monetary arrangements ranging from the conservative gold standard to the more liberal regime of Bretton Woods, the core challenge is the same: how to organize monetary governance in a fashion that reconciles the market logic of efficiency and the political logic of authority.

It bears repeating here that the disjunction between economic and political spheres of action in the contemporary world is not limited to problems of monetary governance. In much of the world, this incongruity is instead a general feature (and indeed a necessary consequence) of advanced economic interdependence among nationally organized societies. But interdependence and especially integration pose especially sharp problems for monetary governance, owing to the peculiar dynamics of international monetary economics.

To a substantial degree, these distinctive problems can be understood in mechanical terms. Governments either pursuing or acquiescing in the deep linkage of financial markets cannot hope to preserve fixed (or pegged) exchange-rate regimes and independent monetary policies, except episodically. The reasoning is straightforward: differences in monetary policies among countries generate different rates of return on financial assets, which lead to exchange-rate movements when capital is free to flow across borders. To the extent that governments accept (or are subject to) high capital mobility, they experience a trade-off between pursuing autonomous monetary policies and targeting their exchange rates.

Following Benjamin J. Cohen, we refer to the three-way trade-off among capital mobility, exchange-rate stability and monetary autonomy as the "Unholy Trinity."[5]

---

[5] B. J. Cohen, "The Triad and the Unholy Trinity: Lessons for the Pacific Region," in R. Higgott, R. Leaver, and J. Ravenhill, eds., *Pacific Economic Relations in the 1990s* (Boulder, Colo.: Lynne Rienner, 1993). Compare T. Padoa-Schioppa, "The European Monetary System: A Long-Term View," in F. Gi-

Recognition of this policy problem draws attention to the important linkage between financial integration and monetary governance. Early approaches to understanding economic interdependence emphasized either the threat to the autonomy of national polities arising from disjunctions between the decision-making domains of business firms and states or the increasing likelihood and magnitude of national payments imbalances as trade and investment grow. But opening or widening channels between national financial markets adds another level of complexity to this story, as the analytics of the Unholy Trinity make abundantly clear.[6]

For students of international monetary relations, then, the Unholy Trinity is the beginning of wisdom. But it cannot be the end thereof. Studies that rely solely on this approach suffer from at least two deficiencies.

The first concerns a narrowness of interpretation. As capital becomes more internationally mobile, as it has during each of the past five decades, the trade-off between pursuing a truly independent monetary policy corresponding to national preferences and stabilizing the exchange rate against some external target undoubtedly becomes more severe. But some observers have pushed this logic to the conclusion that real policy choices have therefore been reduced to two: either rigidly fixing exchange rates or allowing them to float freely. The once-viable "middle" alternatives between these two extremes, including pegging schemes and so-called "dirty floats," are now presumed to be too costly for rational governments to pursue; only the "corner solutions" remain.[7]

Although the parsimonious logic of this approach is appealing, studies in this volume begin with the awareness that the universe of empirically observable and apparently sustainable policy options remains much wider than it suggests. The costs of attempting to balance policy independence and exchange-rate objectives may indeed have risen in a world of heightened capital mobility, but many governments seem both willing and able to bear those costs. The "messy middle" between fixed exchange-rate regimes and free floats remains important, and the political trade-offs implied thereby are important to understand. Put differently, governments—and not only the governments of rich countries—retain substantial discretion in matters of monetary strategy. Globalizing finance does indeed increase constraints on policy makers, but it also creates opportunities. It may, for example, encourage inward investment. Between constraint and opportunity lies the terrain of political choice, terrain that remains to be theorized and explored.

A second deficiency in some analyses of the Unholy Trinity involves narrowness of scope. The modest institutional machinery created to manage monetary and fi-

avazzi et al., eds., *The European Monetary System* (Cambridge: Cambridge University Press, 1988), chap. 12, who includes free trade in his analysis and dubs the resulting framework the "Inconsistent Quartet."

   [6] For analysis along this line, see D. M. Andrews, "Capital Mobility and State Autonomy: Toward a Structural Theory of International Monetary Relations," *International Studies Quarterly* 38, no. 2 (1994): 479–511.

   [7] B. Eichengreen, *International Monetary Arrangements for the 21st Century* (Washington: Brookings Institution, 1994).

nancial relations among states confronts serious problems in reconciling legitimacy and effectiveness. The activities of multilateral economic institutions such as the International Monetary Fund raise basic political questions: governance by whom, for whom, for what purposes, and with what ultimate consequences? Any serious consideration of modern democracy under conditions of economic interdepend- ence must bring such questions to the fore. As Dani Rodrik has recently observed, the logic of the Unholy Trinity in the economic sphere has spawned a more funda- mentally political "trilemma": deep international economic integration, primacy of the nation-state, and mass politics of the sort associated with modern democracy are in fundamental tension.[8] Typically, a policy regime can succeed in achieving only two of these three objectives at one time. Thus the nineteenth-century gold standard gave priority to international markets and strong state institutions at the expense of mass politics.[9] The Bretton Woods regime that followed World War Two provided greater scope for mass politics at the expense of some degree of integra- tion, capital mobility in particular.[10] And in more recent times, regionally organized federalist or multi-level governing arrangements represent—at least in some in- stances—novel attempts to give priority to economic integration and political de- mocracy at the expense of the traditional prerogatives of states.[11]

In short, the questions of how to govern supranational monetary areas effec- tively, and how to render such governance authoritative, remain open. Ensuing chapters explore these issues in depth, with attention to both regional and global applications.

Currency "Deterritorialization" and Regional Monetary Governance

Attention to issues of effectiveness and authority helps shed considerable light on what some leading scholars now call the "deterritorialization" of national curren- cies. In contrast to the conventional view of monetary geography, wherein each state issues a currency whose usage coincides with the national territory, deterrito- rialization refers to the disconnection between the domain of currency usage and the geographic borders of issuing states. As Cohen puts it:

> The traditional Westphalian model of monetary geography discounts the role of mar- kets. . . . Once we acknowledge the growth of cross-border competition, the state-cen-

[8] D. Rodrik, "Governance of Economic Globalization," in J. S. Nye, Jr., and J. D. Donahue, eds. *Governance in a Globalizing World* (Washington: Brookings Institution Press, 2000).

[9] B. J. Cohen, *Organizing the World's Money: The Political Economy of International Monetary Rela- tions* (New York: Basic Books, 1977).

[10] L. W. Pauly, *Who Elected the Bankers? Surveillance and Control in the World Economy* (Ithaca: Cor- nell University Press, 1997). See also B. Eichengreen, *Globalizing Capital: A History of the International Monetary System* (Princeton: Princeton University Press, 1996).

[11] G. Marks and L. Hooghe, *Multi-Level Governance* (Lanham, Md.: Rowman & Littlefield, 2001).

tric model looks increasingly inadequate, if not wholly misleading. The more widely circulated currencies come to be used across, not just within, political frontiers, the more pivotal becomes the independent role of market forces in global monetary governance. Market agents too exercise power, and they increasingly rival governments as direct determinants of currency outcomes. The strategic interaction between public and private sectors, not between states alone, becomes the primary focus of authority in monetary affairs.[12]

Regional monetary integration represents one important aspect of this trend. Most of the scholarship on regional integration was originally inspired by the western European example. During the period after the Treaty of Rome was concluded but before the completion of the Common Market, monetary union was little more than a vision or ideal shared by a small number of politicians, civil servants, and academics. It was in this environment that a few farsighted economists nevertheless began analyzing the case for European monetary integration. Approaching the subject normatively, these economists—among them Robert Mundell, Ronald McKinnon, Peter Kenen, and Max Corden—identified a few key criteria that would determine whether countries would benefit from forming a currency union.[13] Those criteria (including output diversity, labor mobility, real wage flexibility and fiscal transfers) sprang from their theory of optimum currency areas.

Optimum currency area theory was the analytical workhorse of economic approaches to monetary integration, with wide applications to other states and regions. As initially conceived, the theory employed a distinctly Keynesian, two-country framework under conditions of low capital mobility—assumptions that were fairly realistic in the 1960s but hardly appropriate to the 1980s and 1990s. Subsequent development of this approach, inspired in part by the new classical economics, expanded the list of criteria examined by optimum currency area theorists.[14] Even so, when efforts to unify Europe's national monetary systems intensified in the late 1980s and early 1990s, most economists based their empirical work on the classical optimum currency area criteria developed by Mundell and others in the 1960s. The resulting analyses indicated that a broad European monetary area would be far from optimal.[15] The European Union nonetheless created the euro in

---

[12] B. J. Cohen, *The Geography of Money* (Ithaca: Cornell University Press, 1998), 167–68.

[13] R. Mundell, "A Theory of Optimum Currency Areas," *American Economic Review* 51, no. 3 (1961): 657–65; R. McKinnon, "Optimum Currency Areas," *American Economic Review* 53, no. 4 (1963): 717–25; P. Kenen, "The Theory of Optimum Currency Areas: An Eclectic View," in R. Mundell and A. Swoboda, eds., *Monetary Problems of the International Economy* (Chicago: University of Chicago Press, 1969); M. Corden, "Monetary Integration," *Essays in International Finance* 93 (Princeton University, International Finance Section, 1972).

[14] T. D. Willett and C. Wihlborg, "Optimum Currency Areas Revisited," in C. Wihlborg, M. Frattianni, and T. D. Willett, eds., *Financial Regulation and Monetary Arrangements After 1992* (Amsterdam: North-Holland, 1991), 279–97.

[15] L. Bini Smaghi and S. Vori, *Rating the EC as an Optimum Currency Area: Is It Worse Than the U.S.?* (unpublished manuscript, Banca d'Italia, 1990); T. Bayoumi and B. Eichengreen, "Shocking Aspects of European Monetary Unification," in F. Torres and F. Giavazzi, eds., *The Transition to Economic and Monetary Union in Europe* (Cambridge: Cambridge University Press, 1992).

all but cash form in 1999 and introduced notes and coins in early 2002, suggesting that optimum currency area theory is a poor guide to understanding the politics of monetary integration.

The failure of traditional optimum currency area theory to predict behavior in Europe (or elsewhere) was followed by two distinct but related scholarly developments. The first was an effort to save the optimum currency approach by making it consistent with changes in both economic theory and circumstances. The second was a willingness to consider entirely different approaches to understanding the incentives for monetary integration, rather than focusing on the efficiency arguments at the core of the theory. A few words on each of these endeavors are in order.

Among the chief findings of those scholars embarked on the quest for a more complete understanding of monetary integration within the context of optimum currency area theory was that a broader, more dynamic analysis was needed. Changes in one policy or policy field often produce ripple effects in other fields, even when they appear unrelated. Such changes need not be seen in purely functionalist terms, with automatic accommodating adjustments. But awareness of the possibility of dynamic changes across policy areas has led scholars and policymakers to confront a new political economy of *policy endogeneity*.

For example, as outlined more fully below, advanced monetary integration under conditions of internationally mobile capital may create formidable political pressures for government action in economically depressed areas within a currency union. More broadly, monetary integration may induce, after the fact, the very sorts of policies and behaviors that would make it desirable on optimum currency grounds. As a general principle, then, when either policy changes or market behavior help an integrating region satisfy the criteria for optimality—for example, by increasing some combination of real wage flexibility, labor mobility, or fiscal transfers—a currency area is said to be "endogenous."[16]

The magnitude of these endogenous effects is the focus of an emerging empirical literature. For example, Andrew Rose argues that past monetary unions have stimulated trade among members by an average factor of three.[17] Even if such estimates overstate the impact for modern, medium-sized industrial economies, monetary union in Europe is nonetheless likely to have a large economic impact.[18] Nevertheless, specific policy sectors will differ in their amenability to reform in the face of monetary union. Most close observers expect policies related to capital markets to be most responsive, those related to goods markets less responsive, and those related to labor markets to be least responsive. Several of the chapters that follow provide further guideposts for the emerging work on the political economy of the euro area and EMU's "optimality."

[16] J. A. Frankel and A. K. Rose, "The Endogeneity of the Optimum Currency Area Criteria," *Economic Journal* 28 (1998): 1009–25.

[17] A. K. Rose, "One Money, One Market: Estimating the Effects of Common Currencies on Trade," *Economic Policy* 30 (2000): 9–33.

[18] Note that some professional economists disagree. See, for example, T. D. Willett, "Some Political Economy Aspects of EMU," *Journal of Policy Modeling* (2000), 379–89.

In the years since the introduction of optimum currency area theory, but especially in the wake of the recently renewed interest in European monetary integration, political scientists have also addressed the positive and normative gaps left by this policy-optimizing approach. These scholars have typically shared with economists an interest in how the integration of goods and capital markets served as a critically important foundation for the integration movement. Many went further, however, to assess the role of societal preferences and domestic politics and institutions in this process.[19] Others explored bargaining dynamics and issue linkages.[20] Still others examined the role of German dominance and of neoliberal ideological consensus.[21] The effect of instability in the international monetary system has also been the subject of intense analysis and debate.[22] Considered collectively, a weakness of this literature is that it leaves monetary integration in Europe overdetermined. Like other research programs that focus primarily on a single case or region, these writings provide a surfeit of interpretations calling out for additional case studies in order to cull those explanations that are generalizable from those that are not.

Such cases can be found in the numerous regional monetary experiments that were beginning to develop outside of Europe even before EMU was created. Despite emotional resistance to the very idea of a North American monetary union, increasingly voluble debates on this question are rising among the signatory states of the North American Free Trade Agreement (NAFTA). Preliminary ideas along

[19] On societal preferences, see, for example, J. Frieden, "Making Commitments: France and Italy in the European Monetary System, 1979–1985," in B. Eichengreen and J. Frieden, eds., *The Political Economy of European Monetary Unification* (Boulder, Colo.: Westview Press, 1994), a volume which contains a number of other valuable contributions; C. R. Henning, *Currencies and Politics in the United States, Germany and Japan* (Washington: Institute for International Economics, 1994); and J. I. Walsh, *European Monetary Integration and Domestic Politics : Britain, France, and Italy* (Boulder, Colo.: Lynne Rienner, 2000). On domestic politics and institutions, see J. Goodman, *Monetary Sovereignty : The Politics of Central Banking in Western Europe* (Ithaca: Cornell University Press, 1992); T. H. Oatley, *Monetary Politics: Exchange Rate Cooperation in the European Union* (Ann Arbor: University of Michigan, 1997); K. Kaltenthaler, *Germany and the Politics of Europe's Money* (Durham, N.C.: Duke University Press, 1998); D. Heisenberg, *The Mark of the Bundesbank: Germany's Role in European Monetary Cooperation* (Boulder, Colo.: Lynne Rienner, 1999); and P. Loedel, *Deutsche Mark Politics: Germany in the European Monetary System* (Boulder, Colo.: Lynne Rienner, 1999).

[20] D. M. Andrews, "The Global Origins of the Maastricht Treaty on EMU: Closing the Window of Opportunity," in A. W. Cafruny and G. G. Rosenthal, eds. *The State of the European Community, Volume 2* (Boulder, Colo.: Lynne Rienner, 1993); A. Moravcsik, *The Choice for Europe: Social Purpose and State Power from Messina to Maastricht* (Ithaca: Cornell University Press, 1998); and K. Dyson and K. Featherstone, *The Road to Maastricht: Negotiating Economic and Monetary Union* (Oxford: Oxford University Press, 1999).

[21] On the first theme, see M. Kaelberer, *Money and Power in Europe: The Political Economy of European Monetary Cooperation* (Albany: State University of New York Press, 2001), and D. M. Andrews, "Currency Coalitions and the Monetary Balance of Power," *Working Paper* 1–13 (European Union Center of California, Fall 2001); on the second, K. R. McNamara, *The Currency of Ideas: Monetary Politics in the European Union* (Ithaca: Cornell University Press, 1998), and M. Marcussen, *Ideas and Elites: The Social Construction of Economic and Monetary Union* (Aalborg, Denmark: Aalborg University Press, 2000).

[22] C. R. Henning, "Systemic Conflict and Regional Monetary Integration: The Case of Europe." *International Organization* 52, no. 3 (1998): 537–73.

similar lines are being mooted in East Asia and in parts of South America. "Dollarization" has occurred in parts of Latin America and the Caribbean, and the "euroization" of many countries in the geographic vicinity of the EU is widely expected. Even if no other formal monetary unions evolve in the near future, examining variation in the degree and style of adaptation across these regions will improve our understanding of monetary governance.

Indeed, the diversity of regional experience is what makes questions of monetary governance of both theoretical and practical interest. If the central dilemma created by extensive economic cooperation is the increasing disjunction between political and economic spheres of action, two key challenges follow: how can systems of effective monetary governance be developed in a given context, and how can those systems be rendered legitimate? Monetary integration is most advanced in Europe. Accordingly, it is there that the disjunction between the transnational sphere of economic activity and the national sphere of political activity is greatest. Likewise, it is there that questions of institutional architecture (the effectiveness problem) and of democratic representation (the legitimacy problem) have been most thoroughly examined.[23] The fact that the resulting arrangements remain problematic bears mute testimony to the political difficulties inherent in the process of economic integration.

Sometimes, as in the case of the former Soviet Union, the political challenges prove to be insuperable. The delegitimation and collapse of the Soviet state undermined regional economic governance, and the implosion of the ruble zone demonstrated the enduring attractiveness of territorial currencies. Russian policy competence, however, was not sufficient even to sustain the ruble as the sole national currency, and the dollar became widely used within that country.[24] The Russian case reminds us that the effective geographical range of a currency reflects not only the official decisions of national governments but also the personal decisions of thousands or even millions of individual consumers. Thus the analytical framework adopted in this book also applies to cases of monetary disintegration. Governments must continuously earn the loyalty of their citizens by establishing and maintaining institutions of monetary governance that are both effective and authoritative, or else suffer the consequences of their failure to do so. Finally, the regional integration theme developed in this book re-opens basic issues of international monetary cooperation.[25] Robert Lawrence's phrases are apt as we probe whether monetary

[23] On the governance of EMU, see, among others, J. Frieden, D. Gros, and E. Jones, *The New Political Economy of EMU* (Lanham, Md.: Roman & Littlefield, 1998); A. Verdun, "The Institutional Design of EMU: A Democratic Deficit," *Journal of Public Policy*, 18 (1998): 107–32; J. A. Caporaso, *The European Union: Dilemmas of Regional Integration* (Boulder, Colo.: Westview, 2000); C. Crouch, ed., *After the Euro: Shaping Institutions for Governance in the Wake of European Monetary Union* (Oxford: Oxford University Press, 2000); M. G. Cowles and M. Smith, *The State of the European Union: Risks, Reform, Resistance, and Revival* (Oxford: Oxford University Press, 2000); K. Dyson, *The Politics of the Euro Zone: Stability or Breakdown?* (Oxford: Oxford University Press, 2000).

[24] D. Woodruff, *Money Unmade: Barter and the Fate of Russian Capitalism* (Ithaca: Cornell University Press, 1999).

[25] C. R. Henning, *Cooperating with Europe's Monetary Union* (Washington: Institute for International Economics, 1997); P. R. Masson, T. H. Krueger, and B. G. Turtelboom, eds., *EMU and the International Monetary System* (Washington: International Monetary Fund, 1998); R. Mundell and A.

regions are "stumbling blocks" or "building blocks" for the multilateral system.[26] Just as some regard regionalism in the trade arena as threatening to an expansive multilateral trading system, EMU might be viewed as a threat to global monetary stability. Conversely, others see trade regionalism as a sub-optimal but politically feasible means for building a more open global economy. In like fashion, monetary regionalism might create more balanced conditions across the world's main economic regions that could, with wisdom, encourage the construction of new system-stabilizing mechanisms in the monetary arena. How then should the United States respond to policies in Europe or Asia aimed at monetary balancing? What role would the IMF and the other multilateral institutions play in a refashioned, regionalized international monetary order? Much work remains to be done in examining these and related questions.

Global Money and the Changing Contours of Political Authority

The relation between monetary regionalism, the continued deepening of cross-national capital markets, and political authority is complex. An emerging community of scholarship is therefore focusing attention on whether the webs of monetary and financial interdependence now being so tightly woven together will someday constitute the sinews of new forms of governance beyond the territorial state. Simply put, is the raw power inherent in border-spanning capital markets and the intricacy of relationships at the top of what Cohen calls the "Currency Pyramid" reconstructing fundamental political relations across the international system and creating a new kind of governing authority?[27]

If so, the sense of disquiet that global economic integration has long stimulated among traditional defenders of state sovereignty and, more recently, among domestic social reformers promoting equity and distributive justice becomes understandable. The legitimacy of such an order is at issue.[28] While the importance of states in the contemporary global order can be overstated, the practical problems of accountability and fairness within them are nonetheless becoming much more salient.[29] Most historically informed observers now acknowledge that these issues

---

Clesse, eds., *The Euro as a Stabilizer in the International Economic System* (Amsterdam: Kluwer, 2000); C. R. Henning and P. C. Padoan, *Transatlantic Perspectives on the Euro* (Washington: Brookings Institution Press, 2000).

[26] R. Z. Lawrence, *Regionalism, Multilateralism, and Deeper Integration* (Washington: Brookings Institution Press, 1995).

[27] Cohen, *The Geography of Money*.

[28] S. Strange, *Mad Money* (Ann Arbor: University of Michigan Press, 1998).

[29] D. Held et al., *Global Transformations: Politics, Economics, and Culture* (Stanford, Calif.: Stanford University Press, 1999); J. A. Scholte, *Globalization: A Critical Introduction* (Houndmills, U.K.: Palgrave, 2000); and M. Th. Greven and L. W. Pauly, eds., *Democracy Beyond the State? The European Dilemma and the Emerging Global Order* (Lanham, Md./Toronto: Rowman & Littlefield/University of Toronto Press, 2000).

must be addressed simultaneously with the kinds of efficiency-oriented problems that have long dominated research and policymaking in this area.

In the middle of the twentieth century, Karl Polanyi argued that unfettered markets destroyed the very social and political institutions that had spawned them, producing political reactions of the most negative and destructive sort.[30] During the second half of the twentieth century, a politically managed form of capitalism rested on more enduring domestic foundations. The precise formula for managing the social effects of markets differed among countries, but the broad framework of what John Ruggie famously termed "embedded liberalism" appeared to deliver both rapid economic growth and reductions in poverty among the advanced industrial states at the core of the post-war international economy, and indeed among an expanding band of industrializing states.[31] Over time, the system organized around this formula came to dominate competing socioeconomic systems, most notably state socialism. At the dawn of the twenty-first century, it nevertheless remains painfully obvious that the large portion of humanity resident in perennially poor states has never managed to find a promising place in the "global" economy. These individuals lack access to the kinds of domestic systems that once allegedly tamed markets in rich states. Likewise, the future remains far from clear for those resident in some of the so-called "states in transition" from socialist systems.

Contemporary monetary and financial developments could have profound implications for all three groups mentioned above—that is, citizens of the wealthy, the poor, and the post-socialist transition states. If Ruggie was right, the original post-war compromise in the core states depended in significant part on political control of international capital movements aimed at facilitating the redistribution of financial resources domestically, and the deliberate management of international economic engagement. The erosion of such controls throughout the post-war period and the rapid expansion of international capital markets after the early 1970s seemed to resurrect a kind of global liberalism similar in some respects to that which scholars like Polanyi and Ruggie indicted as a key progenitor of the international disorder of the first half of the twentieth century.

Little wonder, then, that the process of financial liberalization has slowed and in some cases even reversed. Meanwhile, activists on the streets of the world's great cities have targeted monetary and financial institutions as the enemy of social democracy, economic stability, and sustainable development. Polemics aside, identifying the sources of social resistance to global markets constitutes a central challenge for international political economists. Even without the anti-globalization backlash, new directions for scholarship are becoming evident.

The research reported in this book provides important indicators of this new scholarship. While each chapter explores different aspects of the changing terrain of global governance, the answers that the authors propose to specific questions—whether concerning international institutional design and selection, monetary uni-

---

[30] K. Polanyi, *The Great Transformation: The Political and Economic Origins of Our Time* (New York: Rinehart, 1944).

[31] J. G. Ruggie, *Constructing the World Polity* (London: Routledge, 1997).

fication and other forms of currency deterritorialization, actor choice and constraint, or hegemonic stability—can be viewed collectively within the overarching context of effectiveness and authority. Scholars and citizens alike need a better understanding of the purposes for which power is being wielded. Knowledge, after all, is a vital part of the process through which raw power is transformed into legitimate authority.

Outline of the Chapters

The relationship between market efficiency and authoritative governance is reciprocal: governmental decisions underpin markets, which in turn influence future decisions deemed authoritative. Claims to legitimacy stabilize the expectations of market actors seeking efficiency gains, while such expectations feed back into systems of rule that require the willing deference of those affected by markets if they are to endure. For students of global governance, a key challenge is to characterize these dynamic processes in a meaningful way and to identify key moments in their evolution.

A number of the chapters in this volume therefore focus on fundamental choice points in history, moments when institutions of monetary and financial governance were designed or redesigned as the competing logics of economics and politics clashed. Such events are rare, but their significance is long lasting. They include the Civil War in the United States; the rise of American hegemony during the mid-twentieth century, consolidated by the Second World War; the end of the Cold War; and the consolidation of the European Union and its monetary union. The character of authoritative monetary governance changed in the wake of these defining moments.

These chapters and indeed all the accompanying contributions use the effectiveness-and-authority framework to structure their collective explorations in the monetary and financial arenas. More specifically, they focus on the overlapping themes of institutional design, regionalization and the transformation of authority. The editors invited prominent scholars known for their interdisciplinary inquiry to contribute original essays highlighting one or another of the themes. Some of the authors are best known as economists, some as international relations specialists and others as economic historians, but all are known for their seminal insights and scholarly breadth. Their contributions to this volume underscore the contemporary breakdown of barriers between international politics and international economics, both in scholarship and in the world of practice. Viewed together, they push forward the frontier for future research in international political economy.

Robert Gilpin provides an orientation for the chapters that follow with a concise review of scholarship in international political economy and its evolution. Gilpin, a leading scholar in the field, analyzes the parallel development of economics and political science since their separation about one century ago and the conditions contributing to their current re-connection. Traditional economics—the science of decision making under constraint and scarcity—developed powerful analytical tools; at the same time, the profession limited its scope to examining the efficient alloca-tion of scarce resources to maximize welfare. Recognizing this limitation, some economists began to re-incorporate social, institutional, and political variables into their theories and models in recent decades. This effort, however, falls well short of re-integrating economics and political science. Gilpin puts the central dilemma succinctly: "Whereas the logic of the market is to locate economic activities wher-ever they will be most efficient and profitable, the logic of the state is to capture and control the process of economic growth and capital accumulation in order to in-crease the power and economic welfare of the nation." Unless analysts engage both of these logics, their inquiries are likely to be seriously incomplete.

Gilpin speaks authoritatively for scholars of international political economy grounded in traditional realist approaches to international relations. This group continues to emphasize the central role of the state and the distributive conse-quences of economic activities. Contrary to the widespread view that global mar-kets are overrunning state authority and undermining the relevance of the state as a unit of analysis, Gilpin contends that it remains important to distinguish between national and international economies. "Political boundaries do and will divide [states'] economies and economic policies. . . . States, and other powerful actors as well, use their power to influence economic activities to maximize their own eco-nomic and political interests." Through such a lens, Gilpin encourages students of international money and finance to examine governing regimes with a degree of skepticism. The institutional manifestations of relevant rules, norms, and princi-ples guiding behavior at any given time and in any given context rest on a structure of power that cannot be ignored.

Notwithstanding their broad appreciation of the differing logics of political power and market efficiency, Gilpin notes that political economists tend to talk past one another by emphasizing different aspects of their shared field of study. Nowhere is this clearer than in the monetary arena, where the essence of policy and the meaning of specific actions are often shrouded by arcane technicalities. Here and elsewhere, Gilpin explains that by the end of the twentieth century the very term "political economy" had come to be used in three distinct senses. The phrase had a substantive meaning (as a subject matter arising from the interaction of states and markets); a conceptual meaning (as the application of specific economic theo-ries to explain social behavior); and a methodological meaning (as a set of tools built on the assumption of methodological individualism or a rationalist model of human behavior). Although elements of each appear in the chapters that follow, most of our authors privilege the first as they trace changing relationships between states, non-state actors, and markets in the monetary and financial domains.

In his chapter, Miles Kahler develops the institutional design theme in an ana-lytical case history of the international monetary regime that followed the end of the Second World War. Kahler examines the selection of the Bretton Woods insti-tutions and the rejection of competing arrangements by the United States, Britain, and their allies. He lays out the dimensions of institutional variation and the explanations for institutional selection, arguing that functional requirements of monetary cooperation—avoiding competitive depreciations while at the same time permitting scope for full-employment policies—substantially account for the adoption of pegged-but-adjustable exchange rates and the organizational architecture deemed necessary to sustain them. But why did the Roosevelt administration agree to the particular institutional design, which included at its core the highly formalized, multilateral International Monetary Fund (IMF) in which finance ministries rather than central banks held sway? Kahler stresses the desire of key American officials to limit free riding on the part of small states and to achieve greater transparency. He also notes the importance of coalitional politics in the United States, which temporarily suppressed the influence of Wall Street. According to Kahler, understanding the logic and the politics behind the birth and the subsequent development of the IMF remains crucial to making informed judgments about the future of international monetary cooperation. His chapter thus contributes to our understanding of the institutionalized bargains that continue to shape analytical and policy debate on reforming the global architecture for money and finance in a new century.

On this same theme, Thomas Willett analyzes the expansion in scope of the activities of the IMF after the breakdown of the Bretton Woods exchange-rate system in the early 1970s. The Fund could very well have gone out of business at that moment, when the central reason for its existence disappeared. Instead, the broadening of its ambition has become a source of controversy and puzzlement. No group of analysts has been more enthusiastic in investigating this puzzle than those working under the banner of "public choice." Willett himself helped pioneer the public-choice approach to this problem, but now argues that much of the analyses of this school are too rigid. He proposes instead to move toward what he labels a "broad" public-choice framework, an approach that is self-consciously eclectic and borrows from recent developments in institutional economics and mainstream IPE. In political terms, Willett's analysis supports the middle ground in an increasingly polarized spectrum of opinion regarding the IMF, running from left-wing critics, who see the Fund as a simple agent of capitalist exploitation, to right-wing critics, who see it as representing a cabal of special interests and self-interested bureaucrats.

Willett's contribution emphasizes the costs of acquiring information, the conceptual difficulties naturally arising from complex situations involving both governments and markets, and the coordination and free-rider problems that deepen when progressively larger numbers of actors are involved. Without abandoning the cause of rigorous analysis and critique, this "broad" approach accepts that both international markets and international organizations remain imperfect. Using this framework for understanding the path of institutional redesign and incremental restructuring, he proposes specific explanations for the phenomenon of IMF "loan-pushing," for the Fund's controversial involvement in Russia in the late 1990s, and for the creeping expansion of its general mission. Although the political obstacles to meaningful reform of the IMF are considerable, Willett's broad public-choice approach offers more ground for optimism than does traditional, narrow public-choice analysis.

The next several chapters focus on the political economy of monetary integration and the implications thereof for the international system as a whole. This account begins with a highly original examination of the costs and benefits of expanding a currency's geographic domain, the preoccupation of monetary economists for the past generation, and the ramifications of doing so for other economic policies. Three studies follow: one on the evolution of the Economic and Monetary Union (EMU) in Europe, one on the unification of the American monetary system in the nineteenth century, and the last on the many challenges that confront national currencies at the start of the twenty-first century.

Peter Kenen offers a rigorous critique of optimum currency area theory and then surveys a generation of conceptual and applied research on that subject. As discussed above, the theory of optimum currency areas identifies the conditions under which a group of countries might benefit from forming a monetary union. As one of the earliest pioneers and key developers of this theory, Kenen is particularly well placed to assess its strengths and weaknesses as well as to estimate its influence over the course of the long policy debate culminating in European monetary unification. Kenen asks whether other groups of countries should follow the European example by adopting monetary unions, currency boards, or the dollar or euro as their local currencies. He argues that the optimality of these alternatives depends on the depth of integration beyond the trade area, in the financial and fiscal areas in particular. He demonstrates that the formation of a monetary union creates formidable pressure for coordination or centralization of fiscal policy while drawing a sharp analytical distinction between the domain of currencies on the one hand and the domain of monetary and fiscal policies on the other. The advanced version of optimum currency area theory that Kenen proposes on this basis opens the analytical and normative space for more optimistic expectations for the future of regional currencies such as the euro than many economists have heretofore been willing to concede.

In a parallel fashion, Pier Carlo Padoan examines the evolution of Europe's monetary union since its creation in 1999, concentrating on the channels through which a monetary union alters policy and economic behavior. By placing pressure on governments, employers and trade unions to be more flexible, he argues that the euro area might well satisfy the criteria for optimality after the fact. Whether European monetary integration is truly "endogenous," as discussed above, is an important analytical and policy question. In Padoan's model, a mix of cooperation and institutional competition drives policy reform among the member states of the euro area, producing different degrees of convergence across policy domains. Because these pressures are likely to persist and even increase, Padoan concludes that the monetary union is at least partially endogenous. In this context, he emphasizes that the evolution of the euro area will continue to be reinforced by international monetary instability and a longstanding European concern that the United States cannot ultimately be relied upon to provide a durable monetary anchor for the world economy.

Kathleen McNamara throws a new light on Padoan's theme by drawing a fascinating and relevant historical analogy: the contribution of a single currency to state building in the United States during the Civil War. To finance that war, the North created a national banking system, mandated internal convertibility of bank notes at par throughout the Union, and issued a new paper currency, the greenback. McNamara argues that the resulting consolidation of monetary union within the United States played a central role in the construction of the modern American state. Specifically, it strongly reinforced the financial capacity of the federal government, helped to unify the national financial market, created constituencies supporting centralized finance, and contributed to the formation of national identity. By extension, McNamara argues that the European Union shares in the decentralized political tendencies exhibited by the American states prior to the Civil War. By creating incentives for centralization of government finance and debt management, the creation of the euro area could powerfully reinforce political integration.

Against the backdrop of arguments connecting monetary integration to parallel political projects, Eric Helleiner examines the decoupling of currencies from territorial states. Helleiner asks whether a retreat from the goals initially sought by the creation of national currencies explains a rising number of episodes involving the deterritorialization of money. He argues that raising revenue and strengthening political identification are less significant at the beginning of the twenty-first century than they were in the nineteenth and early twentieth centuries. Indeed, an array of policymakers in the contemporary period seem to be bending over backward to explain to their publics that alternatives to territorial currencies will not undermine national identities. Whereas policymakers earlier sought to reduce transaction costs within countries by creating national currencies, many are now apparently more concerned with reducing international transaction costs.

The deterritorialization of money, Helleiner concludes, also reflects disillusionment with activist macroeconomic management in the face of international capital mobility. As activist monetary and fiscal policies are deemed to be increasingly ineffective in raising output and employment, an important rationale for state-based money dissipates. Such a realization calls into question the core institutions through which authoritative governance is delivered in a multi-layered global economy. Cohen has asserted that "the growing deterritorialization of money has by no means eliminated a role for public policy in the management of currency relations. It has, however, greatly complicated the task facing governments long accustomed to the privilege of national monetary sovereignty."[32] Helleiner's innovative study suggests that this may understate the problem.

The final two chapters directly challenge the dominant paradigm of rational state actors that continues to guide much of the scholarship examining the politics of an integrating global economy. John Odell's chapter offers a constructive cri-

---

[32] Cohen, *The Geography of Money*, 167.

tique of the theoretical underpinnings of our knowledge about such issues. He points to numerous shortcomings of the particular conception of rational choice that currently dominates economics and most political science scholarship. Rather than objecting to all rationalism, he refocuses attention on Herbert Simon's variant—bounded rationality—and argues that future research built on this alternative premise could improve our knowledge of the world political economy, including its monetary system.

For example, the assumption that individuals use cognitive shortcuts and decision rules other than optimization allows us to make better sense of a wide range of observed behaviors, including speculative bubbles, herd behavior in financial markets, exchange-rate oscillations, interest group pressures and their absence, the behavior of central bankers and politicians, and popular backlashes against them. Odell therefore calls for more empirical research on how individuals and organizations actually make their decisions. He directly engages constructivists as well as their liberal and realist colleagues, contending that bounded rationality could help bridge the canyon separating them while at the same time making IPE scholarship more relevant for practitioners.

In the book's final chapter, Philip Cerny observes the unraveling of a series of grand political compromises following World War II. While the cause of freer trade and more open national markets was once linked to a set of social guarantees and the capacity for authoritative national economic regulation—very importantly including the regulation of international capital flows—to achieve them, Cerny contends that markets are now becoming truly transnational and "disembedded" from their social roots. Other aspects of the regulatory state have also eroded in tandem with the post-war compromise. Governance continues, but in many fields it seems unconnected to duly constituted governments.[33]

In their place, Cerny traces the emergence of "webs of governance" that have a decidedly private character. State apparatuses through which authority has been traditionally grounded and exercised are in his view now enmeshed in wider global structures, including an ever-more-autonomous global capital market. The resulting multi-layered patterns of authority are sometimes compared to those of medieval Europe. Cerny recommends developing the insights coming from such analogies by analyzing changes in global governance along sectoral lines, since "asset specificity" appears to vary by sector. He advocates a macro-sociological approach to international political economy, particularly in arenas such as money and finance where economic approaches have long dominated. Cerny concludes that the real action, both for policymakers and for scholars, lies in an emergent global civil society. A number of constructivist students of international relations have come to similar conclusions, arguing that transnational society must re-embed financial and other markets in a broader solidaristic framework capable of grounding legitimate governing authority in a new era.

---

[33] J. N. Rosenau and E. Czempiel, eds., *Governance without Government: Order and Change in World Politics* (Cambridge: Cambridge University Press, 1992).

Conclusion

This volume makes three principal contributions. First, by mapping the dimensions of institutional variation and examining the creation and evolution of the Bretton Woods institutions over time, the book advances our understanding of institutional selection and adaptation in international monetary and financial relations. Second, the volume deepens our analysis of regional monetary integration by, among other things, extending the theory of optimum currency areas, advancing research on endogenous currency areas, and examining the deterritorialization of money. Finally, this book charts paths for research on the reordering of political authority in a market-oriented global economy, with particular attention to the implications for democracy and accountability. These are promising directions for moving the field of international political economy forward.

Much history and interdisciplinary theory suggest that, while global capitalism flourished in the late twentieth century, it may prove unstable. Indeed, we may well be in the eye of a hurricane.[34] Recurrent financial crises, social disruption, and a backlash against globalization at the dawn of the twenty-first century raise questions among even the most ardent free-market advocates about the stability of the world economy's contemporary organization. But asking whether the institutions designed after World War II can be adapted or whether new institutions that are both more effective and more authoritative need to be crafted make such questions more tractable.[35]

Certainly in rapidly changing monetary and financial arenas, the existing international system is being tested. Monetary matters are now forcing Europeans to ask themselves quite explicitly whether a regional monetary system requires the further development of an accompanying governing structure to bolster effectiveness and legitimacy. In other regions of the world, monetary developments suggest stark choices for governments inclined to resist external pressures. Similar issues arise at the global level. Whether the social and political underpinnings of a truly global economy can be maintained, and for how long, is a looming question for our time. The tensions between the functional logic of global economics and the geographic logic of state-centered politics are becoming more acute. This book provides a rich set of evidence, concepts, and perspectives through which to assess those tensions and the prospects for their peaceful resolution.

---

[34] R. O. Keohane, "Comment," in P. B. Kenen, *Managing the World Economy: Fifty Years after Bretton Woods* (Washington: Institute for International Economics, 1994), 58–63.

[35] See, for example, G. J. Ikenberry, *After Victory: Institutions, Strategic Restraint, and the Rebuilding of Order after Major Wars* (Princeton: Princeton University Press, 2001).

CHAPTER TWO

The Evolution of Political Economy

Robert Gilpin

T he study of political economy in general and international political economy in particular has become very much in vogue among historians, economists, and social scientists.[1] This interest reflects the growing appreciation that the worlds of politics and economics, once thought to be separate (at least as fields of academic inquiry), do in fact importantly affect one another. The polity is much more influenced by economic developments than many political scientists have appreciated, and the economy is much more dependent upon social and political developments than economists in general have admitted. Recognition of the interrelationships between the two spheres has led to increased attention from historians and social scientists to the relationship between politics and economics.

The Nature of Political Economy

During the last two centuries several different definitions of the term "political economy" have been set forth.[2] A brief summary of the changes in those definitions provides insight into the nature of the subject.[3] For Adam Smith in *The Wealth of Nations*, political economy was a "branch of the science of a statesman or legisla-

---

[1] D. K. Whynes, ed., *What Is Political Economy?: Eight Perspectives* (Oxford: Basil Blackwell, 1984). The references to the classical economists discussed below may be found there. For fuller development of themes presented in this chapter, see R. Gilpin, *Global Political Economy: Understanding the International Economic Order* (Princeton: Princeton University Press, 2001).

[2] J. A. Caporaso and D. P. Levine, *Theories of Political Economy* (New York: Cambridge University Press, 1992).

[3] This discussion of the various meanings of political economy is based largely on Colin Wright, "Competing Conceptions of Political Economy," in J. H. Nichols, Jr., and C. Wright, eds., *From Political Economy to Economics—And Back?* (San Francisco: Institute for Contemporary Studies, 1990).

tor" and a guide to the prudent management of the national economy, or as John Stuart Mill, the last major classical economist, commented in a reference to Smith, political economy was the science that teaches a nation how to become rich. These thinkers emphasized the wealth of *nations* and the term "political" was as significant as the term "economy" itself.

In the late nineteenth century, this broad definition of what economists study was narrowed considerably. Alfred Marshall, the father of modern economics, turned his back on the earlier emphasis on the nation as a whole and on the political as important to understanding the nature and dynamics of the economy. In his highly influential *Principles of Economics* (1890), Marshall substituted the present-day term "economics" for "political economy" and greatly restricted the domain of economic science. Following Marshall's precept that economics was an empirical and value-free science, his disciple Lionel Robbins in *The Nature and Significance of Economic Science* (1932) provided the definition to which most present-day economists subscribe: "Economics is the science which studies human behavior as a relationship between ends and scarce means which have alternative uses." In more modern terminology, economics is defined by economists as a universal science of decision-making under conditions of constraint and scarcity.

At the end of the twentieth century, the term "political economy" has come back into fashion even among economists, but there are important differences from earlier usages; also there is considerable controversy even over what the term means. For many professional economists, especially those identified with the Chicago School, political economy means a significant broadening of the *scope* or subject-matter that economists study.[4] These economists have greatly extended the social domain to which the methods or formal models of traditional economics are applicable. The underlying assumptions regarding motivation and the analytical tools of mainstream economics, they argue, are pertinent to the study of all (or at least almost all) aspects of human behavior. For such Chicago School economists as Gary Becker, Richard Posner, and Anthony Downs, the methodology of economics, that is, methodological individualism or the rational-actor model of human behavior, is applicable to all types of human behavior from individuals choosing a sexual partner to voters choosing the American president. According to this interpretation, behavior can be explained by the efforts of individuals to maximize, satisfy, or optimize their self-interest.

"Economic imperialism" has spread among many economists and other social scientists enamored with economics as they attempt to use the individualistic or rational choice methodology of economics to explain social institutions, public policy, and other forms of social activities that have traditionally been regarded as non-economic in nature. This "economic imperialism," identified most closely with the Chicago School, covers a number of specific scholarly areas that include neo-institutionalism, public-choice theory, and what economists themselves call "political

---

[4] W. J. Samuels, ed., *The Chicago School of Political Economy* (University Park, Pa.: Association of Evolutionary Economists, 1976).

economy." The essence of this approach to social institutions and other socio/political matters is to assume that individuals act alone or together to create social institutions and promote other social/political objectives to advance their private interests. Two fundamental positions may be discerned within this broad range of scholarly research. On the one hand, some scholars assume that individuals seek to create social institutions and advocate public policies that will promote overall economic efficiency; the interesting work of Richard Posner on the evolution of the common law is an example of this approach. On the other hand, the term "political economy" is most frequently used by "neo-classical" economists to refer to rent-seeking behavior on the part of individuals and groups.[5] The research of Robert Baldwin and others on trade protectionism is an example of this approach. There is, however, a powerful normative bias among economists that economic institutions or structures are created to serve market efficiency.

The long-term objective of this body of scholarship is to make *endogenous* to economic science those variables or explanations of social phenomena that have traditionally been assumed to be *exogenous* and, therefore, the exclusive province of one of the other social sciences such as psychology, sociology, or political science. By "endogenous," economists mean that a particular human action can be fully explained as a self-conscious effort of an individual to maximize his or her interests; for example, according to the "endogenous growth theory," a firm invests in scientific research in order to increase its profits. By "exogenous," economists mean that a particular action can best be explained by a factor or variable that is external to the model under discussion; for example, Albert Einstein may be said to have been motivated in his work by curiosity or by the desire for fame rather than by a desire to increase his income.

Economic imperialists assume that political and other forms of social behavior can be reduced to economic motives and explained by the formal methods of economic science. Government policies, social institutions including the state itself, and even whole societies, these economists claim, can be explained through the application of formal economic models. For example, economist Edmund S. Phelps broadly defines political economy as "the *choice* of economic systems and public laws and policies that society has available for coordinating and rewarding its members' participation in the economy."[6] Underlying this sweeping definition of political economy is the conviction, expressed by Jack Hirshleifer, that economics is the one and only true social science.[7] The universality of economics, he argues, is due to the fact that its analytic abstractions such as scarcity, cost, and opportunities are themselves universally applicable and can be used effectively to explain both individual behavior and social outcomes. The belief that there is only one universal so-

---

[5] "Rent seeking" refers to the use of a resource to obtain a surplus over the normal economic return to that resource. An example is a tariff.

[6] E. S. Phelps, *Political Economy: An Introductory Text* (New York: W. W. Norton, 1985), xiii–xiv.

[7] J. Hirshleifer, "The Expanding Domain of Economics," *American Economic Review* 75, no. 6 (1995): 53.

cial science, namely economics, is a powerful dogma embraced by many, if not most, economists.

At least three different schools of economists employ an economic approach to human behavior: the public-choice school, neoclassical institutionalism, and what is sometimes called the "new political economy." Neoclassical institutionalism attempts to explain the origin, evolution, and functioning of all types of institutions (social, political, economic) as the result of the maximizing behavior of rational individuals. The public-choice school is also interested in applying the methods of formal economics to analysis of political behavior and institutions, especially to the *political* organization of free men.[8] The new political economy is interested primarily in the political determinants of economic policy.

The public-choice approach is most closely associated with Nobel Laureate James Buchanan and his co-author Gordon Tullock.[9] Using the framework of conventional economics, Buchanan and Tullock in their highly influential *The Calculus of Consent* promoted the important sub-field of public choice.[10] For most economists in the public-choice school, the subject matter is the same as that of political science; they believe they are applying superior methods of economic science to political affairs.[11] What defines the public-choice school more than anything else, however, is its political coloration. With certain important exceptions such as Nobel Laureates Kenneth Arrow and Paul Samuelson, both of whom have made important contributions to the subject of public choice, this school of political economists, especially Buchanan and Tullock themselves, is distinguished by its explicitly normative commitment to unfettered markets and its strong opposition to government intervention in the economy. While some economists emphasize *market failures* as a reason for government intervention in the economy, the more conservative branch of public-choice economics considers *government failures*, that is, economic distortions caused by the policies of governments, to be more of a threat to economic well-being. Politicians and government officials are not the disinterested public servants assumed by many economists and advocates of government interventionism but have interests of their own that they seek to maximize in their public activities. This position asserts that politicians, liberal reformers, and others distort the efficient functioning of the market as they use the apparatus of government to further their own private interests.

Neoclassical institutionalism is one of the most interesting developments in contemporary economics. According to neo-institutionalist economists, economic in-

---

[8] C. Wright, "Competing Conceptions of Political Economy."

[9] D. C. Mueller, *The Public Choice Approach to Politics* (London: Edward Elgar, 1993).

[10] J. M. Buchanan and G. Tullock, *The Calculus of Consent* (Ann Arbor: University of Michigan Press, 1962). The relevance of the public-choice approach to the international economy is set forth in T. D. Willett, *The Public Choice Approach to International Economic Relations* (Charlottesville: University of Virginia, Center for Study of Public Choice, 1996).

[11] The term "positive political economy" is frequently applied to this position. An example is J. E. Alt and K. A. Shepsle, *Perspectives on Positive Political Economy* (New York: Cambridge University Press, 1990).

stitutions (and other institutions, including the state) and their characteristics can
be explained by the methods of neo-classical economics. Nobel Laureate Douglass
C. North, one of the foremost representatives of this school, maintains that economic institutions (like all forms of economic activity) are the consequence of in-
tentional actions by rational individuals to maximize their economic interests.[12]
Economic actions may be motivated by the desire to increase economic efficiency
or may be simply rent-seeking. However, there is a predilection among neo-institutionalists, as well as other economists, to assume that economic institutions have
been produced by rational efforts to increase efficiency.[13] This neo-institutionalist
school is weakened by the fact that it overlooks the non-economic factors responsible for the creation of social institutions and the rules governing societies.

Most mainstream economists frequently use the term "political economy" pejo-
ratively to refer to the self-serving behavior of individuals and groups in the determination of public policy. According to the new political economy, national policy
is most frequently the result of private groups' efforts to employ public means to
further their own private interests rather the result of selfless efforts to advance the
commonweal. Economic policy, this position argues, is the outcome of distributional politics and competition among powerful groups for private advantage. For
example, the economics literature on trade protection (endogenous trade theory)
exemplifies this approach as it argues that tariffs and other obstructions to free
trade can best be understood as rent-seeking behavior by particular interest
groups.

A very different concept of political economy is used by those critics (especially
Marxists) who believe that the discipline of economics has become too formal,
mathematical, and abstract. The study of economics as the development of formal
models, many charge, has become largely irrelevant to understanding and solving
real social and economic problems. A major reason for this isolation of economics
from the real world, they argue, is that economics neglects the historical, political,
and social setting in which economic behavior takes place. As a consequence, some
assert that economics, at least as it is taught and practiced in traditional departments of economics, has little relevance to the larger society and its needs.

Closely associated with this general criticism is what many critics regard as the
pretension of economics to be a "science" modeled on physics and other natural
sciences. Economics, they contend, cannot be value-free, and economists should
not pretend that it is. According to Marxists and other adherents of this view, conventional economics reflects the values and interests of the dominant groups of a
capitalist society. Rather than being value-free, economics is alleged to be infused
with an implicit conservative social and political bias that emphasizes market and

[12] D. C. North, *Structure and Change in Economic History* (New York: W. W. Norton, 1981); D. C.
North, *Institutions, Institutional Change, and Economic Performance* (New York: Cambridge University
Press, 1990).

[13] R. A. Posner, *The Economics of Justice* (Cambridge: Harvard University Press, 1981). A valuable
critique of neo-classical institutionalism is A. Field and J. March, "On the Explanation of Rules Using
Rational Choice Models," *Journal of Economic Issues* 13, no. 1 (1979): 49–72.

efficiency and neglects such social problems as inequality of income and chronic unemployment. In the opinion of Robert Heilbroner and William Milberg, contemporary economics is nothing but a handmaiden of modern Western capitalism, and its primary purpose is to make this troubled system work.[14]

By the end of the twentieth century, the term "political economy" had been given three broad and different meanings. For some scholars, especially economists, political economy referred to the application to all types of human behavior, including behaviors that would not be classified by others as economic, of the *methodology* of formal economics, that is, methodological individualism or the rational-actor model of human behavior. Other scholars used the term to mean employment of a specific economic *theory* or theories to explain social behavior; a good example is found in Ronald Rogowski's use of the Stolper-Samuelson theorem to explain political outcomes over time and space.[15] For those political scientists, including myself, who believe that social and political affairs cannot be reduced to a sub-field of economics, political economy refers primarily to *questions* generated from the interactions of economic and political affairs. Proponents of this broad approach to the subject are eclectic in their choice of subject-matter and methods (economic, historical, sociological, political, and so on).

Distribution of Wealth and Economic Activities

Whereas the science of economics emphasizes the efficient allocation of scarce resources and the absolute gains enjoyed by everyone from economic activities, many state-centric scholars of international political economy emphasize the distributive consequences of economic activities. According to economics, exchange takes place because of mutual gain; were it otherwise, the exchange would not occur. The state-centric interpretation of many state-centric scholars, on the other hand, argues that economic actors are attentive not only to absolute but also to relative gains from economic intercourse, that is, not merely to the absolute gain for themselves but also to the size of their own gain relative to gains of other actors. Governments are concerned about the terms of trade, the distribution of economic returns from foreign investment, and, in particular, the relative rates of economic growth among national economies. Indeed, the issue of relative gains is seldom far from the minds of political leaders. Yet, it should be stressed that the pursuit of both absolute and relative gains are important determinants of international economic affairs.

The significance of relative gains for economic behavior and in the calculations of nation-states was recognized at least as early as the economic writings of the eighteenth century political philosopher David Hume (1711–1776). Hume's mer-

---

[14] R. L. Heilbroner and W. Milberg, *The Crisis of Vision in Modern Economic Thought* (New York: Cambridge University Press, 1995).

[15] R. Rogowski, *Commerce and Coalitions: How Trade Affects Domestic Political Alignments* (Princeton: Princeton University Press, 1989).

cantilist contemporaries argued that a nation should seek a trade and payments surplus, basing their arguments on the assumption that it was only *relative* gains that really mattered. In today's language of game theory, international commerce during the mercantilist era was considered to be a zero-sum game in which the gain to one party necessarily meant a loss to another. Hume himself demonstrated the folly and self-defeating nature of this mercantilist argument by introducing the "price-specie flow mechanism" into economic thought.[16] Subsequently, formulation by David Ricardo (1772–1823) of the law or principle of comparative advantage revealed that every nation could gain in absolute terms from free trade and from an international division of labor based on territorial specialization. Subsequently, John Stuart Mill modified Ricardo's theory and pointed out that states were also interested in the relative gains from trade. Ricardo's demonstration that international economic exchange was not a zero-sum game but rather a positive-sum game from which everyone could gain, led Paul Samuelson to call the law of comparative advantage "the most beautiful idea" in economic science. However, Mill's caveat reminds us that the distribution of these gains is also important in international economic affairs.

A number of political economists have addressed the issue of absolute versus relative gains in international affairs, and the ensuing debate has largely centered on Joseph Grieco's argument that states are more concerned about relative than absolute gains and that this creates difficulties in attaining international cooperation.[17] Although I know of no political economist who dismisses altogether the role of relative gains in international economic affairs, scholars of international political economy do differ on the weight each gives to absolute versus relative gains. Whereas many state-centric scholars stress the importance of relative gains, liberals emphasize the importance of absolute gains and believe that Grieco has overstated the significance of relative gains. Absolute gains, they argue, are more important than Grieco's analysis suggests, and, therefore, international cooperation is easier to attain than he postulates. In my own judgment, there is no final or definitive answer whether absolute or relative gains are more important. As Robert Powell has pointed out, a state's emphasis on absolute or on relative gains depends mainly on the "strategic environment."[18]

---

[16] In oversimplified terms, the "price-specie flow mechanism" states that the flow of specie (gold or silver) into an economy as a consequence of a trade/payments surplus increases the domestic money supply and raises prices of a country's exports. This price rise in turn decreases the country's trade/payments surplus. In short, any attempt to have a permanent trade/payments surplus is self-defeating.

[17] J. M. Grieco, *Cooperation among Nations: Europe, America, and Non-Tariff Barriers to Trade* (Ithaca: Cornell University Press, 1990). An excellent volume on the debate over the importance of relative versus absolute gains is D. A. Baldwin, ed., *Neorealism and Neoliberalism: The Contemporary Debate* (New York: Columbia University Press, 1990).

[18] R. Powell, *The Shadow of Power: States and Strategies in International Politics* (Princeton: Princeton University Press, 1999), 80. An important empirical study of how a state may sacrifice absolute gains for relative gains is Michael Mastanduno's analysis of the American-Japanese trade dispute. M. Mastanduno, "Do Relative Gains Matter? America's Response to Japanese Industrial Policy," *International Security* 16, no. 1 (1991): 73–113.

The importance of absolute versus relative gains in state calculations is actually highly dependent upon the circumstances in which a specific trade-off occurs. While it may be true that states can never be totally unconcerned about the distributive consequences of economic activities for their relative wealth and power, they frequently do, largely for security reasons, ignore this concern in their dealings with others. As Joanne Gowa has demonstrated, states may even sacrifice their own relative gains to benefit an ally. During the height of the Cold War, for example, the United States fostered the economic unification of Western Europe for political reasons despite the costs to its own economic interests. Kenneth Waltz has noted that the conscious decision of the United States to build the power of its European allies at a sacrifice to itself was an historically unprecedented action.[19]

States are particularly interested in the distribution of those gains affecting domestic welfare, national wealth, and military power. When a state weighs absolute versus relative gains, military power is by far the most important consideration; states are extraordinarily reluctant, for example, to trade military security for economic gains. Modern nation-states (like eighteenth century mercantilists) are extremely concerned about the consequences of international economic activities for the distribution of economic gains. Over time, the unequal distribution of these gains will inevitably change the international balance of economic and military power and will thus affect national security. For this reason, states have always been very sensitive to the effects of the international economy on the relative rates of economic growth among national economies in an international system. At the beginning of the twenty-first century, concern is focused on the distribution of industrial power, especially in those high-tech industries vitally important to the relative power position of individual states. The territorial distribution of industry and of technological capabilities is a matter of great concern for every state and a major issue in international political economy.

The Issue of National Autonomy

One of the dominant themes in the study of IPE is the persistent clash between the increasing interdependence of the international economy and the desire of individual states to maintain their economic independence and political autonomy. At the same time that states want the benefits of free trade, foreign investment, and the like, they also desire to protect their political autonomy, cultural values, and social structures. However, the logic of the market system is to expand geographically and to incorporate more and more aspects of a society within the price mechanism, thus making domestic matters subject to forces external to the society. In time, if unchecked, the integration of an economy into the world economy, the intensifying pressures of foreign competition, and the necessity to be efficient in order to survive economically could undermine the independence of a society and force it to

[19] K. N. Waltz, *Theory of International Politics* (Reading, Mass.: Addison-Wesley, 1979).

adopt new values and forms of social organization. Fear that economic globalization and integrating market forces are destroying or could destroy the political, economic, and cultural autonomy of national societies has become widespread.

The clash between the evolving economic and technical interdependence of national societies and the continuing compartmentalization of the world political system into sovereign independent states is one of the dominant motifs of contemporary writings on IPE. Whereas powerful market forces (trade, finance, and investment) jump political boundaries and integrate societies, governments frequently restrict and channel their economic activities to serve the interests of their own societies and of powerful groups within those societies. Whereas the logic of the market is to locate economic activities wherever they will be most efficient and profitable, the logic of the state is to capture and control the process of economic growth and capital accumulation in order to increase the power and economic welfare of the nation. The inevitable clash between the logic of the market and the logic of the state is central to the study of international political economy.

Most economists and many political economists believe that the international economy has a positive impact on international political affairs. The international economy, many argue, creates webs of mutual interdependence and common interests that moderate the self-centered behavior of states. Underlying this benign interpretation is a particular definition of economic interdependence as mutual dependence. However, as Albert Hirschman pointed out in *National Power and the Structure of Foreign Trade* (1969), while economic interdependence may be characterized by mutual dependence, dependence is frequently not symmetrical. Trade, investment, and markets establish dependencies among national societies that can be and are exploited. Integration of national markets creates power relations among states where, as Hirschman notes, economic power is "the power to interrupt commercial or financial relations. . . ."[20] Economic ties among states almost always involve power relations.

Robert Keohane and Joseph Nye extended this analysis of economic power and the political aspects of economic interdependence by distinguishing "sensitivity" interdependence from "vulnerability" interdependence.[21] Most economists really are referring to sensitivity interdependence when they use the term "interdependence"; this entails the responsiveness among economic variables like changes in interest rates in one country that influence interest rates in another. Vulnerability interdependence, on the other hand, is what Hirschman and political economists frequently have in mind when they speak of economic interdependence; this latter term refers to the possibilities of political exploitation of market interdependencies. Individual states have a powerful incentive either to decrease their own dependence

---

[20] A. O. Hirschman, *National Power and the Structure of Foreign Trade* (Berkeley: University of California Press, 1969), 16.

[21] R. O. Keohane, and J. S. Nye, Jr., eds., *Transnational Relations and World Politics* (Cambridge: Harvard University Press, 1972); R. O. Keohane and J. S. Nye, Jr., *Power and Interdependence* (Boston: Little, Brown, 1977).

on other states through such policies as trade protection and industrial policies or, in the case of expansionist states, to increase the dependence of other states upon them through such policies as foreign aid and trade concessions. International economic relations are never purely economic; they always have profound implications for the economic autonomy and political independence of national societies.

The Politics of International Regimes

Every economist and political economist acknowledges the need for some minimal rules or institutions to govern and regulate economic activities; even the most ardent public-choice economist would agree that laws are needed to enforce contracts and protect property rights. A liberal international economy, that is, an international economy characterized (at least in ideal terms) by open markets, freedom of capital movement, non-discrimination, etc. certainly needs agreed-upon rules. A liberal economy can succeed only if it effectively provides a stable monetary system, eliminates market failures, and prevents cheating and free-riding.[22] Although the primary purpose of rules or regimes is to resolve economic problems, many are actually enacted for political rather than for strictly economic reasons. For example, although economists may be correct that an economy benefits from opening itself to free trade whether or not other countries open their own markets, a liberal international economy could not politically tolerate too many free-riders who benefit from the opening of other economies but refuse to open their own markets.

In the past, the rules governing the international economy were quite simple and informal. Insofar as the implicit rules were enforced at all, they were enforced by the major powers whose interests were favored by those rules. For example, in the nineteenth century under the *Pax Britannica*, overseas property rights were frequently upheld by British "gunboat diplomacy,"[23] and the international gold standard, based on a few generally accepted rules, was managed by the Bank of England. Now formal international institutions have been created to manage today's extraordinarily complex international economy. The most important institutions are the Bretton Woods institutions such as the World Bank, the International Monetary Fund, and the General Agreement on Tariffs and Trade, and the world economy would have difficulty functioning without these institutions. Therefore, understanding the functioning of these international institutions has become an extremely important concern of political economists.[24]

[22] In nontechnical language, a public or collective good is one that everyone can enjoy without having to pay for the use of the good. A frequently used example is a lighthouse. Because of this free use, no one usually has an incentive to provide them and, therefore, public goods tend to be "under-provided." The literature on this subject and on proposed solutions to the under-provision problem is extensive.

[23] C. Lipson, *Standing Guard: Protecting Foreign Capital in the Nineteenth and Twentieth Centuries* (Berkeley: University of California Press, 1985).

[24] Many realists would disagree with my belief that international organizations, at least in the area of economic affairs and insofar as they do not infringe on the security interests of powerful states, are important.

The concept of international regimes, defined as "sets of implicit or explicit principles, norms, rules, and decision-making procedures around which actors' expectations converge in a given area of international relations," has been at the core of the research on international institutions.[25] Although a distinction can be made between an international regime as rules and understandings and an international institution as a formal organization, the word "regimes" and the word "institutions" are frequently used interchangeably in writings on international political economy. Moreover, what is really important for the world economy's functioning are the rules themselves rather than the formal institutions in which they are usually embodied. To simplify the following discussion, I shall use "international regime" to encompass both rules and such formal international organizations as the International Monetary Fund or the General Agreement on Tariffs and Trade.

Robert Keohane has been the most influential scholar in the development of regime theory. In his book *After Hegemony*, Keohane set forth the definitive exposition and classic defense of regime theory. He argues that international regimes are a necessary feature of the world economy and are required to facilitate efficient operation of the international economy. Among the tasks performed by regimes are: reduction of uncertainty, minimization of transaction costs, and prevention of market failures. International regimes are created by self-centered states in order to further both individual and collective interests. Even though a particular regime might be created because of the pressures of a dominant power (or hegemon), Keohane argues that an effective international regime takes on a life of its own over time. Moreover, when states experience the success of an international regime, they "learn" to change their own behavior and even to redefine their national interests. Thus, according to Keohane's analysis, international regimes are necessary to preserve and stabilize the international economy.[26]

From its beginning, regime theory has been surrounded by intense controversy. One major reason for the intensity of this debate is that regime theory arose as a response to what Keohane labeled "the theory of hegemonic stability." Proponents of the latter theory had argued that the postwar liberal international economy was based on the economic and political leadership of the United States. Some theorists had argued that the hegemonic stability theory also suggested that the continued existence of a liberal world economy was jeopardized by the relative decline of American power due to the rise of new economic powers and to the slowing of American productivity growth in the early 1970s. As Steven Weber has written, "regime theory developed in the context of the gradual decline of Ameri-

---

[25] The definition appears in S. D. Krasner, "Structural Causes and Regime Consequences: Regimes as Intervening Variables," *International Organization* 36, no. 2 (1982). As Krasner himself points out, there are several variants of regime theory. For this reason, I shall focus on what I consider to be the common denominators in these theories. R. N. Cooper, "Prolegomena to the Choice of an International Monetary System," *International Organization* 29, no. 1 (1975) coined the term "international regime." The term "regime" was introduced into the IPE literature by J. G. Ruggie, "International Responses to Technology: Concepts and Trends," *International Organization* 29, no. 3 (1975).

[26] R. O. Keohane, *After Hegemony: Cooperation and Discord in the World Political Economy* (Princeton: Princeton University Press, 1984).

can power, upon which were superimposed energy price shocks and which brought recession and 'stagflation' to the core of the world economy."[27] Opposing what he labeled the "theory of hegemonic stability," Keohane (1980) and others argued that international regimes and cooperation among the major economic powers would replace declining American leadership as the basis of the liberal international economic order. Thus, the political purpose of regime theory was, at least in part, to reassure Americans and others that a liberal international order would survive America's economic decline and the severe economic problems of the 1970s.

British scholar Susan Strange was the most outspoken critic of regime theory.[28] According to Strange, regime theory was at best a passing fad and at worst a polemical device designed to legitimate America's continuing domination of the world economy. Strange and other critics alleged that such international regimes as those governing trade and monetary affairs had been economically, politically, and ideologically biased in America's favor, that these regimes were put in place by American power, reflected American interests, and were not (as American regime theorists have argued) politically and economically neutral. Susan Strange charged that many of the fundamental problems afflicting the world economy actually resulted from ill-conceived and predatory American economic policies rather than simply being symptoms of American economic decline.

Strange's foremost example of American culpability was the huge American demand in the 1980s and 1990s for international capital to finance America's federal budget and trade/payments deficit.[29] Through the use of what she referred to as "structural power" (such as America's military, financial, and technological power), she alleged, the United States continued to run the world economy during that period and made a mess of it. Susan Strange and other critics also alleged that the regime of the dollar as the key international currency had permitted the United States to behave irresponsibly. More generally, Strange and other foreign critics charged that the American discipline of international political economy, regime theory in particular, has been little more than an effort to defend America's continuing desire to reign economically and politically over the rest of the world. Whether or not we accept these criticisms, they should remind us that regimes and

[27] S. Weber, "Institutions and Change," in M. Doyle and G. J. Ikenberry, eds., *New Thinking in International Relations* (Boulder, Colo.: Westview Press, 1997). The emphasis on regimes also grew out of the realization in the 1970s that international governance was not coterminous with international organizations. Consult F. Kratochwil and J. G. Ruggie, "A State of the Art on an Art of the State," *International Organization* 40, no. 4 (1986): 753–75.

[28] S. Strange, "Cave! Hic Dragones: A Critique of Regime Analysis," in S. D. Krasner, ed., *International Regimes* (Ithaca: Cornell University Press, 1983), 337–54. It is noteworthy that very few non-American scholars have been positively inclined toward regime theory or involved in its development. A major exception is V. Rittberger, ed., *Regime Theory and International Relations* (New York: Oxford University Press, 1993).

[29] S. Strange, *Casino Capitalism* (New York: Basil Blackwell, 1986); S. Strange, *Mad Money* (Manchester: Manchester University Press, 1998).

other social institutions are sometimes created to preserve inequalities as well as to improve coordination and overcome other obstacles to mutually beneficial cooperation.[30] It is desirable to study such important issues as the origins of international regimes, the content, rules, and norms of international regimes, and the history of compliance by affected states, particularly in situations when a regime is perceived as being counter to a state's interests.

Following the lead of Benjamin Cohen, this volume considers the nature and role of monetary and financial regimes in the international economy.[31] The importance of the monetary regime can hardly be overstated; it is the glue that holds the international economy together. Created in 1944 at the Bretton Woods Conference, the postwar regime based on fixed exchange rates was a fundamental stabilizing factor in international economic affairs. In 1971, the content of the monetary regime was changed substantially in response to economic and political developments; this shift from fixed to flexible exchange rates and the development beginning in the 1970s of a global financial system are major concerns of this book. The purpose here is to set forth some the general issues associated with the international regimes that attempt to govern the international economy.

Origins of Regimes

International regimes have originated in a number of different ways. Some have arisen spontaneously and do not involve conscious design; many of the informal rules governing markets are of this type. Others have resulted from international negotiations among states; the postwar Bretton Woods system of monetary regimes, for example, was the result of international negotiations, primarily between the United States and Great Britain (see the chapter by Miles Kahler in this volume). Still other regimes have been imposed by powerful states on less powerful ones; the colonial systems of the nineteenth century are a notorious example. This section will concentrate upon regimes created through international negotiations, especially the Bretton Woods regime for monetary affairs, which was the result of American leadership.

In creating the post-World War II monetary regime, the most important task for American leadership was to promote international cooperation. The United States undertook the leadership role, and other economic powers (Canada, Japan, and Western Europe) cooperated for economic, political, and ideological reasons. These allies believed that a liberal world economy would meet their economic interests and also solidify their alliance against the Soviet threat. In addition, cooperation was greatly facilitated by the fact that these nations shared an ideological commit-

---

[30] A. Schotter, *The Economic Theory of Social Institutions* (New York: Cambridge University Press, 1981), 26.

[31] B. J. Cohen, *Organizing the World's Money: The Political Economy of International Monetary Relations* (New York: Basic Books, 1977); B. J. Cohen, *The Geography of Money* (Ithaca: Cornell University Press, 1998).

ment to a liberal international economy based on free trade and open markets.[32] All three factors—leadership, cooperation, and ideological consensus—were important to the creation of the post-World War II liberal international economy.

Content of Regimes

The content of an international regime, that is, the precise rules and decision-making techniques embodied in a particular regime, is determined by technological, economic, and political factors. The international monetary regime, for example, could not function well if its rules were counter to scientific and technological considerations. Regimes governing international economic affairs must be based on sound economic principles and must be able to solve complex economic matters. The postwar international monetary regime based on pegged exchange rates had both to solve such difficult technical problems as the provision of international liquidity and to provide an adjustment mechanism for nations with balance-of-payments problems—questions that continue to bedevil the IMF (see the chapter by Thomas Willett in this volume).

Economists, however, seldom agree on these complex issues; there are, for example, several competing theories on the determination of exchange rates. It is important to realize that the specific means chosen to solve a given economic problem may have significant consequences for individual states and/or may impinge on their national autonomy. In the early postwar monetary system, the central role of the dollar as a reserve and transaction currency, as Cohen pointed out, greatly facilitated financing of American foreign policy. Thus, while the content of an international regime must be grounded on sound technical and economic considerations, it is important to recognize that regimes do produce political effects.

A number of regime theorists have a tendency to think of regimes in a benign way. Regime theory has emphasized the efficiency and efficacy of international cooperation and problem-solving as well as the fact that regimes are instituted to achieve inter-state cooperation and information sharing, to reduce transaction costs, and to solve common problems. Although these goals do exist, it is also true, as some scholars of institutions point out, that institutions—and regimes—do create or preserve inequalities; regimes can also have a redistributive function.[33] His-

[32] The term "epistemic community," attributed to J. G. Ruggie, has been given to the role of shared ideas or beliefs in promoting international cooperation. A useful discussion is P. Haas, *Saving the Mediterranean* (New York: Columbia University Press, 1990). An important volume on the subject is J. Goldstein and R. O. Keohane, eds., *Ideas and Foreign Policy: Beliefs, Institutions, and Political Change* (Ithaca: Cornell University Press, 1993). Another important study is J. Goldstein, *Ideas, Interests and American Trade Policy* (Ithaca: Cornell University Press, 1993). Although I agree that ideas are very important, they are important politically only insofar as they are supported by the interests and power of important actors such as states or domestic political coalitions.

[33] In his analysis of institutions and, by implication, regimes, Schotter identifies four types of problems whose solution leads to the creation of institutions: coordination problems, prisoners'-dilemma-type games, cooperative-type games, and, most important for my present purpose, the preservation of the status quo. Schotter, *The Economic Theory of Social Institutions*.

tory is replete with such examples as the carving-up of Africa at the Congress of Berlin (1878) and the post–World War I mandate system.[34] Thus, the purpose, content, and actual consequence of every international regime must be closely examined; there should be no assumption that regimes are *ipso facto* of equal or mutual benefit to every participant.

Because international regimes frequently do have distributive consequences as well as implications for national autonomy, the rules, norms, and so on embedded in regimes generally reflect the power and interests of the dominant power/s in the international system. Certainly the liberal trade and monetary regimes following World War II promoted the economic and, I would emphasize, the political and security interests of the United States while also strengthening the anti–Soviet political alliance. Moreover, as American interests changed, the United States used its power to modify one or another of these regimes; the August 1971 Nixon decision to destroy the system of fixed exchange rates because he believed that it no longer suited American interests provided a particularly striking example of this type of behavior.

Nevertheless, it is unlikely that the regimes governing a liberal international economy do or will represent the interests of the dominant power/s and no others. Liberal international regimes must satisfy the interests of all the major economic powers to at least some degree; if they do not, the regimes would neither function nor long survive. The major trading partners of the United States were satisfied with the postwar trade regime and, in fact, benefited economically from the regime more than did the United States. Although a liberal international economic order does reflect the interests of a dominant power, such a power cannot impose a liberal economic order on the rest of the world; ultimately, the regime must rest on international cooperation.

Compliance with Regimes

Although some scholars deny, or at least minimize, the importance of the compliance issue, compliance with international regimes is a major problem, and it is important to understand the reasons for compliance or non-compliance.[35] The compliance or enforcement problem arises because there is no authoritative international government, because states frequently value highly their relative gains and national autonomy, and there is a collective action problem in which individual actors are tempted to cheat and free-ride. Although the compliance problem may be of minor significance for many or even the majority of international re-

[34] Indeed, concern with such matters was the central issue addressed in Cohen's first book, *The Question of Imperialism* (New York: Basic Books, 1973).

[35] Some scholars, for example, argue that as most states do comply with international regimes, compliance is not a serious problem. This position, which Downs, Rocke, and Barsoom label the "managerial school," is criticized by these authors. G. W. Downs, D. M. Rocke, and P. N. Barsoom, "Is the Good News about Compliance Good News about Cooperation?" *International Organization* 50, no. 3 (1996), 379–406.

gimes, when the rules and principles of an international regime have significant distributive consequences for states and powerful domestic groups or when they impinge significantly on the autonomy and security of states, the compliance problem becomes of overwhelming importance. Many of the international regimes governing the world economy, in fact, are of this latter type because they do have important consequences for the distribution of global wealth and national autonomy.[36]

Scholars of international political economy have devoted considerable attention to analysis of possible solutions to this problem. One solution is based on the theory of iterative (or repeated) games and, in particular, on what game theorists call the Prisoners' Dilemma. Another is based on insights from the new institutionalism or "new economics of organization."[37] These approaches fall within the larger category of "theories of international cooperation." Most scholars of international political economy would accept the definition made popular by Robert Keohane that cooperation occurs "when actors adjust their behavior to the actual or anticipated preferences of others, through a process of policy coordination."[38] Although theories of cooperation may be helpful in explicating the nature and difficulties of the compliance problem, they do not really provide an adequate solution.

The Prisoners' Dilemma is undoubtedly very familiar to most readers of this chapter. Nevertheless, I shall provide a brief reminder: Two prisoners are accused of a crime and held separately. If they both confess to the crime of which they are accused, they will both be punished. If neither confesses, that is, if in essence they cooperate with one another, they will both be punished but less severely. However, if only one confesses (or defects), and the other does not confess, the latter will be punished more severely. Thus, although each has an incentive to cooperate with the other by not confessing, each also has an incentive to confess (defect). Uncertainty regarding what the other player will do could lead to a less than optimal outcome for both players.

This type of mixed-motive game in which the players have a motive to cooperate and also a motive to defect is characteristic of almost every aspect of international

---

[36] The reasons why the distribution issue is such a major obstacle to international cooperation is discussed by J. D. Morrow, "Modeling the Forms of International Cooperation," *International Organization* 48, no. 3 (1994): 387–423. The formal treatment by Morrow, Ferejohn, and others on the distributive aspects of international cooperation have not been adequately integrated into the regime literature. I am indebted to George Downs for enlightening me on this scholarship.

[37] The "new institutionalism" is based largely on the research of Oliver Williamson and on the concept of transaction costs, that is, the costs of doing business. For a discussion of the relevance of this literature for IPE, consult B. V. Yarbrough and R. M. Yarbrough, *Cooperation and Governance in International Trade* (Princeton: Princeton University Press, 1992).

[38] Keohane, *After Hegemony*. For a useful and extensive analysis of theories of cooperation consult H. Milner, "International Theories of Cooperation Among Nations: Strengths and Weaknesses," *World Politics* 44, no. 3 (1992): 66–96. Although the literature on game theory and international cooperation distinguishes among different types of problems, such as problems of coordination or of collaboration, I shall use "cooperation" to refer to all the varieties of international cooperation. For a valuable discussion of the issue, see L. Martin, "Interests, Power, and Multilateralism," *International Organization* 46, no. 4 (1992): 765–92.

politics and certainly of international monetary affairs. Although the players would gain from cooperation, each might gain even more by defecting (cheating); yet both would lose if both cheat. For example, a nation could increase its international competitiveness by unilaterally devaluing its own currency. However, if other countries simultaneously devalue their own currencies, everyone loses. Therefore, everyone is better off, at least in absolute terms, as a result of cooperation. Yet the possibility of increasing one's own relative gains by cheating or successfully "free-riding" always provides a powerful temptation in international affairs.[39]

A number of attempts have been made by economists and other scholars to solve the Prisoners' Dilemma. Proposed solutions entail methods or techniques designed to increase the likelihood that players will cooperate and not cheat; they include creating norms of reciprocity, which make each move in the game less distinct and link issues to one another. Such techniques attempt to lessen the incentive to cheat in a particular instance so that the players learn how to cooperate.[40] The most noteworthy effort to solve the Prisoners' Dilemma has been the concept of iterative games developed by Robert Axelrod and others.[41] This concept leads to the conclusion that, if a game is repeated over and over again, and if in each game a participant pursues a "tit-for-tat" strategy in which cooperative moves are rewarded and uncooperative moves are punished, the participants in the game will learn to trust and cooperate with one another.[42]

The literature on the theory of repeated or iterative games has become extensive and has been subjected to intense theoretical criticism and defense. Although scrutiny of the theory has vastly increased our understanding of the compliance problem, this scholarly debate has not yet enabled us to predict when cooperation or defection from (cheating) a regime will in fact occur. The fundamental problem of uncertainty and hence of regime compliance has not yet been solved and probably never will be; a player can never be absolutely sure whether another player will cooperate or defect, and the costs of miscalculation could be extremely high. The absence of an adequate body of research on the actual functioning of specific regimes makes it impossible to be confident that regimes are of decisive importance in the behavior of states. In addition, a fundamental methodological problem makes it difficult to determine whether or not regimes actually make a difference in the conduct of international affairs. As one strong supporter of regime theory has stated, "investigating the consequences of international regimes requires a counter-

[39] B. S. Frey, *International Political Economics* (Oxford: Basil Blackwell, 1984), chap. 7 has a valuable analysis of the "free-rider" problem and why international cooperation matters.

[40] An important discussion of this subject is K. A. Oye, ed., *Cooperation Under Anarchy* (Princeton: Princeton University Press, 1986).

[41] R. M. Axelrod, *The Evolution of Cooperation* (New York: Basic Books, 1984).

[42] Criticisms of Axelrod's approach to the cooperation problem include J. Gowa, "Anarchy, Egoism, and Third Images: The Evolution of Cooperation and International Relations," *International Organization* 40, no. 1 (1986): 67–186, and D. E. Spiro, "The State of Cooperation in Theories of State Cooperation: The Evolution of a Category Mistake," *Journal of International Affairs* 42, no. 1 (1988): 205–25.

factual argument," that is, knowledge of what would happen if the regime did not exist.[43]

The "new economics of organization" or what some scholars prefer to label "neo-institutionalism" has produced another important effort to solve the compliance problem. This theory of international cooperation has been described by David Rocke and George Downs as "a loose composite" of transaction-cost economics and non-cooperative game theory.[44] According to new institutionalism, regimes can provide a solution to such problems as market inefficiencies, economic uncertainties, and market failures. However, as Rocke and Downs point out, this theory of international cooperation makes only a limited contribution to solving the compliance problem, and compliance with international regimes ultimately rests on the domestic and, I would add, the foreign policy interests of individual states.

Contrary to what many scholars believe, the increasing importance of social welfare in state behavior has not substantially changed matters. As James Mayall points out, international regimes have resulted in few, if any, sacrifices of domestic social welfare.[45] Despite much talk of international distributive justice, for example, voluntary sharing by one society of a substantial portion of its wealth with other societies is rare indeed. Foreign aid, for example, has never absorbed more than a small percentage of a nation's GNP and, with a few notable exceptions, such aid has been and is given for national security or economic (rather than humanitarian) reasons. The modern welfare system has actually made states even more attentive to their own economic interests. The nationalistic nature of the modern welfare state is well demonstrated by the singular fact that every state severely restricts immigration, at least in part to restrict access to its welfare system.

While international regimes are useful to provide solutions to technical, economic, and other problems associated with the world economy, they also invariably affect the economic welfare, national security, and political autonomy of individual states. For this reason, states frequently attempt to manipulate regimes for their own parochial economic and political advantage. This concept of international regimes as both technical solution and arena of political struggle diverges from the one held by many economists and liberal scholars of political economy that regimes are economically and politically neutral. The realist interpretation maintains that international regimes are neither above nor outside of the struggle for power and advantage among states. Regimes are both a part and an object of a political struggle. As a consequence, if a regime is to be effective, and if its rules are to be enforced, it must also rest on a strong political base. Due to the central importance to most nations of distribution and autonomy issues, the compliance problem is un-

---

[43] V. Rittberger, ed., *Regime Theory and International Relations* (New York: Oxford University Press, 1993).

[44] G. W. Downs and D. M. Rocke, *Optimal Imperfection? Domestic Uncertainty and Institutions in International Relations* (Princeton: Princeton University Press, 1995), 19.

[45] J. Mayall, *Nationalism and International Society* (New York: Cambridge University Press, 1990), chap.6.

likely to be resolved, and regime rules are unlikely to be enforced unless there is strong international leadership.

Conclusion

Although the science of economics is a necessary foundation for a comprehension of international political economy, this chapter has focused attention on the inter-action of markets and political actors. Economics alone is an insufficient tool for an analysis of such vital issues as the international distribution of wealth and economic activities, the effects of the world economy on national interests, and the effective-ness of international regimes. I reject the popular idea that universal economic laws and powerful economic forces now rule the global economy. Despite increasing economic globalization and integration among national economies, it is still neces-sary to distinguish between national and international economies. Political bound-aries do and will divide the economies and economic policies of one nation from those of another; political considerations also significantly influence and distin-guish economic activities in one country from the next. States, and other powerful actors as well, use their power to influence economic activities in order to maximize their own economic and political interests.

CHAPTER THREE

Bretton Woods and Its Competitors: The Political Economy of Institutional Choice

Miles Kahler

Governments created and deepened regional and global institutions during the 1990s. This burst of institutional innovation and transformation produced two positive ancillary results in research on international political economy. Since states—the final arbiters in realist analysis—have pushed this wave of institution-building forward, one can assume that these institutions "matter" to their creators, ending a long and fruitless debate on the possibilities for international cooperation and the significance of international institutions. At the same time, a more productive and sophisticated investigation of institutional design has centered on this profusion of new and transformed institutions. The new research agenda includes explanations of institutional variation, evaluations of the effects of that variation on interstate cooperation, and assessments of the performance of different institutional designs.

International monetary institutions provide a useful and important field of cases for explaining institutional variation over time and exploring the consequences of that variation for economic performance and state collaboration. They are of particular interest at the present time. The pendulum of scholarly and official opinion has swung back and forth between rule-based, fixed exchange-rate regimes and flexible exchange rates since the 1960s. Opinion is now divided between those favoring various forms of "hard" pegs (regional currency unions, currency boards, dollarization) and those who see floating rates as the best alternative in a world of large-scale private capital flows. A re-examination of the Bretton Woods design, an earlier experiment that sought to combine international oversight of exchange-rate policy with fixed but adjustable pegs, sheds light on the reasons for particular institutional choices in monetary affairs, choices that are driven by political as well as economic logic, as discussed in Chapter 1 of this volume.

The author gratefully acknowledges the research assistance of Pablo Pinto.

Establishing the dimensions of institutional variation in global monetary regimes is a necessary first step, taken in the following section. Those dimensions have seldom been specified clearly, which has hindered efforts to explain and evaluate competing institutions. Competing explanations for the choice of a particular institutional design are presented next. Those that rely on domestic political variables are juxtaposed with functionalist alternatives. A survey of the apparent novelty of the Bretton Woods institutions is prefaced by a description of their competitors: a revived gold standard based on central bank cooperation and a model of informal collaboration among the monetary powers, represented in the Tripartite Agreement. An evolutionary approach to global monetary institutions suggests that these competitors, which were familiar to policy-makers and enjoyed considerable political support, shaped the design of Bretton Woods. An explanation for the particular dimensions of the monetary order negotiated at Bretton Woods is offered in the next section of the paper. A functionalist approach—based on a misreading of inter-war history by the participants—offers some purchase on the eventual outcome. However, the institutional architecture of Bretton Woods is best explained as a solution by two governments—the United States and the United Kingdom—to the economic dilemmas of labor-based political coalitions. Whatever its later political symbolism, Bretton Woods began as a creation of the political left that was meant to sustain both international economic openness and domestic economic activism.

Dimensions of Institutional Variation

The Articles of Agreement of the International Monetary Fund (IMF) that were negotiated in 1944 described an international monetary order that could be distinguished from its predecessors using three key dimensions: membership (the type and number of institutional principals); legalization (the character of rules and the degree of third-party delegation); and methods of rule-making. These dimensions, used here to characterize international monetary institutions, are also applicable to other spheres of international collaboration.

First, international institutions vary according to their membership—the type and number of principals that promulgate the rules and are governed by them. The assumption that states are the only actors that can construct international systems of governance is a neorealist canard. Entire sectors of the international economy, such as petroleum, have been governed for long stretches of time by rules designed and administered by private actors. In contemporary international politics nongovernmental organizations play a role in designing international rules as well as monitoring and enforcing international agreements. The principals in international institutions also provide a domestic anchorage for those institutions and shape the domestic politics in which they are embedded. The ability of governments to serve as successful institutional gatekeepers will often determine the lines of political conflict around particular institutions. Whether international monetary institutions are based on a membership of states alone, of private financial actors, or some combination of the two is an important dimension of institutional variation.

The number of members is also an important variable. Clubs of the major powers are perhaps the oldest mode of governance in the state system. Such clubs often lie at the core of international institutions. In the twentieth century, however, institutions with restricted membership have competed with those whose membership aims at universality. Multilateral institutions with large membership occur with greater frequency after World War I. The International Monetary Fund and the World Bank are representative of such institutions.

As Padoa-Schioppa has shown, a second dimension of institutional variation is the role of formal rules or injunctions as compared with either episodic or rule-governed discretionary bargaining.[1] Robert Mundell distinguishes an international monetary system from an international monetary order in part according to the status of formal rules in governing international monetary affairs.[2] Either domestic or international rules can constrain government behavior within rule-governed systems. A key contrast between the pre-1914 gold standard and the Bretton Woods system—both rule-governed systems—is that the former was grounded in national legislation that bound governments and central banks. There were no formal, international rules of the game in the classical gold standard.[3]

This institutional dimension has been extended recently in the concept of legalization, measured by the level of obligation and precision of rules and the degree of delegation to a third party for interpretation, monitoring, or enforcement of those rules.[4] The delegation of responsibilities for monitoring and sanctioning to a formal organizational core was a central innovation of the Bretton Woods experiment. The creation of the International Monetary Fund at the center of the new monetary regime represented a level of organizational delegation in international monetary affairs that would not be matched until the construction of European monetary institutions four decades later.

A third dimension of institutions is related to legalization: the mode of rule creation. Rules may be created through constitution-making among states in a centralized and historically circumscribed manner, as they were at Bretton Woods. Institutional rules can also evolve over time through decentralized and incremental processes that strengthen conventions. Another label for this distinction is agent-directed design versus Hayekian spontaneous order. Postwar international institu-

---

[1] M. Kahler, "Organization and Cooperation: International Institutions and Policy Coordination," *Journal of Public Policy* 8, no. 3/4 (1989): 375–401; compare to Kenneth A. Oye's distinction between rule-governed systems and those governed by "unrestricted bargaining." K. A. Oye, *Economic Discrimination and Political Exchange* (Princeton: Princeton University Press, 1992).

[2] R. A. Mundell, "The Future of the International Monetary System," in A. L. K. Acheson, J. F. Chant, and M. F. J. Prachowny, eds., *Bretton Woods Revisited* (Toronto: University of Toronto Press, 1972).

[3] K. W. Dam, *The Rules of the Game* (Chicago: University of Chicago Press, 1982), 30–31.

[4] On the definition and application of the concept of legalization, see J. Goldstein, M. Kahler, R. O. Keohane, and A. Slaughter, eds., *Legalization and World Politics* (Cambridge, Mass.: MIT Press, 2001).

tions have colored our ideas of typical institutional genesis: Bretton Woods and San Francisco, the quintessential examples of international constitution-making in fact represent only one pattern of institutional rule-making. According to this deeply engrained model, cooperation is confirmed in formal intergovernmental institutions founded in contractual agreements.

Incremental, bottom-up strategies of hardening "soft" conventions may be equally or more effective over time than top-down rule-making.[5] In international monetary affairs this spectrum of rule-making is a familiar one. Robert Mundell has noted that the gold standard evolved "haphazardly," that it was "never created," in contrast to the Bretton Woods order. Nevertheless, both the gold standard and Bretton Woods constitute two of only three periods in history that Mundell labels international monetary order. In each of these periods, a "constitution" of sorts existed for the monetary system, but the genesis of these constitutions differed.[6]

Explanations for Institutional Variation

Historical accounts of Bretton Woods have offered implicit explanations for the adjustable-peg system of exchange rates, the shape of the International Monetary Fund, and other dimensions of the post-1945 international monetary system. Explicit and transferable hypotheses on the sources of institutional variation are rarer. One powerful approach is functionalist. The dimension of legalization, for example, is associated with the underlying pattern of strategic interaction among states in a particular issue-area. Demand for a particular system of monetary governance arises from an evaluation by key governments of its prospective costs and benefits. (Although functionalist analysis of international institutions is usually framed in terms of evaluation by governments, the same logic applies to private actors as well.) Agents choose institutional alternatives because of their prospective and intended effects. Legalized institutions with substantial delegation to formal organizations—and perceptions of the need for such organizations—often signify the demands of a particular type of strategic interaction: one in which the risks of opportunistic behavior are high.

Functionalist arguments have been criticized for supplying only demand-side explanations for international institutions without offering a clear supply-side explanation for institution building.[7] Charles Kindleberger and others have offered one explanation for the supply of such institutions, particularly stable international monetary orders: the distribution of power. An open trading system and a stable set of international monetary rules are associated with a single dominant international

---

[5] On the emergence of decentralized cooperative regimes to govern common-pool resources, see E. Ostrom, *Governing the Commons* (Cambridge: Cambridge University Press, 1990).

[6] The third case was the Roman-Byzantine order, but that order was not freely constituted among equal political units. Mundell, "The Future of the International Monetary System," 98.

[7] On this point, see R. H. Bates, "Contra Contractarianism: Some Reflections on the New Institutionalism," *Politics and Society* 16, no. 2–3 (1988): 387–401.

economic and financial power such as Britain during the pre-1914 gold standard or the United States during Bretton Woods. A modified version of this argument, based less on economic power consciously applied than on economic weight in the system, has been advanced by Jeffry Frieden; he argues that a major country can provide "a focal point around which actors can converge—in the international monetary realm, perhaps a major trading and investing nation that can lead others toward a mutually beneficial agreement on international monetary norms."[8]

These demand-side and supply-side explanations for global monetary institutions fail to explain a crucial portion of observed institutional variation over time, however. Unless one can assume that dominant or core economic powers have fixed preferences over the substantive content of international monetary regimes (for example, a dominant financial power will always prefer a rule-based regime of fixed exchange rates), then the preferences of key actors must be explained. The very different institutional outcomes before 1914 and after 1945 suggest that dominant economic powers do not share common institutional preferences over time.

Domestic politics and political economy offer a superior baseline for defining state preferences in functionalist models. These include factor endowment models based on relative abundance of capital and labor as well as specific factor models that posit sectoral preferences over both exchange rate levels and their fixity under different levels of capital mobility. Frieden, for example, advances a sectoral explanation for preferences over exchange-rate arrangements. The distributional implications of monetary institutions produce different preferences on the part of domestic interest groups:

> . . . we expect internationally oriented economic actors to favor fixed rates, and domestically oriented economic actors to favor floating or adjustable rates. By the same token, those that favor a devaluation (essentially producers of import or export-competing tradable goods) tend to oppose a fixed-rate system that prohibits devaluation.[9]

Other domestic political explanations assign policy preferences to broader, typically class-based, political coalitions and parties in order to predict national preferences over international monetary arrangements. In her account of inter-war international economic instability, Beth Simmons presents a powerful argument based on the policy choices made by different coalitions in the face of increasingly de-

---

[8] J. Frieden, "The Dynamics of International Monetary Systems: International and Domestic Factors in the Rise, Reign, and Demise of the Classical Gold Standard," in J. Snyder and R. Jervis, eds., *Coping with Complexity in the International System* (Boulder, Colo.: Westview Press, 1993), 137–62.

[9] Frieden, "Exchange Rate Politics: Contemporary Lessons from American History," *Review of International Political Economy* 1, no. 1 (1994), 141. Also, J. Frieden and R. Rogowski in R. O. Keohane and H. M. Milner, eds., *Internationalization and Domestic Politics* (New York: Cambridge University Press, 1996); J. Frieden, "Invested Interests: The Politics of National Economic Policies in a World of Global Finance," *International Organization* 45, no. 4 (1991): 425–52.

mocratized political systems. In dealing with increasingly intractable issues of domestic adjustment to external imbalance, coalitions of Left and Right chose policy mixes that posed different obstacles to international collaboration.[10]

Models based on political economy accounting of this kind have two shortcomings as explanations for national preferences. First, the weight assigned to particular groups or sectors in explaining national preferences can only be estimated if a domestic institutional filter is specified. Helen Milner, for example, argues that the distribution of powers between legislature and executive is a particularly important institutional determinant of whose preferences are most influential.[11] The effects of international institutions on domestic political institutions may also shape the choices of domestic actors. International arrangements may be selected because of their domestic institutional anchors, which award privileged access or predominant influence to particular political actors. For example, private finance, because of its multiple links to central banks, has often preferred systems centered on those domestic institutions rather than intergovernmental alternatives. Domestic political actors may also select international institutions because they add an important increment of credibility to domestic policy commitments made in the face of future political uncertainties.

A simple tally of the institutional preferences of domestic actors is inadequate for a second reason. Preferences over international monetary regimes are not independent of the particular menu of institutional choices that is available politically in a particular epoch: a public international institution to oversee international monetary affairs was simply not an extant institutional choice before 1914. More than one institutional outcome can also satisfy preferences on particular institutional dimensions, such as legalization.

Cognitive and ideational variables often explain the supply and restriction of institutional alternatives. One explanation of this kind complements arguments based on international bargaining. Ideas provide focal points among a number of stable negotiating equilibria established by the play of interests. Geoffrey Garrett and Barry R. Weingast suggest that ideas assist in the coordination of expectations, that ideas must "fit" a particular bargaining environment in order to serve a catalytic role, and that ideas institutionalized successfully provide a normative system that sustains cooperation.[12] The novel intergovernmental option negotiated at Bretton Woods could be seen as such an ideational focal point. An alternative ideational explanation awards a larger role to expert communities. Professional or knowledge-based communities reduce policy-making uncertainty, particularly in spheres of in-

[10] B. Simmons, *Who Adjusts? Domestic Sources of Foreign Economic Policy During the Interwar Years* (Princeton: Princeton University Press, 1994).

[11] H. Milner, *Interests, Institutions, and Information: Domestic Politics and International Relations* (Princeton: Princeton University Press, 1997).

[12] G. Garrett and B. R. Weingast, "Ideas, Interests, and Institutions: Constructing the EC's Internal Market," in J. Goldstein and R. O. Keohane, eds., *Ideas and Foreign Policy* (Ithaca: Cornell University Press, 1993).

creasing technical complexity. By providing interpretations of events, redefining state interests, and participating in policy-making, such expert communities may shape of collaborative bargains in international politics.

G. John Ikenberry has argued the central role of one such community of economic experts in the negotiation of the postwar monetary and trade regimes.[13] Ideational explanations of this kind must be associated with a model of politics, however. Some ideas and their purveyors prevail; others do not. Those that prevail are not always the "best," according to narrowly intellectual criteria. Although the intellectual prestige of John Maynard Keynes added considerable weight to his plan for an International Clearing Union, his position as designated lead negotiator for the British Treasury was even more significant. Neither his bureaucratic position nor his intellectual stature could overcome the influence of the United States in the negotiations, however. The plan produced by Harry Dexter White had many technical weaknesses, but it became the core of the American negotiating position. As such, it dominated negotiations before and during the Bretton Woods conference. A model of "knowledge politics"—assigning weight to bargaining within an expert community as well as the larger politics in which that community is embedded—is an essential corollary of ideational explanations for institutional choice.

Bretton Woods and Its Competitors

Historians and participants have sometimes portrayed the birth of the Bretton Woods monetary system as a unique episode in institutional innovation. After the chaos of the 1930s, an impressive process of learning led governments of good will—particularly those of the United States and the United Kingdom—to forge novel institutions of monetary governance. Those international monetary rules contributed to the longest period of global economic growth and stability since World War I. One of the intellectual architects of Bretton Woods, Edward Bernstein, declared that the Bretton Woods Conference "seemed like a miracle" given the record of inter-war monetary cooperation.[14] Given the scale of the achievement portrayed, relatively little attention has been devoted to the institutional alternatives to Bretton Woods. Few saw a need to investigate solutions of the past when the best institutional alternative had been adopted.

Without denigrating the substantial and radical achievement of the Bretton Woods order, those competitors provide an important part of the explanation for the final adoption of such peculiar institutional design in 1944. For peculiar it was, by the standards of international monetary history, skewed toward one end of each

---

[13] G. J. Ikenberry, "A World Economy Restored: Expert Consensus and the Anglo-American Postwar Settlement," *International Organization* 46, no. 1 (1992): 289–321; G. J. Ikenberry, "The Political Origins of Bretton Woods," in M. D. Bordo and B. Eichengreen, eds., *A Retrospective on Bretton Woods* (Chicago: University of Chicago Press, 1993), 155–82.

[14] S. W. Black, *A Levite among the Priests: Edward M. Bernstein and the Origins of the Bretton Woods System* (Boulder, Colo.: Westview Press, 1991), 104.

institutional dimension described earlier. Bretton Woods created a monetary system based on agreement among governments, divorced from any transnational private network. Membership in the IMF and the World Bank was not limited to the major financial powers; all sovereign states were eligible. The new monetary order was a legalized system of formal rules with a significant international organization at its core, an organization that could mobilize resources and, at least on paper, sanction the conduct of its members. Finally, rules were created in top-down fashion by contract, not by gradual accretion or a hardening of conventions into legal obligations. This design is now so familiar that it is difficult to recollect the political power of one alternative, a gold standard based on domestic legal commitments, in the not-so-distant past, and the political attractions of great-power discretionary bargaining represented in the Tripartite Agreement during the late 1930s. To understand the triumph and design of Bretton Woods, it is necessary to understand these alternatives and why they were rejected.

The Gold Standard and Central Bank Cooperation

The course chosen by the architects of Bretton Woods during World War II stood in stark contrast to the path of policy-makers after World War I. As Peter Temin, Barry Eichengreen, and others have described, the major economic powers worked during the 1920s to reconstruct the gold standard, often at unrealistic parities. The economic shocks that the war inflicted on the international economy were not accommodated by international monetary institutions.[15] This analysis matches that of Edward Bernstein and other architects of Bretton Woods: the Great Depression was caused by "the interaction of the wartime inflation and the traditional gold standard."[16] Those at Bretton Woods also judged the record of international cooperation under the gold standard as deficient. After World War I, a fragile system of central bank cooperation had supported the gold standard. Such collaboration, sporadic before 1914, became more systematic as the central banks of the major powers cooperated to stabilize inflation-ridden European economies. Their weaker clients were often able to create conflict among the major central banks, in part because collaboration was so weakly institutionalized, and in part because the central banks were no longer independent of domestic political pressures.[17] As Stephen Clarke claims, central bankers in the 1920s were "above all national central bankers," and behaved as such. Even if they disagreed with the policies of national governments, their authority was increasingly circumscribed by democratic politics and was in fact delegated authority, in fact if not yet in law.[18] If the central banks

[15] P. Temin, *Lessons from the Great Depression* (Cambridge, Mass.: MIT Press, 1989), 10–11.

[16] Black, *A Levite among the Priests*, 98.

[17] On these stabilization episodes, see R. H. Meyer, *Bankers' Diplomacy: Monetary Stabilization in the Twenties* (New York: Columbia University Press, 1970).

[18] S. V. O. Clarke, *Central Bank Cooperation: 1924–31* (New York: Federal Reserve Bank of New York, 1967), 29–30.

disagreed over the international rules of the game, no impartial interpreter of those rules could be called upon.

Central banks created only one collective institution during this period. The Bank for International Settlements (BIS) was part of a final effort to resolve the problem of German reparations. As a club of central banks, its fortunes were a good indicator of the relative standing of a central bank–centered model of international monetary cooperation. The mandate and resources of the BIS were too limited to deal with the financial disruptions of the Great Depression. The Bank of England's Montagu Norman had proposed a more substantial organization, a plan rejected because of "the unwillingness, which we have seen in certain quarters, to support a scheme of which the control and the funds are truly international."[19]

The BIS did become a valued instrument of the major central banks, however. It sponsored an improved level of research on international financial issues and encouraged informal consultations at regular monthly meetings. In its Annual Reports, strongly influenced by Per Jacobsson, Economic Adviser and Head of the Monetary and Economic Department (and future Managing Director of the IMF), the BIS continued to preach the gospel of international economic collaboration and sound monetary policies. It became the bearer of the old gold standard norms into the more tumultuous and hostile era of the 1930s and the 1940s. Its increasingly isolated role was symbolized in preparations for the World Monetary and Economic Conference in June 1933. The BIS assisted in drafting resolutions in favor of international monetary cooperation; the Conference in fact confirmed an era of monetary unilateralism.[20]

A disappointed Jacobsson noted at the time of Bretton Woods that "the history of the last hundred years showed that it was the more or less independent central banks who were the guardians of the value of the currency" and lamented American unwillingness to rely on central banks for international monetary collaboration.[21] The BIS figured in the Bretton Woods negotiations only as the target of a hostile effort by the United States and other governments to abolish it for collaboration with the Nazis during World War II. Its defenders, who included John Maynard Keynes and other European representatives, argued that its behavior during the war had not been that of a collaborator but that of an apolitical agent attempting to steer its course in an impossible political environment. The opposition managed to win a recommendation for liquidation at "the earliest possible moment," which, as Keynes noted at the time, would not be very early at all.

The symbolic and institutional role of the BIS made it a target for extinction as much as its wartime activities did. Harry Dexter White, who shared with Keynes the principal architectural role at Bretton Woods, was concerned that it might com-

[19] Ibid., 179.

[20] H. H. Schloss, *The Bank for International Settlements: An Experiment in Central Bank Cooperation* (Amsterdam: North-Holland, 1958), 95; E. E. Jacobsson, *A Life for Sound Money* (Oxford: Clarendon, 1979), 95–96.

[21] Ibid., 181.

pete with the new financial institutions. To BIS opponents, the organization represented an alternative, rule-based system (the gold standard) that had been rejected at Bretton Woods. As Jacobsson proudly noted, the BIS remained the principal international spokesman for the "monetary point of view" throughout the 1930s. Because of constraints on American participation, the BIS was also an overwhelmingly European institution. It therefore posed a potential regional alternative in the eyes of the globalist Americans at Bretton Woods.[22] Finally, to many New Dealers, the BIS and its central bank members represented the policy preferences of private finance. This coalition challenged the dominant role of governments in the direction of monetary affairs.[23]

Central bank cooperation and the BIS both persisted into the Bretton Woods era. Despite its near miss with elimination, the BIS prospered after World War II by assuming a useful role in the process of European integration. It agreed to act as the agent of most European governments participating in the Marshall Plan and later became of the agent of the OEEC and the European Payments Union.[24] (The International Monetary Fund had declined this role.) As Jacobsson noted with satisfaction, early links to the Bretton Woods institutions themselves, particularly the World Bank, also secured the position of the BIS. Finally, however, the BIS survived "because the central bankers, who knew it best, decided that they needed the institution."[25]

As an alternative locus for international financial cooperation, the central bank club at the BIS became more important after the Bretton Woods exchange-rate regime had collapsed in the early 1970s. Financial crises in subsequent decades directed attention to the international implications of financial regulation and supervision and promoted central bank collaboration in the Basle Committee on Banking Supervision (BCBS). The recently created Financial Stability Forum, housed at the BIS, confirms the significant role of central banks in the new international financial architecture.[26]

[22] On the Bretton Woods debate over the BIS, Jacobsson, *A Life for Sound Money*, 186–17; A. Van Dormael, *Bretton Woods: Birth of a Monetary System* (London: Macmillan, 1978), 204–6; J. M. Blum, *From the Morgenthau Diaries, Volume III: Years of War, 1941–1945* (Boston: Houghton Mifflin, 1967), 268; Schloss, *The Bank for International Settlements*, 120; R. Mikesell, *The Bretton Woods Debates: A Memoir* (Princeton: International Finance Section, Department of Economics, 1994), 42.

[23] On this point, more below, but see Blum, *From the Morgenthau Diaries, III*, 229, for Morgenthau's view that private bankers "pursuing selfish ends, had caused most of the trouble in the past."

[24] R. Auboin, *The Bank for International Settlements, 1930–1955* (Princeton: International Finance Section, May 1955), 29–32.

[25] Jacobsson, *A Life for Sound Money*, 189–92.

[26] The evolution of central bank cooperation after World War II is described in greater detail in M. Kahler, "Private Capital, Central Banks, and International Monetary Governance" (paper presented at the Political Economy of International Finance Research Group meeting, Cambridge, Mass., 27 October 2000) and in M. Frattianni and J. Pattison, "Reconciling Global Financial Markets and National Regulation: The Role of the Bank for International Settlements" (paper presented at the workshop on Political Economy of International Monetary and Financial Institutions, University of California Berkeley, 2000).

Great-Power Collaboration: The Tripartite Agreement

The League of Nations might have provided an intergovernmental forum for monetary collaboration. The Financial Committee of the League played a significant role in the inter-war years as a provider of statistical information on its members, a function of international monetary institutions that we now take for granted. The Financial Committee also directed European stabilization programs in the early 1920s. Consortia of central banks later claimed its stabilization role, however. By the 1930s, the Financial Committee's contribution to international monetary cooperation had been reduced to research and intellectual consensus-building.[27] As exchange-rate cooperation became politically feasible once again in the 1930s, national governments, not central banks or the League, were the principals. Both Britain and the United States created stabilization funds as national instruments for managing their exchange rates. That experience, in multilateral form, would reappear in Harry Dexter White's plan for a postwar International Stabilization Fund.[28]

In the 1930s, however, the major governments were not yet willing to constrain their policy autonomy through multilateral and legalized institutions. Instead, they engaged in ad hoc bargaining to achieve exchange-rate stabilization. The Tripartite Agreement, negotiated among the British, French, and United States governments in 1936, signaled a resumption of international consultation on exchange-rate policy. It remained a "gentlemen's agreement," whose broad public commitments were neither precise nor legally binding. Detailed negotiations over rates followed those public statements.[29]

Key participants at Bretton Woods as well as later observers viewed monetary collaboration under the Tripartite Agreement of 1936 as a way station to the new monetary regime. Treasury Secretary Henry Morgenthau, Jr., for example, saw the Bretton Woods institutions as "broader than the Tripartite Pact and more powerful, which would provide a central agency for preventing competitive devaluations, etc."[30] Although governments, not central banks or private financial institutions, were the principals of renewed monetary cooperation in the 1930s, their limited collaboration under the Tripartite Agreement diverged from the Bretton Woods agreements on every other institutional dimension. The Tripartite Agreement was

[27] On the League's role in financial and monetary affairs, Jacobsson, *A Life for Sound Money*, 49–52; F. P. Walters, *A History of the League of Nations* (London: Oxford University Press, 1965), 177, 423; L. W. Pauly, *Who Elected the Bankers? Surveillance and Control in the World Economy* (Ithaca: Cornell University Press 1997).

[28] On the creation of the U.S. Exchange Stabilization Fund, see C. R. Henning, *The Exchange Stabilization Fund: Slush Money or War Chest?* (Washington: Institute for International Economics, 1999).

[29] On the Tripartite Agreement's outlines, see S. V. O. Clarke, *Exchange-Rate Stabilization in the Mid-1930s: Negotiating the Tripartite Agreement* (Princeton: International Finance Section, 1977) and K. A. Oye, *Economic Discrimination and Political Exchange* (Princeton: Princeton University Press, 1992), 126–33.

[30] Blum, *From the Morgenthau Diaries, III*, 229. For a scholarly view along similar lines, see Clarke, *Exchange-Rate Stabilization in the Mid-1930s.*

not legalized, and such ad hoc bargaining among governments was unlikely to produce a new international monetary order of binding rules.

The attractions of a more informal set of arrangements could have remained as
powerful in the 1940s as they had been in the late 1930s: fewer limits to national
policy autonomy, no hint of returning to a politically unpopular gold standard. Yet
political elites in the two greatest financial powers chose a very different path, that
of a legalized, multilateral system in which governments undertook binding obligations regarding their exchange rates. Ad hoc intergovernmental collaboration
among the Great Powers, "unrestricted bargaining" (in Kenneth Oye's phrase), no
longer seemed adequate.

It is difficult to understand the negotiations that produced such novel, even radical, monetary institutions without recalling these institutional competitors. Although the competitors were rejected as postwar templates, they lingered in the
minds of those who drafted the plans for a new monetary order and negotiated its
rules. They also persisted as alternative models for organizing international monetary cooperation long after the negotiators had left the rambling hotel in New
Hampshire.

Bretton Woods: The Institutional Mosaic

The choice of a postwar order centered on a public international organization was
surprising given the mixed record of the League of Nations in international economic cooperation and the limited experience of governments with such entities in
the inter-war era. Despite initial hesitation on the part of President Roosevelt (who
recalled the painful failure of League ratification), the British and Americans
agreed quickly on the need for a formal international institution at the core of the
new system. Given their different diagnoses of inter-war monetary problems,
American and British expert teams proposed alternative visions of that organization: White's International Stabilization Fund and Keynes's International Clearing
Union.

The idea of a stabilization fund that would permit adjustment without deflation
had been part of the intellectual debate for some time. Keynes had prepared papers
before the World Economic Conference in 1933 that foreshadowed an institution
with such a role. Before formal Anglo-American negotiations had begun, White
had proposed an International Stabilization Fund for submission to an Inter-
American Conference.[31] These proposals converged on a central and overriding
goal that distinguished both the American and the British sides in the negotiations
from their predecessors: international monetary arrangements must support domestic economic management. Provision of international finance was necessary to
ward off the threat of another depression brought about by synchronized deflation.
Featured prominently among the purposes of the new International Monetary

[31] Mikesell, *The Bretton Woods Debates*, 6.

Fund were the facilitation of international trade in order to maintain "high levels of employment and real income" and "the development of the productive resources of all members as primary objectives of economic policy."[32]

Anglo-American agreement on an intergovernmental institution was coupled with an equally striking acceptance that internationally agreed-upon rules would govern exchange rates for member states, and that gold would continue to play a role in the new system. These issues were of central concern to the Americans, particularly White, who seemed to assign greater weight to the risk of further competitive depreciation than did Keynes and, given the enormous American gold holdings, was far more content to have gold retain a place in the new design. Early versions of the White plan assigned extraordinary powers of national oversight to the proposed International Stabilization Fund, powers that were quickly reduced in interagency discussions within the United States government.[33] Despite explicit exchange-rate rules, however, several features set the system apart from the gold standard.

As Bernstein argued, the International Monetary Fund was not unique in its provision of reserve credits to governments. In an ad hoc fashion, central banks offered such assistance in the past. Rather, the novelty of the Fund lay in "the concept of a system of fixed but adjustable par values without the rigidity of the gold standard."[34] British hostility toward any monetary order based on the pre-Depression gold standard meant that the new regime had to incorporate greater flexibility in the international constraints that it imposed on member governments. As Albert Giovannini points out, this architecture of fixed but adjustable pegs indicates that the rules of the system were not designed to provide a backing for "credible monetary commitments" in the manner of the pre-1914 gold standard.[35] The degree of national policy autonomy was substantially greater in the new system, as the British had demanded.[36] A generous transition period before current-account convertibility was required (much longer, it proved, than originally envisaged) and a willingness to accept capital controls added further to the policy discretion of governments.

Most important, rules under this regime of relatively fixed parities were constructed by governments, for governments. The architects of the Fund had structured its organizational incentives to bias governments, whatever their current external position, toward responding more gently than other financial actors to the predicaments of other governments. Today's creditor might be tomorrow's suppli-

[32] Articles of Agreement of the International Monetary Fund, Article I.

[33] Mikesell, *The Bretton Woods Debates*, 7–8.

[34] Black, *A Levite Among the Priests*, 107.

[35] A. Giovannini, "Bretton Woods and Its Precursors: Rules versus Discretion in the History of International Monetary Regimes," in M. D. Bordo and B. Eichengreen, eds., *A Retrospective on the Bretton Woods System* (Chicago: University of Chicago Press, 1993), 123.

[36] R. G. Hawtrey disputed this view of the Bretton Woods framework, pointing out that an international agreement was potentially far more binding than the domestic legislation on which the gold standard had been based. R. G. Hawtrey, *Bretton Woods for Better or Worse* (London: Green, 1946), 41.

cant. As Peter Kenen has suggested, the model of the Fund as a credit union introduced an element of potential symmetry over time, whatever the conflict between likely surplus and likely deficit countries. The transnational network of central bankers and their private financial allies that had been at the center of the gold standard had been weakened during the Great Depression and World War II. Central banks had become subordinate agents of governments, and cross-border capital flows, a potential constraint on government policy, had fallen sharply.

Despite a broad consensus between the British and the Americans on the shape of a new international monetary order, disagreement persisted over points that broadly reflected the two countries' prospective postwar roles as creditor and debtor. Keynes, in particular, adamantly resisted intrusion by the new organization in national economic policy. He viewed the new institution as an essentially passive dispenser of large-scale credits, governed by rules that prevented substantial discretionary intervention or oversight. Keynes consistently favored a technocratic model of the Fund, not a "political" model; he pressed for a Fund that would award to national monetary authorities alone "the right of initiative." The United States, on the other hand, was more favorable to greater powers of national supervision for the new institution, as it became clear that the United States was unlikely to approach the Fund for resources.[37] White's plan was "explicit and rigid with regard to exchange-rate stability and the elimination of exchange restrictions and discriminatory payments practices. . . ."[38] The British, on the other hand, favored greater freedom to make unilateral changes in exchange rates and a longer transition period before the elimination of restrictive and discriminatory practices.[39]

A final Anglo-American divide over the new monetary institution became public at the first meeting of the Board of Governors and Executive Directors of the IMF and the World Bank at Savannah in March 1946. The proximate causes of conflict were two: the location of the new institutions and the status of their Executive Directors as full-time employees with relatively high salaries. These issues reflected fundamentally different views of the organization in formation, however. The United States delegation wanted an IMF responsive to the direction of national governments. The organization's system of weighted voting meant that its policies and programs would reflect the preferences of its most influential principal, the United States. Keynes, on the other hand, continued to back a more technocratic future for the Fund, one in which the role of national representatives would be reduced in favor of international civil servants. An organization based in New York with part-time Executive Directors was more likely to satisfy this vision of the Fund.[40] The British ultimately lost this bitter debate, but the future IMF combined

[37] Van Dormael, *Bretton Woods*, 102–3, 108, 111–12.

[38] Mikesell, *The Bretton Woods Debates*, 12.

[39] A. Cairncross, "A British Perspective on Bretton Woods," in Orin Kirshner, ed., *The Bretton Woods-GATT System: Retrospect and Prospect after Fifty Years* (Armonk, N.Y.: M. E. Sharpe, 1996), 73–74.

[40] Cairncross, "A British Perspective," 76; Mikesell, *The Bretton Woods Debates*, 52–53.

elements of both models: substantial delegation to the Managing Director and staff under the watchful eye of the major national governments.

Ratifying Bretton Woods

The Bretton Woods conference itself was something of an anticlimax following the often spirited negotiations between the British and the Americans that had occurred over several years; as Bernstein notes, "most of the drama came before the conference. . . ."[41] Conflicts arose at the conference over respective national quotas (and their corollary of voting rights); a decision to move expeditiously toward effective consensus decision-making was one that persisted in the International Monetary Fund after its formation.[42]

More significant than the conference was the process of ratification—winning domestic political approval for the new agreements on either side of the Atlantic. Although the Anglo-American negotiations and the Bretton Woods conference have received close attention from historians, ratification has too often been taken for granted. Final approval of the agreements by lopsided margins in the United States Congress and the British Parliament disguised deeper lines of political division in the preceding ratification debates. Those divisions provide important evidence of the institutional preferences of politically mobilized groups. Anticipated reactions of Congress and key domestic interest groups also shaped Anglo-American discussions from an early stage and forced the Roosevelt Administration and the British government to accommodate opposition that was likely to appear during ratification.

At an early stage in the negotiations with the British (October 1942), Adolph Berle made clear to Keynes and the British delegation that two considerations would influence any plan agreed: "first, would Congress accept it; second, would it fit the financial policies of the Administration."[43] The United States negotiators were often willing to use the threat of Congressional disapproval to win their way—a ploy that angered Keynes (and many later negotiating partners of the United States). Harry Dexter White described himself at one point as "a middleman between two sovereign powers, the American Congress on the one hand and the British Cabinet on the other."[44]

On several key points of institutional design, the Administration's reading of Congressional preferences was crucial. British proposals for an organization that would offer large-scale finance for balance-of-payments adjustment were whittled down by the Americans to meet the Congressional hurdle: Congress was unwilling to become the banker to the world. The supranational powers invested in the orga-

[41]   Black, *A Levite among the Priests*, 45.
[42]   Van Dormael, *Bretton Woods*, 17–18.
[43]   Blum, *From the Morgenthau Diaries, III*, 236.
[44]   R. Harrod, *The Life of John Maynard Keynes* (New York: W. W. Norton, 1951), 560.

nization in early versions of both the British and the American plans, particularly the ability to set exchange rates and compel countries to change them, was, according to some observers, diluted for reasons of Congressional wariness regarding American autonomy.[45] The Roosevelt Administration portrayed the location of the new institutions in the United States and in Washington, D.C., as a *sine qua non* of Congressional support for the Bretton Woods Agreements.[46] The cycle of Congressional elections even influenced the speed with which the Bretton Woods conference was scheduled. A Republican majority in the House of Representatives was a clear possibility in the wake of Congressional elections in November 1944. A Republican Congress was likely to defeat any international monetary proposals that were solely the product of the Roosevelt Administration. An international agreement was viewed as more resistant to Republican hostility.[47] Jacobsson recounted that one American observer even believed that Congress would favor the creation of two international financial institutions rather than one for the best Madisonian reasons—"the peculiar American hope that the Bank and the Fund could watch each other!"[48]

The administration won Congressional approval for the new monetary arrangements through careful incorporation of Congressional representatives in the negotiating process and by mobilization of grassroots political groups through a campaign mounted by the United States Treasury Department. The administration encouraged informal Congressional involvement during the sensitive Anglo-American discussions. Congressional representatives also participated as members of the American delegation to the Bretton Woods conference.[49] Working more powerfully in the Administration's favor was a political reality that Keynes shrewdly noted: for most Congressmen, the electoral connection was much stronger in trade than it was for international monetary affairs.[50] As Helen Milner suggests, the eventual fate of the International Trade Organization demonstrated this difference between political preferences over trade liberalization and attitudes toward international monetary cooperation.[51]

Nevertheless, the Republicans mobilized against the International Monetary Fund with the support of a once-powerful domestic interest group: the financial conservatives of Wall Street, led by the American Bankers Association and their quasi-official spokesman, the Federal Reserve Bank of New York. Some of the New York financial establishment favored a large loan to Britain and an agreement to stabilize the dollar-sterling exchange rate. Others argued for a return to the pre-De-

---

[45] L. Rasminsky in A. L. K. Acheson, J. F. Chant, and M. F. J. Prachowny, eds., *Bretton Woods Revisited* (Toronto: University of Toronto Press, 1972), 36.

[46] Van Dormael, *Bretton Woods*, 207–11.

[47] Blum, *From the Morgenthau Diaries*, III, 246.

[48] Jacobsson, *A Life*, 183.

[49] Blum, *From the Morgenthau Diaries*, III, 240, 248.

[50] D. Moggridge, ed., *The Collected Writings of John Maynard Keynes*, vol. 25 (Cambridge: Cambridge University Press, 1980), 445.

[51] Milner, *Interests, Institutions, and Information*, 147–48.

pression gold standard.[52] Similar skepticism emerged in the London financial sector: a majority of the Bank of England's Board of Directors opposed the postwar monetary plans in early 1944. They feared for the future of sterling and the London financial markets in a world dominated by multilateralism and the dollar.[53]

The Treasury Department met opposition from the internationally oriented New York banks with an unprecedented public-relations campaign in favor of the agreements, one that was carefully distanced from the Treasury and its New Deal image.[54] The campaign mobilized two important constituencies: the American peace movement and the major American export industries. For the first, Bretton Woods was equated with world peace; for the second, it was interpreted as the key to ending discriminatory foreign-exchange arrangements and currency instability. As Raymond Mikesell, a participant in the campaign, recalls: "Virtually every speech touted stable monetary conditions and exchange rates as defenses against future dictators and World War III. International monetary cooperation would somehow guarantee world peace."[55] Managers of the agreements in Congress shrewdly attached the legislation to other, more popular recommendations in international economic policy, such as new lending authorization for the Export-Import Bank. Nevertheless, the Roosevelt Administration was willing to make a number of concessions in an effort to win the approval of Wall Street and its Republican allies: terminating the President's authority to change the gold content of the dollar; requiring Congressional approval of any change in the par value of the dollar; and, in the United States quota, establishing the National Advisory Council on International Monetary and Financial Policy.[56] The ABA insisted as conditions for its support that one person serve as the Executive Director for both organizations, that a board be appointed to advise on the operations of the two institutions, and that Congress lay down explicit guidance for the American representatives. For some officers of the New York Federal Reserve Bank, even these concessions were not adequate.[57]

The administration's effort to placate the big banks finally failed: the ABA was willing to support the World Bank but not the International Monetary Fund. Ironically, in light of latter-day left-wing criticism of the IMF, the Wall Street financial establishment viewed the World Bank in its early years as the respectable, gilt-edged institution (representatives of Wall Street have typically been chosen as its president); the IMF was "feared as a hotbed of left-wing activism."[58] The opposition of Wall Street ultimately could not defeat ratification, however. Congressional opponents in the final votes were reduced to hard-core isolationists; the alliance of Main Street and Wall Street had never been an easy one within the Republican

---

[52] Mikesell, *The Bretton Woods Debates*, 43–44.

[53] Cairncross, "A British Perspective," 74.

[54] Van Dormael, *Bretton Woods*, 246.

[55] Mikesell, *The Bretton Woods Debates*, 44–46.

[56] Black, *A Levite among the Priests*, 50.

[57] Blum, *From the Morgenthau Diaries, III*, 432–33.

[58] R. Chernow, *The House of Morgan* (New York: Simon & Schuster, 1990), 518.

Party. Small banks, oriented toward domestic lending and represented by the Independent Bankers Association, endorsed the Agreements. The American financial sector, segmented by state and federal regulation, was divided in its political stance on a key international policy issue.[59] The opposition of high finance also brought some unexpected support to the Agreements. The residue of the silver bloc in the Senate threw its populist weight behind a plan that continued to incorporate gold. As one Senator put it, "I am against all god-damned New York bankers!"[60]

In Britain, the ratification battle threatened to be more closely fought. Although financial interests in the City carried no more political weight than they did in the United States, the wartime coalition that had negotiated the Bretton Woods agreement had broken down when the Bretton Woods bill was finally brought before Parliament in December 1945. As a matter of strategy, the Labour Government chose to link the Bretton Woods agreement to the more urgent approval of the American loan agreements and to more controversial American proposals on trade. Since the Labour Party enjoyed a large majority in the House of Commons, approval there was guaranteed, despite some vocal left-wing opposition from the backbenches. Labour did not have a majority in the House of Lords, however, and that body posed a greater threat. Although opposition from the City was muted by the financial sector's support for the American loan, a more politically potent, partisan, and vociferous opposition came from Conservative supporters of the sterling bloc and imperial preferences in trade—a pro-imperial and anti-multilateral lobby that had no precise analogue in the United States. Despite this powerful right-wing opposition, final favorable majorities in the Lords were large: opponents and skeptics chose to abstain with few exceptions.[61]

Explaining Bretton Woods

Bretton Woods represented a striking innovation in international monetary governance, a departure on each of the dimensions of institutional variations described earlier: a legalized, multilateral arrangement among contracting governments that was not dependent on the transnational network of central banks and private finance for its operation. Remarkably, the world's two leading financial powers, countries with substantial investments in alternative institutional designs, negotiated the new international monetary arrangements.

Functionalism combined with a misreading of inter-war history explains some of the institutional choices made at Bretton Woods. Both British and American negotiators were concerned with maximizing policy autonomy while constraining that autonomy on one dimension—exchange-rate management. Despite weak evidence that tit-for-tat depreciations were common in the 1930s, the architects of

[59] Van Dormael, *Bretton Woods*, 245.
[60] Blum, *From the Morgenthau Diaries, III*, 435.
[61] Cairncross, "A British Perspective," 77–78.

Bretton Woods interpreted recent history as a collaboration problem.[62] In their view, threats of national defection from agreed-upon exchange rates and a cycle of competitive depreciation required institutional restraints in the form of legalization: precise obligations and delegation to an organization with capabilities to monitor and sanction.

A functionalist account combined with another misreading of the international economy also explains why the great powers of international finance moved beyond the relatively successful bargaining model of the Tripartite Agreement and created a multilateral agreement with wider membership. Multilateralism appears, on the basis of fragmentary evidence, to have served two purposes. First, White seems to have overestimated the economic weight of the smaller countries in the postwar economy. He argued in one of his early memoranda that rounds of depreciation among smaller economies would affect the larger countries if they were not restrained by an international institution.[63] Even if the IMF were based on a minilateral core of great-power collaboration (the shape that it eventually assumed), other smaller powers could not be permitted to free ride. Multilateralism also provided a foreign policy benefit as a convenient veil for American economic predominance; delegation to the IMF relieved the United States of conflict in a number of bilateral financial relationships.

Sectoral explanations for the preferences of Britain and the United States encounter two serious anomalies in the Bretton Woods innovations. First, economic interests that awarded priority to national policy autonomy were ascendant during the 1930s. Closure and controls had weakened financial internationalists; their institutional representatives, the central banks, had been subjected to direct control by national governments. Economic interests that had been suspicious of the gold standard accommodated themselves to a fixed-rate regime under Bretton Woods. Indeed, on the American side (but not the British), they provided core support for its ratification. This apparent about-face could be explained in two ways. The disintegration of international capital markets and widespread imposition of capital controls (accepted at Bretton Woods) had reduced the trade-off between national policy autonomy and stable exchange rates (but those conditions had existed since the early 1930s). The war may also have internationalized sectors of the American economy, transforming their definition of economic interests in the face of a world economy devastated by conflict and demanding American exports.

A second anomaly centers on the behavior of the weakened financial internationalists. Wall Street bankers and the New York Federal Reserve were at the core of opposition to the IMF; the Bank of England was equally skeptical. Stability of exchange rates was not the key dimension of cleavage over the new institutions. The axis of conflict was not fixed versus flexible exchange rates but *whose* system of fixed

---

[62] On the pattern of exchange rate depreciation in the 1930s: B. Eichengreen and J. Sachs, "Exchange Rates and Economic Recovery in the 1930s," *Journal of Economic History* 95, no. 4 (1985): 925–46; Simmons, *Who Adjusts?*

[63] Blum, *From the Morgenthau Diaries, III*, 254

exchange rates: one managed by central bankers and their collaborators in the world of private finance or one managed by the Treasuries of member governments. Defining the principals in the new system was a central issue in the Roosevelt Administration's negotiations with the New York Federal Reserve and the American Bankers Association. The demands of the New York financial establishment all pointed in the same direction—curbing the ability of the executive to act autonomously in exchange-rate and monetary policy and inserting the representatives of private finance into the oversight of policy.

Other internationalist business sectors behaved more predictably. Export sectors in manufacturing were courted successfully by the Roosevelt Administration: their influence over international monetary policy-making had been limited under the gold standard. For exporters, the prospective gains from stable exchange rates and an end to foreign-exchange restrictions that distorted trade were greater than any loss in influence under the new intergovernmental regime. As Milner describes, the failure of export interests to support the ITO was fatal to that organization's ratification. Their support for the IMF and the World Bank contributed to the ratification of the Bretton Woods agreements.

Sectoral preferences cannot provide a complete explanation for the institutions constructed at Bretton Woods, however. Economic internationalists were divided on the new monetary arrangements; surprisingly, those who had formerly endorsed economic nationalism and opposed the gold standard became a core constituency for the new order. The political record of the 1920s and 1930s suggests a more complete domestic explanation for the institutional outcome at Bretton Woods: the new monetary institutions solved the international policy dilemmas of left-wing, labor-based coalitions. Organized labor was a core constituent of the New Deal coalition. Although Winston Churchill, a Conservative, headed the British wartime coalition government, policy moved in the direction of its Labour partners. Labour's overwhelming victory in the 1945 parliamentary elections confirmed that trend. Governments based on such coalitions had been liberal cooperators on trade issues before World War II and equally predictable defectors from the monetary rules of the gold standard under conditions of high unemployment.[64] The Bretton Woods monetary institutions enabled labor-based coalitions, intent on domestic economic policies directed to full employment, to cooperate successfully in the interests of exchange-rate stability. Capital controls, adjustable pegs, and the provision of finance were key elements in the institutional mix for these coalitions. Never before (or since) had two labor-based coalitions achieved such a dominant political position in the world's two leading financial powers. Much of the institutional design of Bretton Woods (and the International Trade Organization) reflected that particular political moment. Had different political coalitions attained power on either side of the Atlantic, the postwar monetary accord would have had a very different outline.

Domestic political institutions served to amplify coalition preferences over monetary institutions. In neither case (despite the Roosevelt Administration's fears),

---

[64] Simmons, *Who Adjusts?*

did the executives in the United States or Britain contend with divided government, with the limited exception of the British House of Lords. Helen Milner emphasizes the importance of divided government in dooming the ITO after the Congressional elections of 1946. The failure of the United States to ratify the Versailles Treaty had weighed heavily on the Roosevelt administration. Ratification was far less troublesome for these new international institutions because of the administration's successful efforts to engage Congress and mobilize public support.

One final institutional feature of the accords was particularly significant. Roosevelt had chosen the Treasury as the lead agency in negotiations for a new international monetary order. In part, Roosevelt followed his standard strategy of pitting agencies against one another; in part, his choice reflected a view that the State Department, involved in international lending during the 1920s, was too closely associated with Wall Street. Under the ambitious leadership of Henry Morgenthau, the U.S. Treasury took its assignment and made the most of it. The Bretton Woods model, not surprisingly, was based on cooperation among the Treasuries of the United Nations, as Morgenthau had prescribed at an early stage. Central banks and their private banking allies were nowhere to be found. As the British Treasury representative in Washington told Jacobsson after the Savannah conference, ". . . the words 'central banks or monetary authorities' were never once mentioned at Savannah. As if these did not exist."[65] Throughout the Bretton Woods negotiations and the Savannah conference, the governmental character of the new monetary order was emphasized, a reflection in part of "New Deal suspicion of the private commercial banker . . . intent on keeping not merely the control but the day-to-day organization of the International Monetary Fund in the hands of governmental representatives."[66] Links between the monetary regime and member societies would be through agencies of elected governments not through transnational networks of central banks and their allies in the private financial sector.

Explaining International Institutional Choice

A decade after the ratification of the Bretton Woods agreements, the international economic order resembled the predictions of its opponents more closely than the hopes of its supporters. The transition to a new monetary order was long, and its lifetime was short. Nevertheless, liberal norms expressed in Article I of the Articles of Agreement remained significant. However circuitous the journey to a new monetary system would be, the destination was clear—removal of exchange controls, international oversight of exchange-rate policies, and financial assistance for needed adjustment. The new institutions were also grounded in a broad political consensus within the industrialized countries. Despite later opposition from the left, a combination of economic openness and active domestic economic manage-

[65] Jacobsson, *A Life*, 184.
[66] Van Dormael, *Bretton Woods*, 302.

ment had finally convinced much of organized labor to support the new rules of the game.

The survival of the International Monetary Fund suggests that the original design for international monetary cooperation, only dependent in part on an exchange-rate regime, was robust. Despite shifting political conditions and a changing international economy, the International Monetary Fund has remained a core international economic institution. Although its initial institutional dimensions reflected a particular reading of the requirements of international monetary order and were based on transient domestic political coalitions, governments continue to endorse the need for a multilateral, intergovernmental monetary institution.

At the same time, an evolutionary view of institutional choice highlights the persistence of institutional competitors to Bretton Woods. Although the alternatives change over time, institutional competition remains. Per Jacobsson, of "sound money" and central bank cooperation, later became Managing Director of the International Monetary Fund, where he contested a revival of great-power discretionary bargaining outside the Fund in the form of the Group of Ten. The temptation of great-power collaboration outside the IMF reemerged in the 1970s as a substitute for the legalized and multilateral Bretton Woods order. Global exchange-rate management—to the degree that it occurs—now takes place sporadically among the G-7.

As growing financial integration threatened dangerous spillovers in domestic financial systems, central banks took charge of coordinating regulatory policies. Divorced from the gold standard, central bank cooperation now appears essential to financial stability in an era of international capital mobility. The rise and decline of these institutional models continues to affect the course of cooperation in international monetary affairs. Their history suggests explanations for institutional variation in other issue-areas as well as lessons for the design of new institutions that will sustain international collaboration.

CHAPTER FOUR

Toward a Broader Public-Choice Analysis of the International Monetary Fund

Thomas D. Willett

The operations of the Bretton Woods twins—the International Monetary Fund and World Bank—have come under increasing public scrutiny in recent years. Indeed, criticisms from the far left and the far right have become so vehement that in 1999, the U.S. Congress almost failed to pass legislation to provide the U.S. share of an internationally agreed increase in IMF funding. In the spring of 2000, organizations that had protested against the World Trade Organization in Seattle turned their attention to Washington, D.C., and attempted to shut down the high-level meetings of the IMF's and World Bank's international oversight committees. And in fall 2001, the IMF first planned to condense the schedule of its annual meetings before finally canceling them altogether in the wake of the disasters at the World Trade Center and the Pentagon.

One common feature of most of the harshest critics from both the left and the right is a strong sense of certainty that how these international financial institutions operate is well understood. It has apparently given these critics little pause that the agreement between the left and the right that the international financial institutions are bad arises only because these two camps hold diametrically opposed views of what these institutions actually do. The left sees the international financial institutions as instruments of global capitalism, forcing excessively harsh austerity on poor nations, whereas the right sees them as examples of bureaucratic inefficiency that help bolster global socialism by providing funds to national governments and thus helping them to postpone necessary economic reforms.

Earlier versions of this chapter were presented at seminars and workshops at Duke University, the Fletcher School of Law and Diplomacy, Princeton University, the University of Southern California, and the University of Toronto. Especially helpful comments and suggestions have been offered by David Andrews, Graham Bird, Martin Edwards, Erica Gould, Lou Pauly, Bob Tollison, James Vreeland, Clas Wihlborg and several economists at the IMF who should perhaps best remain anonymous.

As one turns to scholarly writing, the situation is only a little better. Many authors seem anxious to jump as quickly as possible to policy conclusions and generally take as given some particular assumption about the behavior of the international financial institutions, often bolstered by an example or two. However, while such papers typically consider only one or two behavioral patterns, across these analyses a substantial range of different assumptions about the positive political economy of the international financial institutions can be found. Often the international financial institutions are depicted as being dominated by virtually autonomous international bureaucrats with little or no effective oversight. Alternatively, many in Europe, Japan, and the developing world view the international financial institutions as lackeys of U.S. foreign policy with little independence of their own. A third common view sees the international financial institutions as captured by the rent-seeking activities of the major private financial institutions. Marxists, of course, see these second and third assumptions as equivalent, with big capital running both U.S. foreign policy and the international financial institutions. Moreover, there are still those who assume that the international financial institutions operate primarily according to their concepts of the global public interest. Indeed this view is implicit in many, if not most, discussions by professional economists of international monetary issues.

Clearly, this wide range of views signals the need for better positive political-economy research. However, the number of studies which attempt to carefully develop and/or test hypothesis about the behavior of international financial institutions is distressing small, especially in contrast to the large literature which attempts to evaluate the effectiveness of their specific programs and policies.[1]

This chapter has the dual purposes of calling attention to this important lacuna in international political-economy research and suggesting directions for how this gap might be filled. I argue that adopting a public-choice approach is likely to be fruitful. However, it is important that students and scholars interested in international political economy understand that public choice does not present a specific model of political economy but rather an approach consistent with a whole set of

---

[1] Exceptions include important work by Graham Bird, Tony Killick, and Roland Vaubel. Very recently there has been a substantial increase in quantitative political-economy research on the IMF by political scientists. See, for example, M. Edwards, "Sticking with Yes: Domestic Institutions and IMF Compliance" (paper presented at annual meeting of the American Political Science Association, San Francisco, 2001); E. Gould, "Money Talks: The Role of External Finance in Influencing International Monetary Fund Conditionality" (paper presented at annual meeting of the American Political Science Association, San Francisco, 2001); D. Kapur, "Risk and Reward: Agency, Contracts, and the Expansion of IMF Conditionality" (paper prepared for workshop on the Political Economy of International Monetary and Financial Institutions, Harvard University, October 2000); L. Martin, "Agency and Delegation in IMF Conditionality" (paper prepared for workshop on the Political Economy of International Monetary and Financial Institutions, October 2000); R. Stone, "Lending Credibility: The IMF and the Post-Communist Transition" (paper presented at annual meeting of the American Political Science Association, Washington, 2000); S. Thacker, "The High Politics of IMF Lending," *World Politics* 52, no. 1 (1999): 38–77; J. Vreeland, "Institutional Determinants of IMF Agreements" (paper presented at annual meeting of the American Political Science Association, San Francisco, 2001).

models. For example, some public-choice theories emphasize the role of the public through median voter models, whereas others emphasize the role of special interests and rent-seeking. Recognizing that public choice offers a broad framework suggests that it provides a convenient way to synthesize the various considerations emphasized in popular single-factor explanations of problems in international political economy.

To date, however, there has been relatively little explicit public-choice analysis of the IMF, and the best known of these—by Roland Vaubel—takes a very narrow focus that emphasizes the role of bureaucratic incentives for budget maximization. Here I seek to illustrate how public-choice analysis can be used in a much broader way to take multiple considerations into account. I also emphasize the need for including within the tool kits available to public-choice and political-economy analysts a "softer" set of assumptions about the motives of senior international bureaucrats. Finally, the approach offered here emphasizes the need to consider not only the multiple sources of external pressures on the IMF but also to begin to disaggregate analysis of the IMF itself, at least to the point of distinguishing between the different motivations and relative power of IMF management and staff.

In short, I highlight the advantages of a public-choice approach that is both broader and softer than the hard-core budget-maximization analysis offered by Vaubel and others. The chapter begins with a brief overview of the traditional major political-economy perspectives and how they tend to view the IMF. I then sketch out key elements of the broader public-choice approach as a synthesizing framework and provide illustrations of how this approach can be applied to the issue of possible biases in IMF lending. Furthermore, I argue that bureaucratic incentives for budget maximization play much less of a role at the IMF than in the typical domestic government bureau, but that there are other possible, if softer, sources of bias that are of serious concern as well.

The remaining sections discuss the growth of conditionality, the issue of ownership of IMF programs, and the need for more political-economy analysis at the IMF, before concluding with some general remarks on the policy implications of the analysis. I argue that while many needed reforms will be difficult to achieve, a broader public-choice approach offers a less pessimistic perspective on these possibilities than does the traditional public-choice literature.

Major Political-Economy Perspectives on the IMF

Mainstream economists have traditionally adopted an optimal-policy approach, in which the range of activities a government or organization should undertake and the specifics of the policies it should pursue are analyzed from the standpoint of economic optimization and market-failure theory. This approach assumes a public-interest-based institution that analyzes the need to provide public goods, correct externalities, and compensate for missing or misperforming markets.

While most mainstream economists regard the number of market failures requiring government action as fairly limited, many on the left see massive market failure. Combined with a public-interest view of government, this leads to criticism of the IMF for being insufficiently activist. In contrast to these idealistic approaches, some conspiracy theorists from the left see the Fund as an agent of the global capitalist class, serving special financial interests at the expense of the poor of the world. They typically look upon the Fund as doing actual harm and see massive market failure and the need for major income redistribution from the rich to the poor; thus they advocate radical reform of the IMF.[2]

From the right, applications of hard-core public-choice analysis also conclude that the IMF does harm but for quite different reasons. This approach tends to assume perfect markets, rent-seeking bureaucrats, and powerful special-interest groups. From this perspective the Fund is unnecessary (except as a welfare agency for economists) and should be abolished altogether.[3]

These different traditions have correspondingly different views on the effectiveness of institutions and organizations. The optimal-policy approach assumes an autonomous government that effectively implements policy. Critiques from the left tend to see the IMF as all powerful from the standpoint of imposing its will on poor countries but as very weak from the standpoint of resisting pressures from capitalists' special interests. Hard-core public-choice analysis from the right typically sees the Fund as having a great deal of autonomy from political oversight but (at least in some versions) as subject to considerable pressure from special-interest groups, typically the financial sector and/or U.S. policy officials. Thus while the IMF is viewed by some critics as autocratic and undemocratic, others see it as a lackey of U.S. foreign policy. And while the idealist tradition in the international-relations literature sees international organizations as powerful mechanisms for promoting the public good, realists see them as having little effect.[4]

No wonder, then, that there is widespread disagreement among commentators about the effectiveness of IMF programs. But what does the scientific literature suggest? Although popular criticisms from the left fault IMF policy conditionality for its excessive harshness, most systematic studies find that the ability of the IMF to enforce its conditionality has been quite weak.[5] Thus it has become common-

---

[2] See, for example, K. Danaher, *50 Years Is Enough: The Case against the World Bank and the International Monetary Fund* (Boston: South End Press, 1994).

[3] See, for example, D. Bandow and I. Vasquez, eds., *Perpetuating Poverty: The World Bank, the IMF, and the Developing World* (Washington: Cato Institute, 1994). Another useful collection of critiques from the right combined with defenses from the middle is presented in L. J. McQuillan, and P. C. Montgomery, eds., *The International Monetary Fund: Financial Medic to the World?* (Stanford: Hoover Institution Press, 1999).

[4] For discussion of these perspectives, see P. Dillon, J. Odell, and T. D. Willett, "Future Directions in the Political Economy of Trade Policy," in J. Odell and T. D. Willett, eds., *International Trade Policies: The Gains from Exchange between Economics and Political Science* (Ann Arbor: University of Michigan Press, 1990), 278–83. For perspectives on the recent debates see T. D. Willett, "Understanding the IMF Debate," *Independent Review* (Spring 2001): 593–610, and J. Williamson, "The Role of the IMF: A Guide to the Reports," *Institute for International Economics Policy Brief* (May 2000): 1–5.

[5] See the analysis and references in G. Bird, "The International Monetary Fund and Developing Countries: A Review of the Evidence and Policy Options," *International Organization* 50, no. 3 (1996):

place for critics on the right to argue that the typical effect of IMF programs is to delay rather than promote stabilization and liberalization, although the evidence for such strong formulations has typically been anecdotal rather than systematic.[6]

Toward a Broader Public-Choice Approach

It is still not sufficiently recognized that public-choice analysis is not a specific theory but rather an approach that contains a number of specific theories—many of which are mutually contradictory. For example, median voter theory sees the political process as dominated by the public through the voting process, whereas rent-seeking theory sees government as having considerable autonomy from the general voter but not from specified interests. Thus public-choice analysis should not be seen as one of the specific contending theories within the IPE literature but rather as the name that most economists and some other social scientists have given to political-economy analysis.[7]

It is true that the range of public-choice analysis does not encompass the full array of political-economy approaches. Public-choice analysis typically focuses on rationality, the role of self-interest and issues of collective action, and the influence of institutions; thus it tends to be skeptical both of unified rational-actor models and sociological models that privilege the group over the individual.[8] Still, the range of consideration that it can encompass is quite impressive.

Unfortunately, however, many of the most famous applications of public-choice analysis rest on very strong assumptions and contribute to the false impression that public choice is a specific narrow theory. For example, public-choice analysis of the IMF was pioneered by Roland Vaubel. His work provided a healthy correction to the optimal-policy view implicit in much of the economic literature and offered a number of useful insights into the behavior of the IMF and other international institutions. However, as will be further discussed in the following section Vaubel's analysis was based on the assumptions of great IMF autonomy and a strong organizational interest in budget maximization.[9] This turns out to be misleading in a

---

477–511; T. Killick, "Principals, Agents, and the Limitations of BWI Conditionality," *World Economy* 19, no. 2 (1996): 211–29; T. Killick with R. Gunatilaka and A. Marr, *Aid and the Political Economy of Policy Change* (New York: Routledge, 1998); and A. Krueger, "Whither the World Bank and the IMF?" *Journal of Economic Literature* 4 (1998): 1983–2020.

[6] As noted by Krueger, "Whither the World Bank and the IMF?"

[7] For a more general discussion of the public-choice approach and its relation to other major approaches to the political economy of international economic relations, see T. D. Willett, "The Public Choice Approach to International Economic Relations," Virginia Political Economy Lecture, Center for Study of Public Choice, George Mason University, 1995, and the references therein. See also the contribution by Robert Gilpin to this volume.

[8] This last point should not be taken to mean, however, that the public-choice approach is inimical to sociological considerations, as the later discussion of Bruno Frey's work makes clear.

[9] R. Vaubel, "A Public Choice Approach to International Organization," *Public Choice* 51, no. 1 (1986): 39–57; Roland Vaubel, "The Political Economy of the International Monetary Fund," in R.

number of respects, and much of the evidence offered in support of Vaubel's analysis is equally consistent with other models.[10]

My general point is that it is important to distinguish between criticisms of specific applications of the public-choice and the general approach.[11] Indeed, both the public-choice and IPE literature more generally have tended to be dominated by a variety of narrow approaches that overlook too many important aspects of the situations they analyze. While the proliferation of contending narrow approaches is understandable in terms of the incentive structures of academia, at best it suggests that we are only at the initial stage of a progressive research agenda. A disinterested look at the evidence shows that most of these specific theories have some explanatory power, and that none of them have complete explanatory power. The scholarly community needs to begin to think more systematically about the problem. A helpful start would be to introduce broader frameworks that allow various specific theories as special cases. This should be followed by analysis of the major considerations that influence the relative importance of the specific theories or factors in different situations.[12]

The approach advocated in this chapter is an example of the first of these two projects. It is a middle-of-the-road synthesis of elements of a number of different theories or approaches within the broad public-choice tradition. As such, it recognizes both market and government failure but sees neither as pervasive or necessarily dominant. It views the IMF as dominated by officials who are neither saints nor sinners; they generally seek to do good but are not entirely immune to bureaucratic incentives and external pressures. This approach sees governments as regularly facing both domestic and international pressures but also as having some scope for autonomy, the precise magnitude of which varies in systematic ways over time and across both countries and issue areas. It also recognizes the scope for bureaucratic politics and sees domestic pressures coming from both the general public and special interests.

As such, public-choice analysis stems from rational-choice theory but, unlike many of the formal-game theory applications thereof, it focuses on the costs of acquiring information, the difficulties of understanding complex situations, and the coordination and free-rider problems that occur where the number of actors involved is large. Thus it helps explain why small well-organized groups can often win politically over the interests of much larger but relatively unorganized groups. Public-choice analysis also emphasizes that even where the median voter is domi-

Vaubel and T. D. Willett, eds., *The Political Economy of International Organizations: A Public Choice Perspective* (Boulder, Colo.: Westview Press, 1991), 200–244.

[10] See T. D. Willett, "Upping the Ante for Public Choice Analysis of the International Monetary Fund," *The World Economy* 24, no. 3 (2001): 317–32.

[11] This distinction tends to be overlooked in the general attack on rational-choice theory launched by D. Green and I. Shapiro, *Pathologies of Rational Choice Theory* (New Haven: Yale University Press, 1999). See also the reactions in J. Frieden, ed., *The Rational Choice Controversy* (New Haven: Yale University Press, 1996).

[12] See Dillon, Odell, and Willett, "Future Directions in the Political Economy of Trade Policy."

nant, she may be rationally ignorant. Whereas many hard-core rational-choice modes assume that all relevant actors understand the true structures of the games they are playing, a broader public-choice perspective emphasizes informational complexities, uncertainty, and the role of ideas and differing mental models. Such considerations can help explain the pressures for political business cycles and other policies that create economic instabilities and inefficiencies.[13]

Some have viewed public-choice analysis as being inherently conservative or anti-government.[14] This is not so. Although it is true that many of the most important contributors to the development of public choice have been from the right of the political spectrum, there have been important counter examples (such as Kenneth Arrow and Mancur Olson). More generally, being realistic about the difficulties of policy implementation can only make for more effective policy. If a situation is heavily politicized, then it is folly to advocate policies that can only be implemented effectively in a politics-free environment.

Of course the broader public-choice approach has a serious shortcoming in comparison with many of the more narrow and specific political-economy approaches discussed above: it does not offer easy answers. In the first place, it is a framework rather than a specific theory. It is, in effect, a broad eclectic approach to political economy that sees value in many different ways of gaining knowledge. It sees the tracing out of the implications of a narrow set of assumptions to be quite valuable, but it is hostile to the common tendency to generalize excessively from such focused analysis. It argues that genuine testing must attempt to discriminate among alternative hypotheses, not simply to settle for evidence consistent with one's favored model. It does not offer quick, easy conclusions that apply to all situations—either with respect to diagnosis or prescription. This seeming disadvantage, however, may be its greatest virtue.

Applications to IMF Lending

As noted above, public-choice analysis of the IMF began with an important series of papers by Roland Vaubel.[15] In these, Vaubel makes the assumption—common to much of the public-choice literature—that "bureaucracies are interested in power, prestige, and amenities. To achieve these objectives, they try to maximize their budget, their staff, and their independence."[16]

However, another important contributor to the development of public-choice analysis of international organizations, Bruno Frey, makes a contrary argument. In

[13] On rational ignorance and the difficulties of processing complex information, see John Odell's contribution to this volume.

[14] See, for example, the characterization by Gilpin in this volume.

[15] Vaubel, "A Public Choice View of International Organisation"; Vaubel, "The Political Economy of the International Monetary Fund"; R. Vaubel, "Bureaucracy at the IMF and the World Bank," *World Economy* 19, no. 2 (1996): 195–210.

[16] Vaubel, "Bureaucracy at the IMF and the World Bank," 195.

his view, "the public choice literature is rather mute on the question of how employees in an international organization use the leeway accorded them,"[17] at least as a matter of principle. And in contrast to Vaubel, Frey offers the more sociologically appealing suggestion that "international bureaucrats pursue those policies that give them most prestige and influence within the reference groups with which they are connected."[18]

Frey's call for greater study of the objectives pursued within international organizations is of crucial importance. These are unlikely to be the same across all organizations and situations. Indeed they may well vary at different levels of an organization, as can the degree to which top-level managers control lower-level staff. Depending on the reasons for the observed divergence from "publicly interested" behavior, different reform strategies might be suggested. Furthermore, the prospects for effective reforms may also be affected by the reasons for the observed behavior.

To take a concrete example, there is rather widespread agreement that at least at times the IMF has suffered from tendencies for loan-pushing and insufficient enforcement of loan conditionality. Such behavior is not consistent with the saintly or public-interest view of IMF officials, but there are different ways to understand the observed behavior. In Vaubel's hard-core analysis, loan-pushing by the IMF is seen as a result of budget-maximization objectives. An alternative explanation, however, is that IMF staff's career advancement may be put at risk if they lose access to high-level national officials in the countries they monitor. Given this incentive, the ability of national officials to impede staff access may provide them with leverage to minimize IMF criticisms and thereby secure continued financing.

The problems with such perceived incentives for IMF staff are discussed in the recent IMF external review of its surveillance policies.[19] If the path to advancement is tied to never rocking the boat, then the IMF will always operate as if it were hostage to client states. The report found concerns among IMF staff "that a report that is incisive but offends the [national] authorities is damaging to a mission chief's career while one that is bland and later turns out to be lacking in some important respect will be overlooked."[20] As the report indicates, it is important that those in charge at the Fund "back up staff who give frank advice."[21] More generally, the problems associated with loan-pushing are likely to be much more amenable to correction if we understand why this behavior takes place—that is, if it is due primarily to "soft" considerations like staff-advancement incentives rather than the budget maximization objectives at the center of "hard core" analyses.

[17] Bruno Frey, "The Public Choice of International Organizations," in D. Mueller, ed., *Perspectives on Public Choice* (Cambridge: Cambridge University Press, 1997), 120.

[18] Ibid., 121.

[19] International Monetary Fund, "Conditionality in IMF-Supported Programs—Policy Issues" (paper prepared by the Policy Development and Review Department, International Monetary Fund, February 16, 2001).

[20] Ibid., 90.

[21] Ibid., 91.

As for national monetary policy, I have argued in earlier work that the budget-maximization analysis has a low degree of applicability to relatively independent central banks and suggested that a softer public-choice approach that focused more on the external pressures that affect the monetary discussion-makers would prove more fruitful.[22] This analysis was in the spirit of Chant and Acheson, who provided the first explicit public-choice analysis of the objective functions of monetary authorities.[23] Assuming that central bankers' primary goals were prestige and self-preservation, these papers helped explain a number of aspects of central-bank behavior, especially the emphasis on secrecy.

Applying such analysis to international financial institutions suggests that budget considerations should be more important at the IMF than at national central banks, but less than at the World Bank.[24] As for top IMF officials, budget maximization is likely to be a relatively low priority. An able staff is helpful for monetary officials to accomplish objectives of prestige and influence reputation with relevant peer groups, but this staff need not be a very large one. It is true that the IMF management and top bureaucrats have little incentive to hold down staff salaries, and indeed Fund officials are extremely well paid. But top IMF managers would seem to have relatively low personal incentives to expand staff size either to increase their prestige or their chances for further advancement.[25]

This example illustrates the need to distinguish more systematically between the objectives and autonomy of the Fund's staff (international civil servants) versus its management (the Managing Director and Deputy Managing Directors, who are politically appointed for specific terms) and Executive Board. Neither Martin nor Vaubel distinguish between the Fund's management and staff, but incentives and objectives can differ substantially between the two groups. For example, Vaubel's loan-pushing analysis is likely to be much more relevant for staff than management.[26]

While less cynical than some hard-core applications of public-choice theory, the "soft-core" approach I am advocating here should not be taken as the totally optimistic half brother of the public-interest/optimal-policy approach. Even assuming away greed and major character failures, there are numerous sources of bias to

---

[22] See T. D. Willett, "Studying the Fed: Towards a Broader Public Choice Perspective," in Thomas Mayer, ed., *The Political Economy of American Monetary Policy* (New York: Cambridge University Press, 1990).

[23] J. F. Chant and K. Acheson, "The Choice of Monetary Instruments and the Theory of Bureaucracy," *Public Choice* 12 (1972): 13–33; K. Acheson and J. C. Chant, "Bureaucratic Theory and the Choice of Central Bank Goals," *Journal of Money, Credit, and Banking* 5 (1973): 637–55.

[24] See Willett, "Upping the Ante for Public Choice Analysis of the International Monetary Fund."

[25] The budget maximization assumption has come under general attack in the recent literature on bureaucracy. For valuable reviews, see T. Borcherding and K. Aaiysha, "Organizing Government Supply: The Role of Bureaucracy," *Handbook of Public Finance* (New York: Marcel Dekker, 1998), 43–91; T. M. Moe, "The Positive Theory of Public Bureaucracy," in Dennis Mueller, ed., *Perspectives on Public Choice* (New York: Cambridge, 1997), 455–80; R. Wintrobe, "Modern Bureaucratic Theory," in D. Mueller, ed., *Perspectives on Public Choice* (New York: Cambridge University Press, 1997), 429–54.

[26] Martin, "Agency and Delegation in IMF Conditionality"; Vaubel, "Bureaucracy and the IMF and the World Bank."

which all but saints may be susceptible. One is that humans tend to respond to lobbying pressure. Thus if most of the "advice" that senior officials receive is from a few selective groups of national-policy officials and representatives of the financial community, it is these points of view that are likely to help shape the officials' own perceptions—neither personal threats nor bribery are required. A second powerful motivation is freedom to do one's job. Thus officials will typically prefer discretion rather than rules and prefer to minimize external monitoring of their actions. A third motivation is the fear of failure and the desire to minimize criticism.

Motives two and three–desire for freedom of action and dislike of failure or criticism–combine to yield a preference for lack of transparency in some important areas. This has been a common characteristic in national central banks as well as the Fund. Of course there are quite valid arguments why complete transparency of discussions of monetary policymaking and IMF programs is not desirable either. Certainly a balance must be found. The point made by the public-choice perspective is that, if left entirely to themselves, senior officials would likely have a human tendency to draw the line at less transparency than would the well-informed impartial spectator. Lack of transparency has indeed been a major source of criticism of the IMF, although strong public pressure from the Congress and others in recent years has induced a movement toward substantially greater transparency (a development which surely suggests the limits of the Fund's bureaucratic autonomy).

Fear of failure also suggests that government officials will in general tend to seek excessive insurance against crisis.[27] Thus we would expect the management of the Fund to prefer to err on the side of quota increases and IMF packages that were too large rather than too small. This would also tend to bias Fund officials against pulling the plug on programs quickly enough when compliance has been unsatisfactory and to agree to initiate programs even though the odds for success are not high.[28] Here the early experiences of the new Bush administration are instructive. The new Secretary of the Treasury, Paul O'Neill, strongly signaled the intention of the Bush administration to be much tougher on international bailouts than was the Clinton White House, yet within its first year of office the Bush team ended up supporting bailouts for both Turkey and Argentina that many international economists believed did not meet the IMF's normal standards.

Neither of these instances demonstrated that the principals—the major IMF shareholders—were unable to control an unwieldy bureaucracy.[29] Indeed, in the Argentine case many of the key negotiations took place in the U.S. Treasury.

---

[27] See R. C. Amacher, R. D. Tollison, and T. D. Willett, eds., *The Economic Approach to Public Policy: Selected Readings* (Ithaca: Cornell University Press, 1976).

[28] On the other hand, the Fund has demonstrated considerable willingness to pull the plug on programs, at least for countries without strong geopolitical significance. This certainly falsifies the extreme view that the Fund has made itself a helpless hostage to host countries. It also casts doubts on the strongest forms of Vaubel's loan-pushing hypothesis. Often, however, the IMF reinstates programs without sufficient evidence that policy compliance is likely to be better in the future.

[29] For examples of the principals' failure to control the Fund in terms of the broadening of conditionality criteria, see Gould, "Money Talks."

Geopolitical considerations certainly played an important role in the case of the loan to Turkey. But despite comments on the importance the Bush administration has placed on better relations with Latin America, it is hard to see this explaining the change in the administration's position with respect to Argentina.[30] Nor did the linkage of additional funding to voluntary debt restructuring provide a highly convincing explanation for the policy reversal. A much more important reason, in my judgment, was the high-stakes gamble of the Argentine government to make public its views that Argentina needed a new loan and was highly confident of getting it. Under these circumstances, a rejection by the IMF would have been highly likely to worsen the crisis, with much of the resulting blame laid at the feet of the IMF and the U.S. Treasury. Thus it is top officials' fear of blame, not loan-pushing by career bureaucrats, that best explains the recent loans to Turkey and Argentina.[31]

These examples have the common feature that, from a short-term perspective, the benefits of either implementing or continuing a program exceed the costs, but that by so doing moral hazard incentives and the likelihood of future crises are increased.[32] As any dieter knows, however, when one has operational responsibility for the short run it is very hard to focus adequately on the long term. Likewise, the same type of difficulty applies to proposals that the IMF notify the public when national officials repeatedly fail to heed its warnings. Since doing so would unleash speculative capital flows against recalcitrant governments, the mere threat of notification might encourage more responsible behavior.[33] But this policy tool is unlikely to be employed often. It is hardly realistic to expect the IMF to tilt more than modestly in this direction unless we either replace human officials with robots or make substantial changes in the incentive structures that they face.

In short, I believe that public-choice analysis of the soft motives of top IMF officials have a good deal more explanatory power than Vaubel's simple budget-maximization hypothesis with respect to IMF loan policies. But these are not the only relevant versions of public-choice analysis to be considered. Another hard-core public-choice concern adds to our understanding of the IMF's disastrous experiences with its loan to Russia in 1998.

Contrary to the loan-pushing hypothesis, numerous interviews with Fund officials suggest that the IMF was very reluctant to make this loan and did so only after considerable political pressure from the governments of the major industrial countries. This pressure, however, can easily be explained using standard public-choice analysis to focus on the incentives facing the principals rather than the agent.[34] The

---

[30] The final version of this chapter was submitted in September 2001, prior to the Argentina default and devaluation.

[31] The 1998 loan to Brazil also fits this hypothesis.

[32] On the problems of time inconsistency and short time horizons in attempting to promote external discipline, see G. Bird, "The Effectiveness of Conditionality and the Political Economy of Policy Reform," *Policy Reform* 2, no. 1 (1998): 89–113.

[33] See, for example, B. Eichengreen, *Toward a New International Financial Architecture* (Washington: Institute for International Economics, 1999).

[34] Applying the principal-agent framework to the IMF, it is typical to treat the major shareholder governments or Executive Board as principals and the Fund management and staff as agents. In one of

governments of the major industrialized countries wanted to make loans to Russia on geopolitical grounds, but they didn't want to ask their legislatures to raise funds for such aid through normal budgetary procedures (e.g., competing for tax revenues). There was little support for such assistance, aside from the financial sector, so governments would have had to use up a good deal of their political capital to pursue this objective. Far better, from the standpoint of short-term political popularity, was to channel aid to Russia on the cheap by using the IMF. The long-run cost of this strategy in terms of further damaging the credibility of the IMF was likely to be considerable, but this carried little weight in the classic "benefits now, costs later" political-incentive structure.[35]

The Growth of Conditionality

One of the most notable features of the evolution of IMF programs has been the huge increase in the average number of conditions included and the great expansion of the range of policies to which policy conditionality have been attached. This proliferation of policy conditions has attracted a great deal of criticism.[36] From public-choice and constitutional-political-autonomy perspectives, the question is not just what policy should be but who should make this determination. With respect to the IMF, this suggests the need for institutional self-restraint and careful delineation between policy advice and the terms of policy conditionality. The Fund's management, staff, and Executive Board should consider not only whether a particular policy would be good for the country in question but also whether making the adoption of that policy a formal condition for funding—instead of just being an object of recommendations—is appropriate for an international body. Thus, for example, one might believe that capital controls are bad and hence recommend against them but also believe that the negative externalities they generate are typically not sufficiently large to make their adoption subject to international sanctions.

It is doubtful that we could ever develop a set of objective criteria that could automatically answer all questions of the appropriate scope for IMF activities, but explicit discussion of the criteria for reaching judgments in the area needs much more emphasis. To its credit, the IMF has recently begun to take seriously the criticism of expanding conditionality. Shortly after the selection of a new Managing Director, Horst Köhler, the need for streaming conditionality became the IMF's official

---

the earliest applications to the IMF, however, Killick, "Principals, Agents, and the Limitations of BWI Conditionality," treated the Fund as the principal and borrowing country governments as the agents.

[35] See, for example, Willett, "Understanding the IMF Debate."

[36] See M. Feldstein, "Refocusing the IMF," *Foreign Affairs* (March 1998): 20–33; IMF, *Conditionality in IMF-Supported Programs;* H. James, *International Monetary Cooperation Since Bretton Woods* (New York: Oxford University Press, 1996); D. Kapur, "The IMF: Cure or Curse?" *Foreign Policy* (Summer 1998): 114–31; J. J. Polak, "The Changing Nature of IMF Conditionality," *Princeton Essays in International Finance* (1991).

mantra, and a substantial review of the Fund's conditionality was initiated with public comment invited.[37]

A great deal of analysis has been presented about the potential pathologies of conditionality. The recent external review of the IMF's external surveillance policies concluded that straying from its core competencies hurt the quality and credibility of Fund analysis, and that the emphasis on too many objectives diluted the effectiveness of Fund recommendations. Furthermore, there is a danger that "the proliferation of conditionality has tended to undermine government ownership, which may well be the most important determinant of program success."[38]

If expansion of conditionality is so suspect, what accounts for it? There is such a rich menu of plausible explanations that it is likely to prove quite difficult to determine their relative explanatory power.[39] But while there is now widespread agreement that for a variety of reasons IMF conditionality needs to be "streamlined," there is little agreement yet on how far this scaling-back should go or what criteria should be employed. A recent paper by Martin Feldstein makes an important start, however.

Feldstein argues that "the legitimate political institutions of the country should determine the nation's economic structure and the nature of its institutions. . . . The IMF should provide the technical advice and the limited financial assistance necessary to deal with a funding crisis and to place a country in a situation that makes a relapse unlikely. It should not use the opportunity to impose other economic changes, however helpful. . . ."[40] These objectives, he suggests, lead to three criteria for evaluating potential IMF programs of policy conditionality, namely:

(1) Is this reform really needed to restore the country's access to international financial markets?

(2) Is this a technical matter that does not interfere unnecessarily with the proper jurisdiction of a sovereign government?

(3) If the policies to be changed are also practiced in the major industrial economies of Europe, would the IMF think it appropriate to force similar changes in those countries if they were subject to a Fund program?[41]

Feldstein argues that the actions should be taken only if all three criteria are met. Although this analysis is a fruitful starting point, the issues raised require considerable further study. In many cases, reasonable people may differ about the answers to Feldstein's questions with respect to specific policy areas. Whether financial-sec-

[37] See IMF, *Conditionality in IMF-Supported Programs*.

[38] Killick, "Principals, Agents, and the Limitations of BWI Conditionality," 218.

[39] For recent discussions of explanations for the expansion in IMF conditionality see Gould, "Money Talks"; IMF, *Conditionality in IMF-Supported Programs;* Kapur, "Risk and Reward: Agency, Contracts, and the Expansion of IMF Conditionality"; Martin, "Agency and Delegation in IMF Conditionality."

[40] Feldstein, "Refocusing the IMF," 27.

[41] Ibid., 2.

tor reforms meet Feldstein's three criteria is a case in point. Another example is the degree of specificity of fiscal-policy changes. The original conception of IMF policy was that the Fund should determine the maximum allowable size of the budget deficit and leave it up to the country to determine the mix of revenue increases and spending cuts necessary to achieve this objective. Over time, however, IMF condi-tionality has expanded to include in many cases details of how deficit reductions should be brought about. This would appear to violate the Feldstein criteria and may in some cases have been due to factors that violate the spirit of Feldstein's approach. But some degree of specificity may be necessary for effective implementation. Given the history of overly optimistic projections of stabilization programs by national governments and the substantial degree of slippage in the IMF's ability to enforce policy conditionality, IMF officials should be confident that a government has a rea-sonable strategy for implementing its plans before a program is approved. Proposals for unspecified budget savings seldom carry much credibility. Thus the IMF does have a legitimate interest in more than just the projected bottom line of the budget.

Feldstein's analysis implicitly assumes that the IMF is dealing with a country that is a unitary actor. Public-choice analysis stresses that although this is useful for some purposes, in many cases the unitary actor assumption leads to seriously faulty analy-sis. Furthermore, even if this simplifying assumption is retained we are left with a somewhat paradoxical situation: if the "good" government is sufficiently strong rel-ative to various "bad" short-run political pressures, there is likely to be little need for IMF programs, whereas if the government is extremely weak, IMF programs are likely to do little good. Between these two extremes, however, are cases in which the IMF and a national government with "good" intentions can form a benign coalition that seeks to counter the operation of domestic political biases.

In some cases IMF programs may provide the leverage to tip the balance of do-mestic political forces in the direction of stabilization and reform. When the as-sumption of benign intentions on the part of the client government is relaxed, how-ever, then the analysis can become quite complex. The Fund may become subject to "inappropriate" pressures, thereby involving management and staff in numerous multiple-level games involving both the Fund's owners and its clients. On top of this, in the absence of "ideal" internal institutional structures, particular actors within the Fund and national governments may face private incentives that differ from "the public interest" (consider Mr. Suharto in this regard), which may lead to further complexities.

For example, there is a widespread perception in South Korea that Japan and the United States took advantage of Korean weakness during the Asian financial crisis of 1997–98 to use the IMF as a lever to force liberalization in areas that were unre-lated to either the causes of or the solutions to the crisis. Such behavior from major powers is just what would be expected from realist analysis and fits as well with public-choice analysis of governments as do the agents of powerful rent-seeking economic groups. In either interpretation, such perceptions undermine the politi-cal legitimacy of Fund programs and can substantially weaken their effectiveness. Our challenge is to see if we can develop some workable, albeit imperfect, criteria for evaluating these questions. Even if no general consensus can be achieved, a focused debate about such questions should prove fruitful.

Ownership and the Need for More Political-Economy Analysis

It is now widely accepted that national "ownership" of the international financial institutions' programs is essential for their effective implementation.[42] The meaning of ownership in this context is far from clear, however, and there has been little serious grappling with this issue, perhaps because in the context of a unified-actor model the answer is straightforward. In a world of multiple actors, however, the issue of how broadly ownership needs to extend becomes quite crucial. As noted in the recent staff study on conditionality, the IMF has traditionally assumed "that the program is fundamentally the [national] authorities' own."[43] The same study recognizes, however, that if "one views conditionality as a mechanism by which the Fund uses financial leverage to induce the authorities to implement reforms they do not endorse, any expansion in conditionality implies a reduction in national ownership."[44] The document goes on to note that the relationship between conditionality and ownership is complex; it raises the important question of "whose ownership is relevant?"[45] but makes little progress in suggesting either an answer or even how to go about analyzing how to try to get an answer.[46]

While from some normative perspectives ownership might be designed so broadly as to include almost all residents, a pragmatic approach to ownership would argue that its breadth be defined in terms of what is necessary to secure implementation of the programs. In the terminology of modern political science, then, ownership should include all potential veto players. The IMF has traditionally dealt primarily with central banks and finance ministries, but even for narrow fiscal-policy issues the relevant authorities may include the national legislature and, as in the recent cases of Argentina and Brazil, regional governments as well. It was the fail-

---

[42] On the importance of government "ownership" of programs see Killick, "Principals, Agents, and the Limitations of BWI Conditionality." He stresses the important role which intellectual persuasion by the IMF and World Bank has played in the process toward liberalization and macroeconomic stabilization in developing countries and argues that this function can be undercut by too much emphasis on conditionality. He also suggests that governments should take on a much larger role in drafting letters of intent.

[43] IMF, *Conditionality in IMF-Supported Programs*, 18.

[44] Ibid.

[45] Ibid., 19

[46] Their brief discussion does note that there are many stakeholders in society and suggests that the range of relevant parties is greater for many of the structural policy areas than for the traditional IMF core of monetary, fiscal, and exchange-rate policies. C. Calomiris, "The IMF's Imprudent Role as Lender of Last Resort," *CATO Journal* 17 (1998): 275–94, gives an excellent discussion of how the extent of special interests in the "intermediate" area of financial-sector reform makes implementation there much slower and more difficult than in the core areas.

ure of the Russian legislature to pass the budget measures on which the IMF and the Executive Branch had agreed that ignited the Russian crisis in 1998.

The Fund appears to be beginning to pay more attention to such issues, but progress is slow. The IMF has relatively little expertise in political-economy analysis, and taking such considerations explicitly into account runs against the traditional culture of the Fund. Understandably, the IMF staff is dominated by economists who specialize in giving advice on optimal economic policies. It does little good, however, to get a government to agree to such policy strategies if it does not have the intention or the capability to implement them. A purely "economic" (that is to say, optimal-policy) approach to designing the initial agreement, followed by a "political" approach to forgiving implementation failures, is not a good strategy for dealing with the complex interactions that inevitably surround IMF programs.

The External Surveillance Review reports a widespread, albeit not universal, perception among senior IMF staff that they "did not see it as their function to come up with policies that, while less than first best, moved the country in the right direction and were politically and institutionally acceptable."[47] The report likewise notes that IMF staff ". . . appear in general to be reluctant to give advice . . . that takes into account the political and institutional constraints within which policymakers need to operate."[48] Given the training of most economists, such reluctance is quite understandable. Economists have no particular expertise in making such judgments. What is needed is additional capability at the Fund so that it can engage in the necessary political-economy analysis.

Toward this end, the report recommends that a higher proportion of the senior staff at the Fund be selected from among economists who have had significant national policy experience. This is a worthwhile recommendation, but it does not go far enough. Unlike the situation twenty years ago, there is now a substantial group of political scientists and a smaller number of economists trained in the study of the intersection of politics and economics. For some time, political economy has been a highly active research field. Although (like traditional economics) it does not have a monopoly on the solutions to these matters, it nevertheless now contains a substantial body of useful knowledge that could be easily drawn upon by the IMF in the development of its programs. Among the benefits likely to result from developing an explicit political-economy capacity at the Fund would be wider consultations within the host country, including the different components of the national government. Likewise, one of the most crucial aspects of designing an IMF program is how to package it to sell best to the legislature and the public. While such packaging must be primarily the responsibility of the national government, this is an area where a political-economy group at the IMF could be quite helpful in offering advice based on previous Fund experience and the growing body of professional literature on political economy.

[47] Ibid., 43.
[48] Ibid., 95.

Concluding Remarks

One of the banes of traditional public-choice scholarship is that the very same analyses that identify possibilities for improvements of public policy also usually suggest that it would be extremely difficult to get these reforms through the political process.[49] However, to the extent that the softer elements stressed in this chapter are relevant, the chances for meaningful reform in at least some areas may not be quite so bad after all.

Identifying potential biases is much easier than correcting them. Still, the identification effort can be worthwhile. Increased awareness of such potential biases may in itself have some effect. There has been a substantial increase in the transparency associated with IMF programs over the last several years; there may also be methods of revising institutional structures and/or management practices to reduce some of the major problems of loan-pushing and insufficient enforcement. For example, if Fund country officers are susceptible to partial capture by client governments and have become too cautious in recommending the termination of programs where policy conditions are being insufficiently met, then an internal review board could vet the recommendations of missions before they were sent to the Executive Board. The same would hold with respect to crisis bailouts designed to limit contagion.

The Fund did create just such a mechanism some time ago, in the form of its Department of Policy Development and Review.[50] However, discussions with IMF staff and the research studies on the enforcement of IMF programs suggest that the effectiveness of this review mechanism has been limited.[51] Although the review department serves as a strong potential counter to possible biases of area department staff, the department has little independence from senior management who, after all, still control the career paths of officials staffing the department. This suggests the possibility that the senior management of the Fund, even though they are appointed directly by the IMF member governments for limited terms, may be a greater source of policy bias than the career staff. If so, it would be particularly useful to devise ways of strengthening the Executive Board relative to management and especially to develop ways of limiting management's ability to informally commit the IMF before discussions by the Executive Board are held.[52]

Prescriptions for reform of the Fund of course rest heavily on perceptions of the

[49]   See, for example, R. D. Tollison, "Rent Seeking," in D. Mueller, ed., *Perspectives on Public Choice* (New York: Cambridge University Press, 1997), 506–25.

[50]   The Research Department also plays such a role to some extent. Policy Development and Review was not started from scratch but rather was based on the long-standing Department of Exchange and Trade Relations, which had been the de facto coordinating group for the area departments.

[51]   In response to recent criticisms, the IMF has announced that it will establish a new independent evaluation unit. The precise institutional structure of this new unit will be of considerable importance, but this is certainly a desirable step.

[52]   Engelen suggests this has been a major problem. See Klaus Engelen, "Why Germans Still Hate the IMF," *International Economy* (September/October 1998): 42–45.

problems that need to be corrected. Our available evidence does not yet allow us to say with much confidence the relative importance of the various types of potential biases discussed in the literature on the political economy of the IMF. It is clear, however, that multiple factors are important, and thus simple remedies may not be easy to find. Because of the problems of political manipulation by national governments, there is a strong case for giving the IMF more protection from short-run political pressures along the same line as the case for independence of national central banks. Because of the types of bureaucratic problems identified by Vaubel and others, however, giving the Fund management complete discretionary autonomy would likely not be a good idea.[53]

The mechanics of governance at the IMF are now under debate, with the French pushing for greater political oversight through strengthening the role of the ministerial level Oversight Committee relative to the Executive Board, which is staffed by lower-level political appointees. (An uncharitable interpretation of the French motivation, however, is to develop a stronger political counterweight to the influence of the United States.) So far, there appears to have been little consideration of what kinds of principles should guide discussion of the Fund's governance structure. This is clearly an important topic to which the literature on public choice and constitutional political economy should be highly relevant.

Public-choice analysis suggests that the most difficult problem to solve is the use of the Fund by the major powers for political purposes. Even here, however, there may be some basis for optimism. It is in the longer-term self-interest of the major powers not to undercut the effectiveness of the IMF. Of course, it is a pipe dream to think that the IMF, any more than national central banks, can be fully depoliticized. But as has now occurred in the central banking legislation of many industrialized countries, there is some hope that governments might be willing to lengthen their time horizons and to embrace approaches that stress medium-term stability over short-term expediency. Governments' willingness to rise to such occasions is, of course, in scarce supply, but sometimes it does happen.

---

[53] For a specific proposal to give the Fund much greater independence, see J. De Gregorio, B. Eichengreen, T. Ito, and C. Wyplosz, "An Independent and Accountable IMF," *Geneva Reports on the World Economy* 1 (London: Centre for Economic Policy Research, 1999).

CHAPTER FIVE

Currency Unions and Policy Domains

Peter B. Kenen

Some contributions to recent scholarship in international monetary relations have focused on the concept of the *currency domain*.[1] This chapter, by contrast, stresses the role of the *policy* domain—the area over which policy is targeted—and argues that the concept deserves more attention than it usually receives. The comparative merits of the various ways in which countries can fix their exchange rates—unilateral dollarization, a currency board, or a full-fledged monetary union—depend largely on the monetary-policy domains that correspond to those regimes. The case for reinforcing a monetary union with a fiscal federation also depends on the policy domain of the monetary union.

Exchange-rate arrangements and views about their merits have changed dramatically in the last half-century, reflecting the joint influence of actual experience with various regimes, changes in macroeconomic theory, and changes in policy priorities. A number of analysts and policymakers now believe that the fixed-to-flexible continuum of currency regimes has been replaced by a stark binary choice: exchange rates must either float or be given up completely.[2] Unfortunately, the insti-

---

[1] B. J. Cohen, *The Geography of Money* (Ithaca: Cornell University Press, 1998), develops the concept of the currency domain.

[2] For the first formulation of this binary view, see B. Eichengreen, *International Monetary Arrangements for the Twenty-first Century* (Washington: Brookings Institution, 1994). Similar views have been expressed by the official community. See Group of Seven (G-7) Finance Ministers, *Strengthening the International Financial Architecture: Report to the Köln Summit*, 1999. There are of course dissenters. Williamson argues cogently that wide-band target zones are viable and sensible. See J. Williamson, "Crawling Bands or Monitoring Bands: How to Manage Exchange Rates in a World of Capital Mobility," *International Finance* 1 (1998): 59–79; and J. Williamson, "Exchange Rate Regimes for Emerging Markets: Reviving the Intermediate Option," *Policy Analyses in International Economics* 60 (Washington: Institute for International Economics, 2000). J. A. Frankel, "No Single Currency Regime Is Right for All Countries or at All Times," *Essays in International Finance* 215 (Princeton: International Finance Section, Princeton University, 1999); and F. Larrain and A. Velasco, *Exchange Rate Policy for Emerging*

tutionalization of fixed exchange rates is often recommended without close attention to the basic economic issues. Emerging-market countries show a growing interest in immutably fixed rates, which reflects their concern about vulnerability to
future currency crises and their revealed preference for exchange-rate stability,
what Calvo and Reinhart describe as "fear of floating."[3] Little is heard about the issues raised by the theory of optimum currency areas (hereafter, OCA theory) or the
concept of the monetary-policy domain.

The first part of this chapter sets out the core of OCA theory, following
Mundell.[4] It shows how his formulation was shaped by assumptions and concerns
that dominated macroeconomic theory in the 1950s and 1960s, and then traces the
subsequent evolution of OCA theory. The chapter goes on to examine how OCA
theory was used to evaluate the potential benefits and costs of Economic and Monetary Union (EMU) in Europe. The role of the monetary-policy domain is considered next, by contrasting the effects of monetary policies under unilateral dollarization and a monetary union. The chapter then turns to complementarities
between a monetary union and a fiscal federation, and it concludes with comments
on the benefits and costs of a currency board or unilateral dollarization, compared
with those of a monetary union.

The Theory of Optimum Currency Areas

To understand OCA theory, we must go back to its birth. It was a by-product of
Keynesian macroeconomics, which assumed that wages and prices are sticky and
that international capital mobility is too low to influence the functioning of domestic policies. Under these assumptions, the nominal exchange rate determines the
real exchange rate, which determines the current-account balance. Therefore, the
nominal rate can be used to maintain *external balance* (i.e., the desired state of the
current-account balance), while monetary and fiscal policies are used to maintain
internal balance (i.e., the highest levels of output and employment consistent with
price stability). In language used by Johnson, the exchange rate is an expenditure-
switching instrument, and an exchange-rate change is thus the optimal response to
an expenditure-switching shock, whereas monetary and fiscal policies are expenditure-changing instruments, and a change in one of them is the optimal response to
an expenditure-changing shock.[5]

Markets: One Size Does Not Fit All (1999, processed) warn that no single exchange-rate regime can be
right for every country and for every situation.

[3] G. A. Calvo and C. M. Reinhart, "When Capital Inflows Suddenly Stop: Consequences and Policy
Options," in P. B. Kenen and A. K. Swoboda, eds., *Reforming the International Monetary and Financial
System* (Washington: International Monetary Fund, 2000).

[4] R. A. Mundell, "The Theory of Optimum Currency Areas," *American Economic Review* 51 (1961):
509–17.

[5] Harry G. Johnson, "Towards a General Theory of the Balance of Payments," in H. G. Johnson,
ed., *International Trade and Economic Growth* (Cambridge: Harvard University Press, 1962).

This is a simplified summary of the story told by the open-economy version of the basic Keynesian model, but it captures the main features, and it can be used to make important points about the functioning of monetary unions. It is, indeed, the framework used by Mundell in his seminal paper on OCA theory, which had an extraordinary influence on the subsequent development of that theory. To see what Mundell said—and did not say—let's examine a world comprising two countries and ask how the two types of shocks, expenditure-changing shocks and expenditure-switching shocks, affect those countries' incomes and the current-account balance between them.[6]

A Two-Country Keynesian Framework

Consider an increase of expenditure in country *1*. It will raise both countries' incomes, but country *1*'s income will rise by more than country *2*'s income, and country *1*'s current-account balance will deteriorate, producing a reserve flow from country *1* to country *2*. These will be "bad things" when both countries enjoy internal and external balance initially. But they can regain that blissful state if country *1* adopts an expenditure-reducing policy. Furthermore, all other policy responses are second-best from one standpoint or another. If, for instance, country *1* fails to respond appropriately, country *2* can adopt an expenditure-reducing policy for internal balance, but it will not bring country *1* back to internal balance, and it will drive both countries further from external balance.

Consider a switch in expenditure from country *2*'s good to country *1*'s good. Country *1*'s income will rise, and it will experience inflationary pressures; country *2*'s income will fall, and it will experience unemployment; and country *1*'s current-account balance will improve, producing a reserve flow from country *2* to country *1*. But both countries can return to their initial states by adopting an expenditure-switching policy—a devaluation of country *2*'s currency. If, instead, they adopt expenditure-changing policies for internal balance, they will move further from external balance, and if they adopt expenditure-changing policies for external balance, they will move further from internal balance.

OCA Theory in the Keynesian Framework

Suppose, now, that countries *1* and *2* fix their exchange rate irrevocably, without adopting a single currency or replacing their national central banks with a supranational central bank. In effect, they create what Corden called a pseudo-monetary

---

[6] For a formal presentation of the Keynesian framework and elaboration, see P. B. Kenen, "Currency Areas, Policy Domains, and the Institutionalization of Fixed Exchange Rates," *Discussion Paper* 467 (London: Centre for Economic Performance, London School of Economics, 2000), available at http://www.cep.lse.ac.uk.

union.[7] In the absence of capital mobility, both countries can pursue independent monetary policies, at least in the short run, and can deal as they should with expenditure-changing shocks. But they cannot use the nominal exchange rate to offset expenditure-switching shocks. And they must pay attention to the current-account balance, because they cannot count on endogenous capital flows to finance a current-account imbalance; they must use reserves or set up reserve-credit lines to mimic the financing of interbank imbalances that occurs endogenously in a full-fledged monetary union.[8]

This, then, is the problem considered by Mundell: How can these countries cope with an expenditure-switching shock once they undertake to keep their exchange rate fixed? It is, indeed, the main case studied in his paper, and the peculiarities of that case had a profound influence on the evolution of OCA theory. Here is Mundell's answer:

With a switch in expenditure from country *2*'s good to country *1*'s good, country *1* will run a current-account surplus; there will be an excess supply of country *2*'s good and excess supply in its labor market, and there will be an excess demand for country *1*'s good and excess demand in its labor market. If prices and wages were perfectly flexible and could thus respond to these excess demands and supplies, the price of country *2*'s good would fall, the price of country *1*'s good would rise, and the change in relative prices would reverse the switch in demand, restoring equilibrium in each country's markets and ending the imbalance in their trade. If prices and wages were perfectly rigid, but the nominal exchange rate were flexible, the switch in demand to country *1*'s good would raise the demand for its currency and cause it to appreciate. This, in turn, would raise the relative price of country *1*'s good and reverse the switch in demand.

When prices and wages are rigid, however, and the nominal exchange rate is fixed, the two countries face an intractable problem unless there is another way to clear their labor markets—a movement of workers from country *2* to country *1*. And that movement would also redress the imbalance in the countries' trade. Workers who moved to country *1* would continue to consume both countries' goods. But their demand for country *1*'s good would be domesticated, becoming part of domestic demand in country *1* and ceasing to be part of the import demand coming from country *2*. Conversely, their demand for country *2*'s good would be internationalized, becoming part of the import demand coming from country *1* and

[7] W. M. Corden, "Monetary Integration," *Essays in International Finance* 93 (Princeton: International Finance Section, Princeton University, 1972).

[8] J. C. Ingram, "State and Regional Payments Mechanisms," *Quarterly Journal of Economics* 73 (1959): 619–32, was the first to describe the endogenous financing of bilateral imbalances in a monetary union; see also J. C. Ingram, "The Case for European Monetary Integration," *Essays in International Finance* 98 (Princeton: International Finance Section, Princeton University, 1973), and my treatment in P. B. Kenen, *Economic and Monetary Union in Europe: Moving Beyond Maastricht* (Cambridge: Cambridge University Press, 1995), chap. 2.

ceasing to be part of domestic demand in country *2*. Therefore, perfect labor mobility can automatically resolve the intractable problem posed by an expenditure-switching shock, and the domain of labor mobility becomes the defining characteristic of an optimum currency area: it can contain many countries but only one unified labor market.[9]

Note that Mundell's story has three special features:

(1) Because the model with which he worked allows each member of a currency union to pursue an independent monetary policy, expenditure-changing shocks play no role in defining an optimum currency area, although they may be asymmetric in origin and impact. When high capital mobility prevents the members of a union from adopting independent monetary policies, those shocks become important.

(2) Because Mundell dealt with a two-country union, the expenditure-switching shock that he studied evinces a unique *mirror-image* asymmetry; it raises output in one country and reduces output in the other. That would not be true of an expenditure-switching shock involving a member of the union and a third, outside country.[10]

(3) Because of this same mirror-image asymmetry, a unified, union-wide fiscal system can cushion the impact of an expenditure-switching shock with little effect on the stance of the unified system. The increase in tax revenue collected in country *1* is similar in size to the decrease in tax revenue collected in country *2*, and the former tends to offset the latter in a unified fiscal system.[11]

Mundell went on to note, however, that optimality is not uni-dimensional and that, for this reason, his labor-market criterion "hardly appeals to common sense." If we applied it strictly, we would have to treat every pocket of unemployment due to imperfect labor mobility as an optimum currency area. It is therefore necessary

[9] Mundell, "The Theory of Optimal Currency Areas."

[10] Faced with such a shock, a currency union can change its external exchange rate, but that will affect output elsewhere in the union. This complication led J. Mélitz, "A Suggested Reformulation of the Theory of Optimum Currency Areas," *Open Economies Review* 6 (1995): 281–98, to suggest that the optimality of a currency union is diminished to the extent that its members are differently involved with the outside world. A similar point is made by J. Maloney and M. Macmillen, "Do Currency Areas Grow Too Large for their Own Good?" *Economic Journal* 109 (1999): 572–87. It can be shown, however, that an expenditure-switching shock coming from outside a currency union closely resembles an expenditure-changing shock originating inside the union. The appendix to Kenen, "Currency Areas, Policy Domains, and the Institutionalization of Fixed Exchange Rates" sets out a three-country model in which an omnibus variable contains expenditure-switching shocks coming from outside a currency union as well as expenditure-changing shocks arising inside the union. It thus shows that the effects of the foreign shocks on each member of the union can be offset fully by expenditure-changing policies.

[11] I made this point in my early papers on OCA theory but did not realize that the self-balancing fiscal outcome reflected the special nature of the shock Mundell had analyzed. P. B. Kenen, "Toward a Supranational Monetary System," in G. Pontecorvo, R. P. Shay, and A. G. Hart, eds., *Issues in Banking and Monetary Analysis* (New York: Holt, Rinehart, and Winston, 1967); P. B. Kenen, "The Theory of Optimum Currency Areas: An Eclectic View," in R. A. Mundell and A. K. Swoboda, eds., *Monetary Problems of the International Economy* (Chicago: University of Chicago Press, 1969).

to weigh the macroeconomic benefit of having a great many currency areas, even subnational areas, against the efficiency cost of reducing the domain of each currency and thus reducing its usefulness as a unit of account and medium of exchange. From a microeconomic perspective, indeed, "the optimum currency area is the world," although it may comprise many separate labor markets.[12]

Completing the Core of OCA Theory

Two other papers are often cited along with Mundell's as being early building blocks of OCA theory. Both were concerned with the implications of country size and structure.

McKinnon argued that a small open economy cannot use the nominal exchange rate to neutralize expenditure-switching shocks. A devaluation of a small country's currency is bound to raise its domestic price level, which will have two consequences. First, it will reduce real wages, generating pressures to raise nominal wages; those pressures, in turn, will vitiate the effect of the devaluation on the real exchange rate. Second, it will reduce the usefulness of the domestic currency as unit of account and store of value. Accordingly, a small open economy, by itself, cannot be an optimum currency area. In McKinnon's own terms, an optimum currency area must be big enough to have a large body of nontradable goods, the prices of which are defined in domestic currency and serve therefore to stabilize its purchasing power for the inhabitants of the area.[13]

Kenen dealt with several issues, including connections between the fiscal domain and currency domain. If the fiscal domain were larger, complex questions would arise. How would taxes be collected if a single fiscal system spanned a number of currency areas, each of them entitled to alter its exchange rate? Which currency would the government use to buy goods and services?[14] Goodhart suggests that the problems posed by having more than one currency within a single fiscal domain may explain why we rarely ask whether the regions of a single country should have separate currencies. Currency unions do not usually break up unless their countries break up too.[15]

---

[12] The same point is stressed by B. J. Cohen, "Optimum Currency Area Theory: Bringing the Market Back In," in B. J. Cohen, ed., *International Trade and Finance: New Frontiers for Research* (New York: Cambridge University Press, 1997), but an interesting qualification is offered by K. Dowd and D. Greenaway, "Currency Competition, Network Externalities, and Switching Costs: Towards an Alternative View of Optimum Currency Areas," *Economic Journal* 103 (1993): 1180–89. Although network benefits and economic welfare increase with the domain of a currency, a world currency may not develop endogenously and may not raise welfare, because of regime-switching costs.

[13] R. I. McKinnon, "Optimum Currency Areas," *American Economic Review* 53 (1963): 717–25.

[14] Kenen, "The Theory of Optimum Currency Areas: An Eclectic View."

[15] C. A. E. Goodhart, "The Political Economy of Monetary Union," in P. B. Kenen, ed., *Understanding Interdependence: The Macroeconomics of the Open Economy* (Princeton: Princeton University Press, 1995).

My paper also argued that a fiscal system spanning several regions can help to maintain internal balance and thus compensate in part for the macroeconomic disadvantage of having a currency area that spans many labor markets—one that is not optimal in the Mundellian sense. This is what I wrote:

It is a chief function of fiscal policy, using both sides of the budget, to offset or compensate for regional differences, whether in earned income or in unemployment rates. The large-scale transfer payments built into fiscal systems are interregional, not just interpersonal, and the rules which regulate many of those transfer payments relate to the labor market, just like the criterion Mundell has employed to mark off the optimum currency area.[16]

Credit or blame for making this point is often assigned to the MacDougall Report, which said that a European monetary union would require a large increase in the budget of the European Community, in order to make room for endogenous fiscal transfers.[17] But I can find no mention of it prior to my own.

My paper is most often cited, however, for stressing the relevance of product diversification for OCA theory. First, a diversified economy will not have to undergo large changes in its real exchange rate. Each of its export goods may be subject to exogenous shocks, reflecting changes in foreign demand or changes in technology, but the law of large numbers will come into play if it exports many goods and if the shocks are independent. Second, diversification reduces the size of the change in the real exchange rate needed for adjustment to a single shock. In a completely specialized economy, workers who lose their jobs due to a fall in exports have nowhere to go, and the depreciation of the real exchange rate must offset the whole fall in demand. In a two-product economy, with an export good and an import-competing good, the depreciation of the real rate will also stimulate the demand for the import-competing good and can therefore be smaller.[18]

[16] Kenen, "The Theory of Optimum Currency Areas: An Eclectic View."
[17] Commission of the European Communities, *Report of the Study Group on the Role of Public Finance in European Integration* (Luxembourg: Office for Official Publications of the European Communities, 1977).
[18] I did not say that the degree of diversification should be the only OCA criterion; in fact, my paper set out to provide an "eclectic" approach to OCA theory. Yet J. A. Frankel and A. K. Rose, "Economic Structure and the Decision to Adopt a Common Currency," *Seminar Paper* 611 (Stockholm: Institute for International Economic Studies, 1996), appear to believe that I viewed diversification as the only appropriate OCA criterion, and they go on to argue that this criterion crumbles:

Stipulate that the joining of two or more regions forms a larger unit that tends to be more highly diversified as a whole than are the regions considered individually. Then if an individual region is sufficiently diversified to pass the Kenen test for pegging its currency to a neighbor, it follows that the larger (more diversified) unit that is thereby created will pass the test by an even wider margin. It thus will want to peg to other neighbors, forming still larger units. . . . The process will continue until the entire world is on one currency.

What if the individual regions are not sufficiently diversified to pass the Kenen criterion to begin with? Then, under the OCA logic, they should break up into smaller currency units (say, provinces) that float against each other. But these smaller units will be even less diversified, and

OCA Theory and EMU

Although there was a flurry of interest in European monetary integration after the Werner Report,[19] there were few contributions to OCA theory in the 1970s.[20] Interest in the subject did not revive until the Delors Report,[21] but most of the new work thereafter tried to apply empirically the analytic framework provided by Mundell and others in the 1960s. There was a rush to measurement—to ask whether Europe constitutes an optimum currency area—rather than an effort to update the OCA framework by taking account of innovations in open-economy macroeconomics, including the development of rigorous microfoundations to underpin assumptions about wage and price behavior, the advent of the rational expectations hypothesis, and research on the implications of asset-market integration.[22]

This empirical work on EMU dealt with four issues. One body of work sought to assess the cost to European countries of giving up exchange-rate changes by measuring the co-variation of the exogenous shocks affecting those countries so as to ascertain the extent to which they are subject to symmetric or asymmetric shocks.

---

thus will fail the Kenen criterion by an even wider margin, and will thus decide to break up into still smaller units (say, counties). The process of dissolution will continue until the world is down to the level of the (fully-specialized) individual.

The first half of their argument holds, but only up to a point. Enlarging a currency area by adding more entities—countries, provinces, or counties—will, of course, tend to diversify its output but will also make it bigger geographically and more heterogeneous culturally. Hence, it is apt to reduce labor mobility within the area, which Mundell rightly identified as being crucially important for low-cost adjustment to expenditure-switching shocks. But to the extent that the first half of the Frankel-Rose argument has any validity, it undermines the validity of the second half. If a particular entity is too small and specialized to be an optimum currency area, chopping it up into smaller entities will make matters worse and reduce the usefulness of the currencies of those new entities.

[19] Council of the European Communities, *Report to the Council and the Commission on the Realization by Stages of Economic and Monetary Union in the Community* (Luxembourg: Office for Official Publications of the European Communities, 1970).

[20] E. Tower and T. D. Willett, "The Theory of Optimum Currency Areas and Exchange-Rate Flexibility," *Special Papers in International Economics* 11 (Princeton: International Finance Section, Princeton University, 1976), who surveyed and synthesized OCA theory by stressing the influence of economic openness on the benefits and costs of currency unification, cited more than 160 papers, but only a quarter of those had titles mentioning currency areas or monetary integration. Of those that did, moreover, several have been cited here and several more appeared in a single conference volume: H. G. Johnson and A. K. Swoboda, eds., *The Economics of Common Currencies* (London: Allen and Unwin, 1973).

[21] Commission of the European Communities, *Report of the Committee for the Study of Economic and Monetary Union* (Luxembourg: Office for Official Publications of the European Communities, 1989).

[22] There was some new analytic work, including a paper by M. B. Canzoneri and C. A. Rogers, "Is the European Community an Optimal Currency Area? Optimal Taxation Versus the Costs of Multiple Currencies," *American Economic Review* 80 (1990): 419–33, which warned that a monetary union could interfere with the optimal use of seigniorage for tax smoothing, and the papers by Dowd and Greenaway, "Currency Competition, Network Externalities, and Switching Costs," and Mahoney and Macmillen, "Do Currency Areas Grow Too Large for Their Own Good?" cited above. By and large, however, there was an oddly uncritical acceptance of the original OCA framework.

Another body of work tackled the same question by examining the degree of diversification in each European country or decomposing output shocks into place-specific and industry-specific shocks.[23] A third body of work examined the role of labor mobility in international and interregional adjustment. And a growing body of literature has examined the ways in which a monetary union might itself affect the size and nature of shocks, the extent of intra-European labor mobility, and so on. This is not the place to review all that work. But it is worth drawing attention to the conceptual problems involved and to unanswered questions.

The Characteristics of Shocks

Early work on the measurement of shocks looked at the cross-country co-variation of changes in real output or real exchange rates.[24] But these are endogenous variables, and their cross-country co-variation depends on the co-variation of the truly exogenous shocks, the endogenous and policy-induced responses to them, and the "thickness" of the various channels through which they travel from country to country. (These include both real channels, whose thickness depends in part on trade integration, and monetary channels, whose thickness depends in part on the exchange-rate regime itself.) This methodology, moreover, cannot distinguish expenditure-changing shocks, which may be asymmetric in origin and impact but can be offset by expenditure-changing policies, from expenditure-switching and productivity shocks, which can be offset only by altering real exchange rates or moving factors of production from one country to another.

Bayoumi and Eichengreen tried to deal with these problems by adapting a technique devised by Blanchard and Quah.[25] It allows one to disentangle exogenous shocks from their effects on endogenous variables and to separate two types of

[23] Unless otherwise indicated, I will refer to place-specific shocks when describing comparisons between region-specific shocks in the United States and country-specific shocks in Europe.

[24] See D. Cohen and C. Wyplosz, "The European Monetary Union: An Agnostic Evaluation," in R. C. Bryant et al., eds., *Macroeconomic Policies in an Interdependent World* (Washington: International Monetary Fund, 1989); A. A. Weber, "EMU and Asymmetries and Adjustment Problems in the EMS," in "The Economics of EMU," *European Economy*, Special Edition 1 (1991); P. De Grauwe and W. Vanhaverbeke, "Is Europe an Optimum Currency Area? Evidence from Regional Data," in P. Masson and M. Taylor, eds., *Policy Issues in the Operation of Currency Unions* (Cambridge: Cambridge University Press, 1993). For a thorough survey and critique of this and subsequent literature, see T. Bayoumi and B. Eichengreen, "Operationalizing the Theory of Optimum Currency Areas," in R. E. Baldwin, D. Cohen, A. Sapir, and A. J. Venables, eds., *Market Integration, Regionalism, and the Global Economy* (Cambridge: Cambridge University Press, 1999). See also K. M. Kletzer, "Macroeconomic Stabilization with a Common Currency: Does European Monetary Unification Create a Need for Fiscal Insurance or Federalism?" *Policy Paper* B97–04 (Bonn: Zentrum für Europäische Integrationsforschung, 1997), who notes that some apparently exogenous shocks may be artifacts of the exchange-rate regime—that asset-market shocks impinge directly on goods markets under flexible exchange rates.

[25] T. Bayoumi and B. Eichengreen, "Shocking Aspects of European Monetary Integration," in F. Torres and F. Giavazzi, eds., *Adjustment and Growth in the European Monetary Union* (Cambridge: Cambridge University Press, 1993); O. J. Blanchard and D. Quah, "The Dynamic Effects of Aggregate Supply and Demand Disturbances," *American Economic Review* 79 (1989): 655–73.

shocks: "supply" shocks, which have permanent output effects, and "demand" shocks, which do not. But the difference between supply shocks and demand shocks, in size and cross-country co-variation, has been shown to be less striking than the difference between shocks affecting European countries and those affecting U.S. regions. Supply shocks are somewhat larger for European countries, and demand shocks are smaller. Yet the cross-country correlations for both types of shocks are lower for European countries than the cross-regional correlations for U.S. regions, which suggests that European countries are further from being an optimum currency area than are U.S. regions.

The earliest work on domestic diversification was done by Bini Smaghi and Vori and by Krugman, who found that European countries are less specialized than U.S. regions and, by implication, less vulnerable to industry-specific shocks.[26] Further work was done by Bayoumi and Eichengreen in the context of a broader effort to test the explanatory power of OCA theory—the degree to which countries' actual exchange-rate regimes match the predictions of theory. They found that the country characteristics featured in OCA theory have significant effects on actual exchange-rate behavior. They also found, however, that exchange-rate policies are influenced less heavily by the dissimilarity of exports—their proxy for vulnerability to industry-specific shocks—than by the variability of output, economic openness, or economic size.[27]

Various methods have been used to decompose output fluctuations into aggregate shocks, industry-specific shocks, and place-specific shocks, but the results are not very sensitive to the methods used. Examining fluctuations in U.S. output growth, Bayoumi and Prasad found that country-wide shocks account for a slightly larger share than industry-specific shocks, while place-specific shocks are somewhat less important. Turning to Europe, they found the same ordering.[28] In a broader study of OECD countries, Funke, Hall, and Ruhwedel found that country-specific shocks have been more important in explaining output changes than international shocks or industry-specific shocks (which have been about equally important). They also found, however, that international shocks have grown in importance relative to country-specific shocks.[29] Hence, my earlier work on OCA theory may have attached too much importance to output diversification.

[26] L. Bini Smaghi and S. Vori, "Rating the EC as an Optimal Currency Area," in R. O'Brien, ed., *Finance and the International Economy* 6 (Oxford: Oxford University Press for the Amex Bank Review, 1992); P. Krugman, "Lessons of Massachusetts for EMU," in F. Torres and F. Giavazzi, eds., *Adjustment and Growth in the European Monetary Union* (Cambridge: Cambridge University Press, 1993).

[27] T. Bayoumi and B. Eichengreen, "Optimum Currency Areas and Exchange Rate Volatility: Theory and Evidence Compared," in B. J. Cohen, ed., *International Trade and Finance: New Frontiers for Research* (New York: Cambridge University Press, 1998); T. Bayoumi and B. Eichengreen, "Exchange Rate Volatility and Intervention: The Implications of the Theory of Optimum Currency Areas," *Journal of International Economics* 45 (1998): 191–209.

[28] T. Bayoumi and E. Prasad, "Currency Unions, Economic Fluctuations and Adjustment: Some New Empirical Evidence," *IMF Staff Papers* 44 (1997): 36–58.

[29] M. Funke, S. Hall, and R. Ruhwedel, "Shock Hunting: The Relative Importance of Industry-Specific, Region-Specific and Aggregate Shocks in the OECD Countries," *Manchester School* (Supplement 1999), 49–65.

The Role of Labor Mobility

Research on the size and nature of shocks has identified significant differences between European countries and U.S. regions. But those differences, by themselves, are not big enough to raise grave doubts about the long-run viability of EMU. That view is reinforced by the results just cited, which indicate that industry-specific shocks do not account for much of the variability in total output. There is much more reason to worry about the lack of labor mobility in Europe.

In their well-known study of regional adjustment in the United States, Blanchard and Katz found that interregional labor mobility plays a crucial role:

> A negative shock to employment leads initially to an increase in unemployment and a small decline in participation. Over time, the effect on employment increases, but the effect on unemployment and participation disappears after approximately five to seven years. Put another way, a state typically returns to normal after an adverse shock not because employment picks up, but because workers leave the state.[30]

Turning to the roles of wages and prices, they found that nominal wages fall strongly after an adverse shock and take some ten years to return to normal. The fall in nominal wages contributes to the gradual recovery of employment but not by enough to offset fully the initial shock. Furthermore, consumption wages do not fall very much because housing prices respond strongly to employment shocks. Hence, Blanchard and Katz conclude that the outward migration of labor, which takes up the remaining slack, cannot reflect the influence of relative consumption wages. It must be ascribed to the lack of job opportunities—to unemployment itself.

It is impossible to know what would happen if labor were less mobile in the United States—whether there would be longer-lasting increases in unemployment or larger changes in relative consumption wages. We do know, however, that labor mobility is lower within Europe countries, that changes in relative wages are not much larger, and that labor-market shocks tend thus to last longer.[31] We also know that labor is far less mobile between European countries than it is between U.S. regions.

---

[30] O. J. Blanchard and L. F. Katz, "Regional Evolutions," *Brookings Papers on Economic Activity* 1 (1992):3.

[31] On labor mobility, see B. Eichengreen, "Labor Markets and European Monetary Unification," in P. Masson and M. Taylor, eds., *Policy Issues in the Design of Currency Unions* (Cambridge: Cambridge University Press, 1993), who shows that wages and unemployment have larger effects on labor movements in the United States than in Britain or Italy. On the persistence of labor-market shocks, see M. Obstfeld and G. Peri, "Regional Non-adjustment and Fiscal Policy," *Economic Policy* 26 (1998): 207–59, who also provide a critique of other studies, including one by J. Décressin and A. Fatás, "Regional Labor Market Dynamics in Europe," *European Economic Review* 39 (1995): 1627–55, who applied the Blanchard-Katz methodology to European countries, found that labor-market shocks are not more persistent in Europe, and concluded that labor mobility plays a significant role in Europe.

On the Endogeneity of Optimality

When Krugman pointed out that European countries are less intensively specialized than U.S. regions, he also noted that the joint effects of the single European market and monetary union might lead to more specialization, increasing the vulnerability of European countries to industry-specific shocks.[32] Thus far, empirical evidence supports his supposition. Here are the main findings of recent work on trends in the location of European industry from 1970–73 to 1994–97:

> Most European countries showed significant convergence of their industrial structure during the 1970s, but this trend was reversed in the early 1980s. There has been substantial divergence from the early 1980s onward, as countries have become more different . . . from most of their EU partners. The most dramatic changes in industry structure have been the expansion of relatively high technology and high skill industries in Ireland and in Finland. However, the specialization process has occurred more generally, with nearly all countries showing increasing difference from the early 1980s onward.[33]

This study also found interesting changes in the location of individual industries. Some that were spatially dispersed initially are now more concentrated; these are mainly slow-growing industries using low-skilled labor. Of those that were spatially concentrated initially, many have stayed that way, but dispersion has occurred in several medium- and high-technology industries.

These trends began too early to be attributable to the single market, much less monetary union. Furthermore, the effects predicted by Krugman may not be too worrisome. Studies summarized above suggest that industry-specific shocks have not been the main cause of output fluctuations. Whatever the reason for it, however,

---

[32] Krugman, "Lessons of Massachusetts for EMU." See also B. Eichengreen, "Should the Maastricht Treaty Be Saved?" *Princeton Studies in International Finance* 74 (Princeton: International Finance Section, Princeton University, 1992), and G. De la Dehesa and P. Krugman, "Monetary Union, Regional Cohesion and Regional Shocks," in A. Giovannini, M. Guitián, and R. Portes, eds., *The Monetary Future of Europe* (London: Centre for Economic Policy Research, 1993). The point is often made by predicting that the growth of inter-industry specialization will dominate the growth of intra-industry specialization; see, e.g., J. A. Frankel and A. K. Rose, "The Endogeneity of the Optimum Currency Area Criteria," *Economic Journal* 108 (1998): 1009–24. But this formulation may be misleading. It assumes implicitly that exogenous shocks affect broad product groups rather than individual products. A switch in demand from road travel to plane travel will harm car producers and benefit aircraft producers. With that sort of switch in mind, it makes sense to ask whether monetary union will induce a country to specialize in cars or aircraft. But a switch in demand from passenger cars to sport utility vehicles will not harm car producers that make all sorts of vehicles. This second example, however, raises another question: How rapidly can a firm or plant switch between individual products? Substitutability in production may be more helpful than labor mobility or wage flexibility in achieving low-cost adjustment to various shocks, including the entry of new competitors and the advent of new technologies.

[33] K. H. Midelfart-Knarvik et al., *The Location of European Industry* (Brussels: European Commission, 2000), 1.

the increase in specialization calls into question the inference drawn by Frankel and Rose that the OCA criteria are really endogenous.[34]

Working with data for twenty-one industrial countries, Frankel and Rose found that the degree of economic integration, measured by the size of the trade links between pairs of countries, is strongly associated with the size of the time-series correlation between their output fluctuations. Their results are quite robust, but their interpretation of them is somewhat confusing. At times, they seem to be saying that openness per se is an OCA criterion. For the purpose at hand, however, openness must be deemed to represent the extent of integration—the exogenous variable that is driving something else. And the "something else" at issue, the correlation between output fluctuations, must be deemed to represent the endogeneity of the OCA criterion. I noted earlier, however, that the correlation between output levels depends on the sizes and characteristics of the exogenous shocks, the endogenous responses to them, and the thickness of the channels through which they travel. Frankel and Rose are aware of these complications and refer repeatedly to the importance of the transmission process. Nevertheless, they interpret their results as bearing exclusively on the nature of the shocks. They conclude that shocks become more symmetric under the influence of close integration, so that countries which opt for close integration become better candidates for close integration. This is a questionable reading of their empirical work.[35]

Unanswered Questions

Although Frankel and Rose are too quick to conclude that closer integration reduces the cost of integration by reducing the dissimilarity between the countries involved, there *are* reasons to believe that a monetary union will lead to closer integration and may indeed be needed to achieve and sustain "deep integration" of the sort taking place in the European Union.

Many attempts have been made to measure the effects of exchange-rate risk on trade, production, and investment. Some of them have found trade-depressing effects but not very large ones. Yet several recent papers have shown that national borders matter, even for members of free-trade areas. More generally, international markets appear to be less tightly integrated than domestic markets. Using a gravity model, McCallum has shown that trade between two Canadian provinces is twenty times larger on average than trade between a Canadian province and a U.S. state,

[34] Frankel and Rose, "The Endogeneity of the Optimum Currency Area Criteria."

[35] In Kenen, "Currency Areas, Policy Domains, and the Institutionalization of Fixed Exchange Rates," I show why their results must be interpreted cautiously. Using a model based on the same Keynesian framework used here, I show that the correlation between two countries' output levels increases unambiguously with the thickness of the channels linking their economies (and that this relationship is reinforced when the thickening occurs at the expense of trade with the outside world). But I also show that the correlation between the countries' output levels is not always raised by reducing the sizes of the asymmetric shocks affecting their economies; the outcome depends on the particular characteristics of the shocks at issue.

after controlling for size and distance.[36] Furthermore, Engel and Rogers have shown that price differences between pairs of Canadian cities are smaller and less volatile than price differences between Canadian and U.S. cities, after controlling for distance and for fluctuations in the nominal exchange rate between the two countries' currencies.[37] Turning from goods markets to asset markets, several studies have shown that private capital flows between subnational regions play a significant role in smoothing the regions' incomes, whereas capital flows between countries play a less important role in smoothing the countries' incomes.[38]

It must be noted, however, that none of these studies seeks to ascertain whether the results obtained reflect the presence or absence of a currency union. Comparisons between interregional and international outcomes, whether they pertain to goods or assets, reflect the presence or absence of many institutional arrangements. Rose has tried to isolate the influence of currency unions and finds that they are very important. Pairs of countries having the same currency trade three times as much as pairs of countries having different currencies. But most of the countries involved in those unions are very small.[39]

We may know more soon, once Europe has adjusted to the euro, but we will not be able to measure precisely the contribution of EMU to the significant structural changes occurring in Europe. Nor will we ever know what would have happened if EMU had not happened—whether the EMS could have survived in one form or another to maintain a modicum of exchange-rate stability or whether, as Eichengreen and Goodhart suggest, trade tensions resulting from exchange-rate changes would have halted or reversed Europe's progress toward a single market.[40]

[36] J. McCallum, "National Borders Matter: Canada-U.S. Regional Trade Patterns," *American Economic Review* 85 (1995): 615–23.

[37] C. Engel and J. Rogers, "How Wide Is the Border?" *American Economic Review* 86 (1996): 1112–25.

[38] See, e.g., B. E. Sørensen and O. Yosha, "International Risk Sharing and European Monetary Unification," *Journal of International Economics* 45 (1998): 211–38, and J. F. Helliwell and R. McKitrick, "Comparing Capital Mobility Across Provincial and National Borders," *Working Paper* 6624 (Cambridge: National Bureau of Economic Research, 1998). See also S. Kalemli-Ozcan, B. E. Sørenson, and O. Yosha, "Risk-Sharing and Industrial Specialization," *Discussion Paper* 2295 (London: Centre for Economic Policy Research, 1999), who find that regions and countries that engage in substantial risk sharing tend to be more specialized, and that causation runs from risk sharing to specialization. Because the ability to engage in risk sharing via portfolio diversification depends on the extent of capital mobility, these authors suggest that a monetary union will intensify specialization by raising capital mobility and portfolio diversification.

[39] A. K. Rose, "One Money, One Market: Estimating the Effects of Common Currencies on Trade," *Economic Policy* 30 (2000): 9–33. It should be noted, however, that this currency-union effect survives even when Rose omits the smallest countries, pairs of countries with unusually large differences in incomes or incomes per capita, and pairs whose bilateral trade is unusually large relative to their total trade. See also A. K. Rose and C. Engel, "Currency Unions and International Integration," *Working Paper* 7872 (Cambridge: National Bureau of Economic Research, 2000).

[40] B. Eichengreen, "A More Perfect Union? The Logic of Economic Integration," *Essays in International Finance* 198 (Princeton: International Finance Section, Princeton University, 1996); C. A. E. Goodhart, "The Political Economy of Monetary Union."

The Domain of Monetary Policy

Most of the early contributions to OCA theory dealt with *currency* unions not full-fledged *monetary* unions. They could do that analytically because they assumed that capital mobility was low, and they could make that assumption realistically because it was quite low when OCA theory was born. Countries might fix their exchange rates immutably without giving up their ability to pursue independent monetary policies. That is no longer the case. Until recently, however, there was not much analytical work on the effects of forming a full-fledged monetary union and thus transferring control over monetary policy to an institution like the European Central Bank (ECB).[41] The problem can be posed in several ways, but one formulation is especially relevant to the choice between unilateral dollarization and a monetary union. How does the *domain* of monetary policy affect the way in which exogenous shocks impinge on individual members of a currency union? We can answer this question by looking at three policy regimes:

Under the first regime, capital mobility is low, and each member of a two–country currency union can conduct an independent monetary policy. This is the regime studied by Mundell.

Under the second regime, capital mobility is too high for that, and there can be no more than one monetary policy in the currency union. But one country's central bank makes all of the monetary-policy decisions and has a *national* policy domain. It seeks to stabilize its own country's output. This leader-follower regime is a stylized representation of the EMS under German leadership and of unilateral dollarization.

Under the third regime, capital mobility is also high, but a new institution replaces the members' central banks and has a *union-wide* policy domain. It seeks to stabilize output in the union as a whole. This supranational regime is a stylized representation of EMU.[42]

[41] See, however, P. Bofinger, "Is Europe an Optimum Currency Area?" in A. Steinherr, ed., *Thirty Years of European Monetary Integration: From the Werner Plan to EMU* (London: Longman, 1992), who argued that EMU might benefit all its members, not merely high-inflation countries, as transferring responsibility to the ECB could reduce the influence of politicians on the making of monetary policy. See also the discussions of policy domains in Kenen, *Economic and Monetary Union in Europe*, and P. B. Kenen, "Preferences, Domains, and Sustainability," *American Economic Review* 87 (May 1998): 211–13.

[42] In the simple Keynesian framework adopted again in this section, stabilizing output is a proxy for maintaining price stability; recall the assumption made earlier that pursuing internal balance involves stabilizing output at a level compatible with price stability. The issue raised by Corden, "Monetary Integration" and others, whether the members of a monetary union might have different Phillips curves or policy preferences, does not arise here, although it is still germane to the conduct of monetary policy in a monetary union. (It lurks in a question often asked about EMU—whether a single monetary policy can "fit" all of its members.) In what follows, moreover, we ignore the current-account balance between the members of the union. Under low capital mobility, this amounts to assuming that they have reserves or reserve-credit lines with which to finance current-account imbalances. Under high capital mobility, it amounts to assuming that endogenous capital movements and interbank settlements finance those imbalances.

In a currency union with low capital mobility, the first-best response to an expenditure-raising shock in a country is, as before, a tightening of monetary policy by that country's central bank. It stabilizes country *1*'s income and also stabilizes country *2*'s income. The second-best response is a tightening of monetary policy by country *2*'s central bank sufficient to stabilize country *2*'s income. Analogous results obtain for an expenditure-raising shock in country *2*.

With an expenditure-switching shock, by contrast, both central banks will modify their policies, whether they cooperate or act independently; with a switch in expenditure from country *2*'s good to country *1*'s good, country *1*'s central bank will tighten its monetary policy and country *2*'s central bank will loosen its monetary policy. No other response will stabilize both countries' incomes.

In currency unions with high capital mobility, there can be only one monetary policy, whether its domain is national or union-wide. We analyze the impact of that policy by assuming that an interest-rate change has the same expenditure-changing effect in both members of the currency union.

Consider first the leader-follower regime, in which country *2* is the leader and country *1* is the follower, and country *2*'s central bank adjusts its monetary policy to stabilize its own country's income. This case yields these results:

An expenditure-raising shock in country *1* has a relatively small effect on country *2*, so the requisite change in monetary policy by country *2*'s central bank is too small to stabilize country *1*'s income. It merely reduces the increase in country *1*'s income.

An expenditure-raising shock in country *2* has a relatively large effect on country *2*, so the requisite change in monetary policy by country *2*'s central bank is too large to stabilize country *1*'s income. Instead, it causes country *1*'s income to fall.[43]

A switch in demand to country *1*'s good drives the two economies in opposite directions, so the requisite change in monetary policy by country *2*'s central bank destabilizes country *1*'s income. It causes country *1*'s income to rise by more than it would have risen had there been no policy change whatsoever.

In brief, this regime is unsatisfactory from country *1*'s standpoint. Why then did we hear so much about the advantages of "tying one's hands" by joining an EMS led by the Bundesbank? Because, it was said, there was no better way for central banks in

[43] Note the resemblance between this outcome and the one faced by several EMS countries in 1991–92, when the Bundesbank pursued a tight monetary policy to combat the direct and fiscal-policy effects of German unification and its EMS partners experienced severe recessions. (Note further that this result differs from the one obtained in the low-mobility case, where the stabilization of country *2*'s income served also to stabilize country *1*'s income. The reason resides in a difference between the domain of the policy *target* of country *2*'s central bank and the effective domain of its policy *instrument*. In the high-mobility case, country *1*'s interest rate changes whenever country *2*'s interest rate changes. Hence, a change in country *2*'s interest rate affects expenditure in country *1* as well as in country *2*. That did not happen in the low-mobility case. Note finally that country *2*'s central bank acts as a Stackelberg leader. When setting its own interest rate to stabilize its own country's income, it takes account of the resulting change in country *1*'s expenditure and the impact on country *2*'s income.)

other European countries to acquire the credibility needed to combat inflation.[44] The choice they faced was not the one implicit in this exercise, between following sensible policies on one's own and following those of the Bundesbank. It was instead the choice between the deplorable effects of following home-grown policies and "importing" the unsatisfactory side effects of the Bundesbank's policies.

Consider, next, the supranational regime, in which the single central bank of the monetary union sets its monetary policy to stabilize the sum of its members' incomes. In this case:

> An expenditure-raising shock in country *1* calls for a tightening of union-wide monetary policy to stabilize union-wide income but not by enough to stabilize country *1*'s income and by too much to stabilize country *2*'s income.
>
> An expenditure-raising shock in country *2* likewise calls for a tightening of union-wide monetary policy. Here, however, there is not enough tightening to stabilize country *2*'s income but too much to stabilize country *1*'s income.
>
> As always, a switch in expenditure to country *1*'s good drives the two countries' incomes in opposite directions, and the union's central bank cannot mitigate the effect of the shock on one country's income without reinforcing the effect of the shock on the other country's income.[45]

As the supranational regime stabilizes the sum of the countries' incomes, it does not stabilize each country's income completely. It is therefore inferior to a leader-follower regime from the leader's standpoint, but it is superior to that regime from the follower's standpoint. The signs of the changes in country *1*'s income are the same as they were under the leader-follower regime, but all of the changes are smaller absolutely. Furthermore, the supranational regime has an attractive property. Although it does not stabilize either country's income in the face of an expenditure-changing or expenditure-switching shock, it imparts to the income effects of *all* shocks the mirror-image feature characteristic of an expenditure-switching shock.[46] This attribute of a supranational union has important implications for fiscal

---

[44] D. Gros and N. Thygesen, *European Monetary Integration*, 2d ed. (New York: Addison Wesley Longman, 1998) survey the relevant literature.

[45] It can, as usual, stabilize the sum of the two countries' incomes, but the sign of the requisite change in its monetary policy will depend on the difference between the countries' marginal propensities to save. If country *2* has the larger marginal propensity to save, the central bank must tighten its monetary policy to stabilize the sum of the two countries' incomes, because the expenditure-switching shock will raise the sum of their incomes. In that case, however, the central bank will reinforce the expenditure-reducing effect of the shock on country *2*'s income and mitigate the expenditure-raising effect on country *1*'s income. If country *1* has the larger marginal propensity to save, the central bank must loosen its monetary policy and the effects on the countries' incomes will then be reversed. If, finally, the two countries have identical marginal propensities to save, the shock will not affect the sum of the two countries' incomes, so the central bank will have no cause to alter its policy.

[46] In fact, it perfects that feature by equalizing fully the absolute sizes of the income changes caused by an expenditure-switching shock, even when countries *1* and *2* have different marginal propensities to save.

arrangements and policies. It strengthens the case for adopting a union-wide system of built-in stabilizers. When the union's central bank stabilizes the sum of its members' incomes, the members' income changes must always sum to zero. Therefore, the corresponding changes in income-tax collections must also sum to zero, and a union-wide system of built-in stabilizers cannot affect the stock of debt.

Fiscal Policy in a Monetary Union

Debate on the implications of a monetary union for the conduct and functioning of fiscal policy has focused on two questions: Does the formation of a monetary union raise the need to constrain or coordinate national fiscal policies? Does it require a centralized, union-wide system of built-in fiscal stabilizers? The first question spawned a large body of theoretical work and a great deal of empirical work on the fiscal policies of U.S. states and of subnational entities in other countries.[47] The framework used in this chapter, however, does not lend itself to the analysis of that question. The second question spawned empirical work on the extent to which national fiscal systems having built-in stabilizers reduce fluctuations in output or income in individual regions.

The Need for a Centralized System of Built-in Stabilizers

It is, of course, important to have a way of stabilizing national economies in a monetary union if its members are exposed to large asymmetric shocks. That is why the MacDougall Report proposed a system of union-wide built-in fiscal stabilizers to transfer funds automatically from prosperous countries or regions to less fortunate countries or regions—those that are the victims of adverse asymmetric shocks.[48] Such transfers might be made between governments; alternatively, they might be made between households or firms, which would pay higher taxes when they prospered and get smaller transfer payments from the central government.[49]

---

[47] See, among other works, W. H. Buiter, G. Corsetti, and N. Roubini. "Excessive Deficits: Sense and Nonsense in the Treaty of Maastricht," *Economic Policy* 16 (1993): 57–100; M. B. Canzoneri and B. T. Diba, *The Stability and Growth Pact: A Delicate Balance or an Albatross?* (Georgetown University, processed, 1999); B. Eichengreen and J. von Hagen, "Fiscal Policy and Monetary Union: Is There a Trade-off between Federalism and Budgetary Restrictions?" *Working Paper* 5517 (Cambridge: National Bureau of Economic Research, 1996); B. Eichengreen and C. Wyplosz, "The Stability Pact: More Than a Minor Nuisance?" *Economic Policy* 26 (1998): 67–104; M. Goldstein and G. Woglom, "Market-Based Fiscal Discipline in Monetary Unions," in M. Canzoneri, V. Grilli, and P. R. Masson, eds., *Establishing a Central Bank: Issues in Europe and Lessons from the U.S.* (Cambridge: Cambridge University Press, 1992); and Goodhart, "The Political Economy of Monetary Union."

[48] Commission, *Report of the Study Group on the Role of Public Finance in European Integration.*

[49] On intergovernmental schemes for Europe, see Kenen, *Economic and Monetary Union in Europe;* for a scheme that seeks to address the moral-hazard problem raised by C. A. E. Goodhart and Stephen

Many attempts have been made to measure the extent of income stabilization resulting from interregional fiscal flows. The results differ from country to country and from study to study. The first such study, by Sala-i-Martin and Sachs, found that regional tax payments to the U.S. government fall by 34 cents when regional income falls by one dollar, while transfers to the region rise by 6 cents.[50] Hence, the net change in the federal "take" offsets about 40 cents of each one-dollar fall in regional income. Von Hagen pointed out, however, that this large number has two parts; it combines redistributional transfers from high-income to low-income regions with stabilizing transfers from regions experiencing beneficial shocks to those experiencing adverse shocks. To distinguish between the two parts, he used cross-sectional regressions to measure the redistributional transfers and time-series regressions to measure the stabilizing transfers, and he found that the latter offset no more than 10 cents of every one-dollar fall in income.[51]

Subsequent studies followed von Hagen in trying to distinguish between the two types of transfers. They found that the change in the federal take lies somewhere between the high number obtained by Sala-i-Martin and Sachs and the low number obtained by von Hagen.[52] It must be noted, moreover, that the distinction between distribution and stabilization is somewhat arbitrary. Recall the finding by Blanchard and Katz that it may take several years for a region to recover fully from an adverse shock and that emigration plays a large role in the adjustment process.[53] The methods usually used to separate redistribution from stabilization are bound to ascribe much of the fall in the federal take to redistribution, when it could equally well be ascribed to stabilization.

Some countries are committed explicitly to making redistributional transfers between subnational governments. Canada does that extensively, and the effects show up clearly in some of the studies cited above, where the redistributional effects of the fiscal system exceed the stabilization effects. Many transfers, however, includ-

Smith, "Stabilization," in *The Economics of Community Public Finance* (European Economy: Reports and Studies 5, 1993), see Obstfeld and Peri, "Regional Non-adjustment and Fiscal Policy."

[50] X. Sala-i-Martin and J. Sachs, "Fiscal Federalism and Optimum Currency Areas: Evidence for Europe from the United States," in Canzoneri et al., *Establishing a Central Bank: Issues in Europe and Lessons from the U.S.*

[51] J. von Hagen, "Fiscal Arrangements in a Monetary Union: Evidence from the U.S.," in C. de Boissieu and D. E. Fair, eds., *Fiscal Policy, Taxes, and the Financial System in an Increasingly Integrated Europe* (Deventer: Kluwer, 1992).

[52] See the survey in Goodhart and Smith, "Stabilization" and more recent papers: T. Bayoumi and P. R. Masson, "Fiscal Flows in the United States and Canada: Lessons for Monetary Union in Europe," *European Economic Review* 39 (1995): 253–74, and J. Mélitz and F. Zumer, "Regional Redistribution and Stabilization by the Centre in Canada, France, the United Kingdom and the United States: New Estimates Based on Panel Data Econometrics," *Discussion Paper* 1829 (London: Centre for Economic Policy Research, 1998), all of which suggest that the net change in the federal take amounts to about 20 cents of each one-dollar fall in income or output. But D. Gros and E. Jones. "Fiscal Stabilisers in the U.S. Monetary Union," *Working Document* 83 (Brussels: Centre for European Policy Studies, 1994), and A. Fatás, "Does EMU Need a Fiscal Federation?" *Economic Policy* 26 (1998): 165–92, come up with numbers closer to von Hagen's although they use different methods.

[53] Blanchard and Katz, "Regional Evolutions."

ing those most closely identified with stabilization, are the by-products of fiscal centralization—the fact that the tax revenues of the central government fluctuate endogenously with the incomes of households and firms and that certain transfers, especially unemployment-insurance payments, also vary endogenously with the recipients' incomes. Regional incomes are stabilized to the extent that personal incomes are stabilized. Hence, redistribution requires social cohesion but stabilization does not.

Yet stabilization requires more centralization, which entails a larger loss of local control over both sides of the budget.[54] For this reason, if no other, European governments have been unwilling to contemplate the requisite centralization. Hence, those who have sought to devise built-in fiscal stabilizers for the E.U. have tended to favor single-purpose schemes, such as the centralization of unemployment insurance. For that same reason, moreover, other groups of governments that might form monetary unions will have reservations about forming fiscal unions.

There is a strong case for fiscal centralization, however, and it is especially strong when the countries involved are members of a monetary union, because a monetary union alters the debt effects of built-in fiscal stabilizers. First, it may cause less debt creation. Second, it may produce a different distribution of debt burdens and thus a different distribution of the resulting Ricardian effects on private-sector spending. This point has been stressed by Buiter and Kletzer, and its relevance has been confirmed by Bayoumi and Masson.[55] Examining fiscal transfers to Canadian provinces, they show that transfers which impose province-specific debt burdens have smaller effects on consumption and thus do less to stabilize income and output than transfers which do not impose debt burdens.

The Domain of Fiscal Policy

The effects of fiscal policies on household behavior, output, and income cannot be analyzed rigorously in a simple Keynesian model. They should be studied in an intertemporal model where households optimize consumption over time, given the present discounted values of their future incomes and future tax payments, their freedom to borrow and lend, and their utility functions. But the simple Keynesian model used in this paper can still be used to show how the income-stabilizing effects of national tax systems differ from those of a centralized tax system.

To approximate the outcomes obtainable from an optimizing model, suppose

[54] For indirect evidence, see A. Fatás and I. Mihov, "Government Size and Automatic Stabilizers: International and Intranational Evidence," *Discussion Paper* 2259 (London: Centre for Economic Policy Research, 1999), who find a negative correlation between the size of government and the instability of output; it holds for both national and subnational governments.

[55] W. H. Buiter and K. M. Kletzer, "Monetary Union and the Role of Automatic Stabilizers," *Working Paper* 382 (Santa Cruz: University of California at Santa Cruz, 1997); T. Bayoumi and P. R. Masson, "Liability-creating versus Non-liability-creating Fiscal Stabilization Policies: Ricardian Equivalence, Fiscal Stabilization, and EMU," *Economic Journal* 108 (1998): 1026–45.

that shocks are too small and short-lived to have significant effects on the present value of a household's income stream. If the household could borrow and lend to smooth its consumption, it would borrow to offset an income-reducing shock. If it cannot borrow, however, the government can borrow for it—which is what governments do automatically when tax collections fall with a fall in income and governments borrow to cover the resulting budget deficit. In both cases, however, households must allow for the need to repay debt—their own or that of the government—and this requirement interferes with the functioning of built-in fiscal stabilizers.

Suppose that a shock reduces households' incomes. It will also reduce their tax payments, and their disposable incomes will fall by less than their earned incomes, diminishing their need to cut back their consumption. The government, however, will have to borrow to cover the shortfall in tax payments, and it will have to raise taxes later in order to service the increase in its debt. Knowing that they will have to pay more taxes in the future, households will spend less than they would if they did not contemplate this unhappy prospect, and the debt-creating side-effect of the reduction in tax payments will therefore diminish the extent to which an immediate reduction in tax payments can stabilize consumption in the face of an income-reducing shock.

This so-called Ricardian debt effect will occur in a monetary union if there is no fiscal union. The effect will not impair the functioning of the monetary union but will weaken the union members' ability to stabilize their own countries' incomes. When, for example, there is an expenditure-raising shock in country 1, that country's income will rise, even though the union's central bank stabilizes the sum of the members' incomes. Furthermore, country 2's income will fall, because the tightening of monetary policy by the union's central bank will more than offset the increase in country 2's income caused by the expenditure-raising shock. Each country's built-in fiscal stabilizers will, of course, compress the change in that country's income. But the Ricardian debt effect will reduce the extent to which they do so. In country 1, where income rises, tax payments will rise too, allowing country 1's government to reduce its debt and thus foretelling a future tax reduction. Hence, country 1's households will spend more than they would if they did not expect lower taxes in the future, and this higher level of spending will partially offset the income-stabilizing effect of the immediate increase in households' tax payments. In country 2, where income falls, tax payments will fall too, raising the government's debt and foretelling a future tax increase. Hence, country 2's households will spend less than they would if they did not expect higher taxes in the future, and this lower level of spending will partially offset the income-stabilizing effect of the immediate decrease in households' tax payments.

Recall, however, the way in which a supranational monetary union affects its members' incomes. Shocks do not affect the sum of the members' incomes. If, then, they pool their tax receipts by forming a fiscal union, those shocks will not alter the stock of debt, and the influence of the built-in fiscal stabilizers will not be reduced by a Ricardian debt effect. The potential impact of that debt effect is, in fact, the chief rationale for centralizing built-in fiscal stabilizers in a monetary union.

The Institutionalization of a Fixed Exchange Rate

Much of this chapter has dealt with applications of OCA theory to European monetary union, but the issues examined and framework used are also relevant to a comparative evaluation of arrangements that might be adopted by a country wanting to move from an ordinary pegged exchange rate to a firmly fixed exchange rate or to abolish the exchange rate completely by de jure dollarization. We start with two unilateral arrangements—a currency board and dollarization—and then compare the two together with a full-fledged monetary union.

Comparing a Currency Board with Dollarization

A country adopting a currency board retains its national currency but relinquishes the ability to pursue its own monetary policy. An ordinary central bank holds assets denominated in its own currency, as well as foreign-currency assets, and it can raise or reduce its domestic-currency assets to influence the liquidity of the banking system. A currency board does not hold domestic-currency assets; the monetary base is backed entirely by holdings of foreign-currency assets. Furthermore, a currency board must buy or sell foreign currency at a fixed exchange rate whenever someone else wants to swap foreign currency for domestic currency. Although those transactions affect the liquidity of the banking system, they are initiated by the public, not by the currency board. Hence, a currency board cannot have any discretionary influence on bank liquidity. It cannot "sterilize" the money-supply effects of its foreign-currency transactions, act as lender of last resort to the banking system, or assist in the financing of a budget deficit.

Williamson draws an analogy between the case for central-bank independence and the case for a currency board; both of them insulate monetary policy from political influence.[56] Yet the two arrangements are profoundly different. An independent central bank can formulate its own monetary policy; a currency board cannot. There are nevertheless two reasons for establishing a currency board. The first was invoked by Rodrik. When a country's history suggests that an ordinary central bank is more likely to produce economic instability than promote stability, a currency board may make sense.[57] The second reason derives from the new binary view of

---

[56] J. Williamson, "What Role for Currency Boards?" *Policy Analyses in International Economics* 40 (Washington: Institute for International Economics, 1995).

[57] Dani Rodrik, *Institutions for High-Quality Growth: What They Are and How to Acquire Them*, draft prepared for the IMF Conference on Second-Generation Reform (1999, processed).

exchange-rate regimes—that exchange rates may either float freely or be firmly fixed but cannot be firmly fixed without being institutionalized.

Yet currency boards are not immortal. Like most other governmental arrangements, including central-bank independence, they are creatures of law and can be abolished by changing the law. That is why dollarization may be the better way to institutionalize exchange-rate fixity. A country having a currency board retains its own currency and can abandon the currency board without taking the steps and time required to introduce a new domestic currency. A country that has dollarized fully and formally cannot move as swiftly and may therefore be vulnerable to capital flight and financial disruption after deciding to introduce a new domestic currency. Accordingly, it is less likely to abandon its fixed-rate regime.

There is a price to be paid, however, for the more credible exchange-rate commitment conferred by de jure dollarization. A country that moves to a currency board retains its foreign-currency reserves and the interest income on them. A country that opts for dollarization must use its reserves to redeem its currency and forgoes the interest income it had earned before. It may even have to borrow foreign currency if its reserves are too small to redeem its domestic currency.[58]

Comparing Unilateral Arrangements with a Monetary Union

The principal differences between unilateral arrangements and a full-fledged monetary union can be grouped under two rubrics: (1) governance and accountability, and (2) optimality and the policy domain. Let us consider those differences briefly.[59]

The Maastricht Treaty could not have been drafted if the Rome Treaty had not been adopted first. It would have been extremely hard to devise a workable plan for EMU if the institutions of the European Union were not already up and running—the Commission, the Council, and the European Parliament. It is, indeed, hard to believe that monetary union would have occurred without the influence of the political and economic imperatives that produced the Common Market and Single European Act. Had they not been members of the EMS, moreover, Euro-

[58] It has been suggested that the United States compensate countries for the interest-income loss due to de jure dollarization; see, e.g., Steve H. Hanke and Kurt Schuler, *Currency Boards for Developing Countries* (San Francisco: International Center for Economic Growth, 1994). Robert J. Barro, "Let the Dollar Reign Supreme from Seattle to Santiago," *Wall Street Journal* (March 8, 1999), actually suggests that the United States print the necessary dollars and hand them over gratis, so that dollarizing countries can keep their reserves, earn interest on them, and use them to support their banks in a liquidity crisis.

[59] For a similar comparison, see Willem H. Buiter, "The EMU and the NAMU: What Is the Case for North American Monetary Union?" *Discussion Paper* 2181 (London: Centre for Economic Policy Research, 1999), who also attaches great importance to the unique constitutional arrangements in Europe and to the difference between the monetary-policy domain under a currency board or dollarization and under a monetary union.

pean governments might have viewed monetary union as an expensive sacrifice of national autonomy.

Other groups of countries, such as the members of NAFTA or Mercosur, do not have decision-making bodies of this sort and would have much trouble creating them. Would the U.S. Senate ratify a treaty under which it would have to share with the Canadian Parliament and Mexican Congress the power to choose the Chairman and Board of Governors of the Federal Reserve System? Would the Canadian Parliament and the Mexican Congress ratify a treaty that did not give them a comparable decision-making role or, for that matter, the right to insist that the Chairman testify before their committees?

It is tempting to stop right here. Political constraints may suffice to prevent a proliferation of monetary unions in the next few years. Political prognostication is perilous, however, and it is therefore useful to compare on their merits a monetary union with arrangements that a country can adopt unilaterally in order to institutionalize a fixed exchange rate.

Advocates of currency boards and dollarization invariably recommend that emerging-market countries back or replace their own currencies with one of the key currencies—the dollar, the euro, or, less frequently, the yen. This is a sensible strategy when the main aim of the regime change is to forestall future currency crises. It would silly from that standpoint to tie Ecuador's *sucre* to Brazil's *real* or to substitute the *real* for the *sucre*.

The use of a key currency also makes sense from another standpoint—reducing domestic financial fragility. Hausmann notes that governments and firms in emerging-market countries have trouble issuing long-term debt in their own currencies; expectations of future inflation and currency depreciation have inhibited the development of the requisite debt markets. Therefore, those countries must choose between issuing foreign-currency debt or relying heavily on short-term debt—options that tend to perpetuate financial fragility and condemn emerging-market countries to periodic crises, whether they have floating or pegged exchange rates. The solution, Hausmann says, is de jure dollarization, which would promote the development of domestic debt markets and thereby reduce vulnerability to financial and currency crises alike.[60]

There are more reasons for using a key currency. First, currency boards and dollarization transfer to a foreign country the responsibility for monetary policy. Therefore, it makes sense to choose a foreign currency and thus a foreign country that can be expected to pursue a sensible monetary policy. Second, many emerging-market countries have already experienced de facto dollarization and several more countries pursue exchange-rate policies that "track" the dollar closely.[61] Should

---

[60] Ricardo Hausmann, "Should There Be Five Currencies or One Hundred and Five?" *Foreign Policy* 116 (1999): 65–79.

[61] See Honohan and Lane (1999), who also show that some dollar trackers do not trade heavily with the United States. But most members of that subgroup trade heavily with other dollar trackers or compete with them intensively in third markets.

they choose to introduce a currency board or opt for formal dollarization, they can perhaps minimize domestic opposition by basing the new regime on the familiar key currency.

It is important, however, to distinguish between positive and normative issues. Market forces help to explain why key currencies play important roles in the economies and economic policies of emerging-market countries. But they do not provide a basis for ranking exchange-rate regimes. That is the role of OCA theory, augmented by attention to the implications of the corresponding policy domains.

The two-country models commonly used in OCA theory are not satisfactory for this purpose. Nevertheless, they pose an important question: Should a particular pair of countries form a monetary union by fixing the exchange rate between their currencies or adopting a new common currency? And they help us to answer that question by posing another: Are the countries apt to experience large asymmetric shocks and, if so, is there enough labor mobility between them—or wage flexibility within them—to let them relinquish the use of the nominal exchange rate? A two-country model, however, tends to focus our attention on expenditure-changing shocks arising within those countries and to expenditure-switching shocks between their goods. We are led to ignore or pay little attention to shocks from the outside world, including shocks arising from exchange-rate changes involving third countries' currencies—those of major trading partners and those of close competitors.

A monetary union can give its members some protection from these external shocks if its external exchange rate is flexible. It cannot protect them completely, however, if they have different partners or competitors in the outside world. But unilateral fixing to a single foreign currency cannot protect a country from external shocks and is a major disadvantage of that regime, especially for countries that have several important partners or competitors.

A monetary union cannot protect its members from currency crises, because its external exchange rate can be attacked. Yet a monetary union may be less vulnerable than its members would be separately. For reasons given earlier, a monetary union must have an independent central bank, which is likely to conduct a better monetary policy than those pursued individually by its member countries. Furthermore, a monetary union is less likely than its members to adopt a pegged exchange rate. It can be more tolerant of exchange-rate changes, because those changes will not have differential effects on its members' exports—except to the extent that their exports are differentially vulnerable to exchange-rate changes vis-à-vis third currencies. Market forces reinforced by monetary policies and by prudent intervention can mitigate the impact of fluctuations in key-currency exchange rates.

An attack on a flexible rate, moreover, may be less damaging than an attack on a pegged rate. As governments tend to defend pegged rates until they run out of reserves, they can rarely engineer a modest devaluation; by the time they are ready for that, they have insufficient reserves to defend the new pegged rate. They are then forced to let it float, and it depreciates precipitously. That is what happened to the lira in 1992, when Italy left the EMS, to several Asian currencies in 1997, and to the ruble and *real* when Russia and Brazil abandoned pegged rates in 1998 and 1999.

Furthermore, a flexible rate may discourage domestic banks and others from assuming large, unhedged foreign-currency debts of the sort that played a major role in precipitating the Asian crisis and led thereafter to a huge fall in output, which occurred because insolvent banks faced insolvent borrowers, and there was a sharp contraction of essential credit flows.

Finally, currency boards and dollarization have asymmetric monetary-policy domains. The monetary policy of the key-currency country is aimed at stabilizing its own economy or at price stability within that economy. Its central bank need not behave as a Stackelberg leader, which is how it behaved in the model used above, but its decisions are normally based on domestic conditions.[62] In a monetary union, by contrast, monetary-policy decisions would presumably be based on economic conditions in the entire union. As a practical matter, of course, a union between big and small countries cannot be fully symmetrical. When decisions are made on the basis of union-wide aggregates or averages weighted by country size, the results will be asymmetric. Smaller countries will be under-represented in a monetary union, no matter how many votes they may have in the decision-making bodies of the central bank. But under-representation is better than none.

If solutions can be found for the problems of governance and accountability raised in the previous section, some groups of emerging-market countries should perhaps form regional monetary unions. They could fare better than they would by linking themselves unilaterally to the dollar, euro, or yen. Such unions might not be less optimal than EMU, given the desiderata supplied by OCA theory.[63]

Conclusion

The coming of EMU has raised two questions: Should other groups of countries set up similar arrangements? Must those that have already formed trade blocs go on to form monetary unions in order to reap the full benefits of regional free trade? This chapter has answered the first question agnostically. Other economists have answered the second one decisively. Eichengreen argues persuasively that customs unions and free trade areas need not form monetary unions.[64] A monetary union may be needed by a group of countries that seek to pursue deep integration—the

---

[62] See Lawrence H. Summers, *Statement Before the Subcommittee on International Trade and Finance of the Senate Banking Committee* (Washington: U.S. Treasury, 1999), who said that it would not be appropriate for the U.S. authorities "to extend the net of bank supervision, to provide access to the Federal Reserve discount window, or to adjust bank supervisory responsibility or the *procedures or orientation of U.S. monetary policy* in light of another country deciding to adopt the dollar" (emphasis added).

[63] For a test of this hypothesis, see Tamim Bayoumi and Barry Eichengreen, "One Money or Many? Analyzing the Prospects for Monetary Unification in Various Parts of the World," *Princeton Studies in International Finance* 7 (Princeton: International Finance Section, Princeton University, 1994).

[64] Barry Eichengreen, "Does Mercosur Need a Single Currency?" *Working Paper* 6821 (Cambridge: National Bureau of Economic Research, 1998). See also Goodhart, "The Political Economy of Monetary Union." But Eichengreen ("A More Perfect Union?") and Goodhart ("The Political Economy of Monetary Union") both warn that trade tensions arising from exchange-rate changes can undermine a

unification of capital markets, a common competition policy, and so on. It is not necessary for free trade.

But a related question still requires thought: Is deep integration needed to form and sustain a monetary union? Whatever one's doubts about fiscal arrangements in Europe—the Stability Pact and all that—those arrangements raise an important issue. Can a monetary union function efficiently if its members are free to manage—or mismanage—their own fiscal policies? Debate continues in Europe, moreover, about bank supervision—whether it should be conducted at the national level or transferred to the EU level—and about the ability and willingness of the ECB to serve as lender of last resort to the banking system of the euro area. In fact, this debate will intensify as the consolidation of banking enters the next phase, in which domestic mergers give way to transnational mergers.

Similar questions are raised by de jure dollarization. We have already seen that there can be no lender of last resort in a country that turns its central bank into a currency board or adopts a key currency as its own. It cannot expect the central bank of the key-currency country to take on that task. It is for this reason that advocates of dollarization often recommend that a country adopting another country's currency open up its banking system to foreign ownership—which is, of course, another form of deep integration.[65]

The institutionalization of a fixed exchange rate may sound simple. It is not. The best method for a particular country will necessarily depend on that country's circumstances and the availability of other methods. A group of small countries may be too small collectively to form a monetary union. A more promising group of middle-sized countries, even those belonging to a free-trade area, may be unable to solve the problems of governance and accountability attending the formation of a monetary union. And many emerging-market countries may well conclude that a flexible exchange rate would be better than the best possible way to institutionalize a firmly fixed exchange rate.

---

regional trading arrangement by producing political pressures to impose new trade barriers or resort to subsidies to provide covert protection.

[65] Other, less drastic steps can nevertheless be taken to safeguard domestic banks. Argentina was able to assist its crisis-stricken banks after the Mexican crisis of 1994–95; see, e.g., Gerard Caprio, Michael Dooley, Danny Leipziger, and Carl Walsh, "The Lender of Last Resort Function under a Currency Board: The Case of Argentina," *Open Economies Review* 7 (1996): 625–50.

CHAPTER SIX

EMU as an Evolutionary Process

Pier Carlo Padoan

Early critics of EMU argued that the project had two major drawbacks, one economic and the other institutional. From the economic point of view, they argued that the euro would not meet the requirements of an optimum currency area and, therefore, that costs would exceed benefits for its members. Second, they argued that EMU would be plagued by an institutional disequilibrium between a supranational, unaccountable central bank and national governments. If these arguments proved to be valid, EMU would probably fail.

This chapter examines these two critiques, and interrelated issues, from an evolutionary perspective. It argues that both critiques are misplaced because the evolution of the economic structure of EMU as well as its economic policy machinery will eventually bring forward an efficient, viable European economic and institutional model. We discuss the optimality of the monetary union by referring to the concept of "endogenous currency areas," in which monetary integration spurs transformations in the integrating economies that make the adoption of a single currency more suitable. We provide some evidence with respect to several aspects discussed in the optimum currency area literature, such as cyclical convergence, regional convergence, specialization, and labor markets. We consider the evolution of these aspects under different monetary regimes in Europe since the introduction of the European Monetary System (EMS) in the late 1970s.

We discuss the relationship between the European Central Bank (ECB) and national governments by referring to the concept of policy spillover. We argue that

I would like to thank, with the usual disclaimer, Peter Kenen, Beth Simmons, Thomas Willett, and the editors of this volume for comments that greatly helped me improve the original draft. I also acknowledge financial support from the University of Rome "La Sapienza."

centralization of monetary policy in Europe leads to changes in other policy areas, such as coordination between the single monetary policy and national budget policies, coordination of national budgets, and convergence toward a "stable budget regime" (understood as the fulfillment of the requirements of the Stability and Growth Pact). Convergence in other policy areas, such as tax policy and labor-market policy may also be expected to increase over the foreseeable future.

This chapter also argues that, over the past decades, economic-policy regimes in Europe have evolved under the pressure of macroeconomic and structural integration. The transformation of economic structures has created a configuration more supportive of monetary union (we refer to this process as endogeneity). The transformation of the European policy regime toward a new model of EU governance holds the promise of improving policy outcomes. These two transformative processes have mutually influenced and possibly reinforced each other and will probably continue to do so in the future.

Costs and Benefits of Monetary Union

Collignon provides a simple yet useful approach, based on the literature on monetary unions, for analyzing the impact of these processes on the costs and benefits of the euro area.[1] Benefits from monetary union increase with the expansion of the union, in terms of the number of participating countries and of economic size. This arises from the fact that the larger the size of the union, the greater are the benefits accruing to each member from the elimination of transaction costs and exchange rate uncertainty, besides those stemming from lower variability of interest rates.[2] These advantages, furthermore, increase with the degree of openness of the member economies. If these two elements are applied to the European case, it follows that EMU's benefits grow with (a) the number of member countries, (b) the EMU's GDP, and (c) the degree of integration of the single market.

Costs increase with dispersion in the preferences of the area's policy-makers regarding stabilization policies. In other words, the costs of union membership for a country with a high preference for containing inflation increase if other union members hold a strong preference for output-stabilization-oriented monetary policies. In general, the higher the convergence of the member countries' preference for low inflation and stability-oriented monetary policy, the lower the costs. From this point of view, EMU's composition becomes crucial, but it is equally evident that the process of convergence toward the Maastricht parameters suggests that the

---

[1] S. Collignon, *European Monetary Union, Convergence and Sustainability* (Paris: Association pour l'Union Monétaire en Europe, 1997).

[2] Ibid. Costs and benefits of monetary unions are amply discussed in the literature. For an overall evaluation, see, for example, P. De Grauwe, *The Economics of Monetary Integration* (New York: Oxford University Press, 1992).

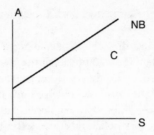

Figure 1: Costs and benefits of a monetary

costs of EMU will be quite moderate. Even the least disciplined among the union's members have implemented rigorous anti-inflationary and fiscal-reform policies.

Graphically, costs (see fig. 1) rise with the value of A, which indicates the propensity of the Union's members to use monetary policy for output stabilization. Increasing values of A fuel the union's inflation and hence diminish monetary stability. Benefits rise as S, the extension of the union, grows because of economies of scale from the use of a common currency. Line NB is the locus of the points where benefits and costs offset each other (net benefits equal zero). NB is increasing because more monetary activism may be offset by an expansion of the union's size. The slope of NB reflects the degree of integration of the union's member economies. Points above NB indicate net negative benefits: there is no incentive to create a monetary union. The opposite occurs below the line. Increasing propensity toward monetary activism for a given size of the union clearly results in net negative benefits and must be offset by enlarging the union and/or by a growing degree of integration (increasing slope of NB) in order to raise the scale benefits.

EMU is "successful" as long as it is described by a point below the NB schedule, such as point C. That success depends on two variables: intensity of integration and convergence of policy preferences toward stability. As long as EMU is endogenous in terms of the intensity of integration, point C will move to the right, while policy convergence will move point C downwards.

While figure 1 is useful to provide an intuition of the general point, it must be supplemented in several respects. Both extension of the union and policy convergence are variables with multiple dimensions. The first variable relates to the evolution of national economic structures toward an "optimal" configuration from the point of view of optimum currency area theory. The second variable relates not only to macroeconomic convergence but, more importantly, to the definition of a coherent and well-functioning structure of governance of EMU, in short, a EU-wide model of economic policy. Indeed, the weakness of the euro during its second year of life and the first half of its third is frequently attributed to unsatisfactory performance in both aspects: a still-not-fully-integrated and inflexible economy and a fragmented and often non-coherent system of governance plagued by excessive conflicts among member states (a sign of non-converging policy preferences). This chapter will consider both aspects in some depth.

Endogeneity: Growth, Convergence, and Specialization

The most serious doubts regarding the sustainability of a common exchange-rate policy in Europe are based on the traditional approach to optimum currency areas. According to the basic tenets of this theory, the changeover to a single currency delivers net benefits only if the countries involved are not subject to asymmetric shocks. Whenever such a condition does not apply, the optimal choice is maintenance of independent monetary policies that can offset the lack of synchronism of business cycles and absorb country-specific shocks.

The conclusions drawn on the basis of the theory of optimum currency areas may, nevertheless, be questioned regarding (a) the correctness of the methodologies and (b) the practical relevance of the issues raised. With respect to the first point, Frankel and Rose emphasize that trade integration and synchronization of business cycles will most likely increase with monetary integration, so that the criteria suggested by the literature on optimum currency areas would be met *ex post* by the countries joining EMU.[3]

The literature on "endogenous currency areas" is still in its infancy, yet it represents a useful approach to assess the perspectives of EMU. In what follows, we provide some further evidence of the endogeneity of EMU as a currency area, looking at macroeconomic and regional convergence. In reviewing the evidence, an important caveat must be kept in mind. The evidence covers a period during which two integration processes have taken place: monetary integration (from the introduction of the EMS to the run up to EMU) and real integration accelerated by the Single Market process. It is extremely difficult, if not simply impossible, to disentangle the effects of the two processes. Because the two processes are complementary and mutually reinforcing, however, disentangling them may not be necessary.

Convergence of Economic Cycles

One of the preconditions for sustainability of a monetary union is convergence of national economic cycles. Different cyclical patterns would point at differences in sensitivity to exogenous shocks, which would produce asymmetrical consequences.[4] The endogenous currency area approach suggests that monetary integration deepens trade integration and leads to converging cyclical profiles. Some evidence is already available in this respect.[5]

Figures 2a and 2b present some further evidence.[6] Correlation coefficients

---

[3] J. Frankel and A. K. Rose, "The Endogeneity of the Optimum Currency Area Criteria," *NBER Working Paper* 5700 (1996).

[4] T. Bayoumi and B. Eichengreen, "Shocking Aspects of Monetary Unification," *CEPR Discussion Paper* 643 (1994).

[5] Frankel and Rose, "The Endogeneity of the Optimum Currency Area Criteria."

[6] Drawn from P. C. Padoan, ed., *Employment and Growth in European Monetary Union* (Cheltenham, U.K.: Edward Elgar, 2000).

with the German cycle

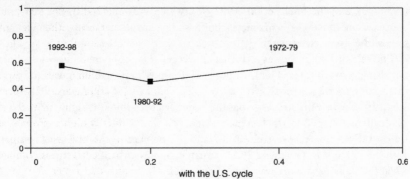

Figure 2a: Cyclical correlation in EU countries

with the French cycle

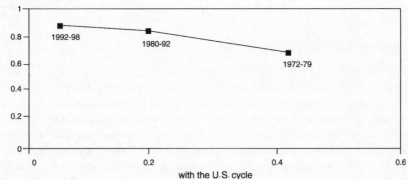

Figure 2b: Cyclical correlation in EU countries

among European GDP cycles are compared for three different sub-periods. Specifically, the cycles of Euroland's largest countries are compared to Germany and to the United States.[7] Furthermore, as the evolution of the German cycle is distorted by the process of unification, the correlation with the French cycle is also presented. Points shown on the curves indicate a marked diversification over time with respect to the U.S. cycle. Note that, in the case of correlation with the French cycle, the curve shifts upwards, indicating a higher coefficient of correlation with the other European economies. This is not present in the German case because of the consequences of unification.

The data confirm the presence of an "emerging" European economic cycle as a consequence of deepening monetary integration. The three periods considered relate to different economic policy regimes in Europe: an initial period of flexible ex-

[7] A similar analysis was developed by M. Artis and W. Zhang, "International Business Cycles and the ERM: Is There a European Business Cycle?" *CEPR Discussion Paper* 1191 (1995).

change rates following the collapse of Bretton Woods (1972–79), the EMS years (1980–92), and the final period (1992–98), which were marked by the substantial depreciation of several currencies but also by an acceleration of convergence toward the single currency.

The relevant point, however, is that convergence was obtained toward declining, not rising, growth rates. The European GDP growth rate declined over the period in question (average growth rates were 3.3 percent in 1972–79, 2.4 in 1980–92, and 1.6 in 1992–98). This suggests that the countries with initially higher growth rates gradually converged to the German economy's slower rate: while the French and Italian GDP grew, respectively, at 3.3 and 3.7 percent in the seventies compared with 2.9 percent in Germany, the German economy expanded faster in 1980–92, when the Italian economy was growing more slowly.

In the immediate aftermath of the introduction of the euro, GDP cycles have begun to diverge, suggesting a separation between fast-growing small economies, and slow-growing large economies. During 2000, however, convergence increased as the large economies started to grow faster.

Exchange Rates and Growth

In a currency area experiencing increasing trade integration such as EMU, two factors need to be examined to assess its sustainability: the sensitivity of growth to exchange-rate changes and the elasticity of employment with respect to exports and growth. The sensitivity of growth to exchange-rate changes is one of the topics that is commonly discussed in connection with the evaluation of costs and benefits of a single currency. It is usually assumed that there are differences among the EMU countries' preferences for exchange-rate management that could create coordination problems in the management of the common monetary policy. To the extent that the growth model of the "Mediterranean" members of EMU is relatively more dependent on the exchange rate, for example, these countries would be suffering higher costs in terms of growth and employment by giving up the exchange rate. In other words, currency unification would be biased by a structural divergence in policy preferences.[8]

Evidence reported in *Employment and Growth in European Monetary Union* sheds some light in this respect.[9] In the first place, the elasticity of exports to intra-European exchange rates is highest in Germany and lowest in Italy. This implies that, contrary to what is often believed, the German economy will benefit from the creation of the single currency as it interrupts the real long-term appreciation of the D-mark. At the same time, the cost to Italy of giving up intra-European exchange-

---

[8] From a long-term perspective, export-led growth should matter less than productivity-led growth. However, for a number of European countries the advent of flexible exchange rates presented the possibility of competitive devaluations, which provided a temporary boost to exports and growth and, to the extent they were unanticipated, significantly influenced business attitudes toward investment.

[9] Padoan, *Employment and Growth in European Monetary Union.*

rate variability is limited, as the elasticity of its exports to this variable is relatively small (less than 0.5).

Germany, next to Spain, also displays the highest export elasticity to the real extra-EU exchange rate. An appreciation of the euro would depress German exports more than those of France and Italy. On the other hand, Italy displays the highest export demand-elasticity, vis-à-vis both the European aggregate and the rest of the world. A demand shock would thus affect Italy to a proportionally greater extent. The relevance of this has been confirmed in 1999 and in 2000 as the depreciation of the euro has largely benefited German growth through exports.

Nonetheless, export elasticities are only a partial confirmation of an export-led model. Table 1 reports some causality tests between employment, exports, and growth in the four large euro countries as well as in the United Kingdom.[10] With the important exception of Germany, there does not seem to be a causal link between exports and employment, nor between exports, investments, and productivity. These links are, on the contrary, observable in the case of Germany, suggesting that an export-led growth model is applicable only in the center economy of EMU.[11] In this respect as well, Germany's economy would be the most negatively (positively) affected by an appreciation (depreciation) of the euro.

As a whole the evidence reported above suggests that, for most of the European countries, the loss of the exchange-rate instrument would not seriously affect long-term growth as we find little evidence of export-led growth and little evidence of exchange-rate sensitivity of exports. While these results support the idea of a sustainable EMU, however, other results presented above suggest that convergence toward the German cycle has not favored investments and employment. Further evidence reported in *Employment and Growth in European Monetary Union* provides additional insights. Deceleration of investment in Europe, which can be seen, to some extent, as the cost of monetary and cyclical convergence, has been accompanied by an increase of the labor-saving (capital-deepening) share of capital accumulation over total capital formation, implying that, partially at least, a cost of (getting to) monetary union might be foregone employment opportunities.[12]

Regional Catching-up

An additional set of evidence relates to regional catching-up.[13] Using a standard model we report tests of the hypothesis that monetary convergence has a positive

---

[10] The same tests have been used in A. Belke and D. Gros, "Estimating the Costs and Benefits of EMU: The Impact of External Shocks on Labour Markets," *CEPS Discussion Paper* 9795 (1997).

[11] There is here a clear difference from the Bretton Woods system, which was focused on the central country's (the U.S.) trade deficit.

[12] Padoan, *Employment and Growth in European Monetary Union.*

[13] Evidence reported in this paragraph also draws on Padoan, *Employment and Growth in European Monetary Union.* Available data on regional per capita output did not allow estimates beyond 1995.

Table 1: Exports and economic growth in selected countries: Granger causality tests

	Germany	France	Italy	Spain	United Kingdom
Exports > employment	11.3*	0.7	1.5	4.2**	1.7
Exports > gross fixed capital formation	7.9*	0.5	2.7***	0.1	1.5
Exports > productivity	0.0	1.6	0.7	0.8	2.0
Gross fixed capital formation > exports	0.6	0.1	1.6	1.6	0.1
Productivity > exports	8.6*	0.3	0.2	0.8	3.5**
Gross fixed capital formation > productivity	3.0***	0.2	4.7	2.6	1.3
Productivity > gross fixed capital formation	8.4*	1.2	6.3*	1.4	4.6**

Source: Padoan, *Employment and Growth in European Monetary Union.*
Asterisks indicate cases for which the null hypothesis of non-causality is rejected.

effect on regional catching-up in Europe.[14] A measure of the rate of convergence in a neoclassical model of exogenous growth is obtained by log-line arising the movement of the capital-stock around its steady state; in the case of a Cobb–Douglas production function, the rate of growth of income per capita is a fixed proportion of the rate of growth of the per-capita capital stock, so that the convergence parameter can be estimated within the following equation:

$$D \log y \cong -\text{\ss} \log \left(\frac{y}{y^*} \right)$$

where $D \log y$ is the rate of growth of per-capita income over the period, y indicates the per capita income of the i-th region at the beginning of the time interval (in our case, 1980–95), y^* is the per-capita income of the richest region, and ß is the measure of regional convergence. The method of estimation is non-linear least squares. We report the values of ß, the convergence parameter (see table 2). We first look at convergence over the whole sample period. We obtain a significant, but very small, convergence parameter.

We then consider the effect of the exchange-rate regime for the convergence process: that is whether, and to what extent, the introduction of the EMS in 1979 may have affected the regional convergence process in Europe. For this purpose, we consider three separate periods: the first EMS period (1980–87), the "hard EMS" period (1987–1992), and the period following the 1992 crisis.

Over the 1980–87 period, which was marked by a regime of fixed, yet adjustable exchange rates, there is no evidence of income convergence among the European regions as parameter ß is not significantly different from zero. Conversely, regional convergence is not rejected during the period of the "hard EMS," 1987–1992, featuring strict nominal exchange rigidity. The value of ß is not significantly different from that obtained from the equation covering the entire period. In the following period, 1992–1995, which was marked by a more flexible exchange regime and by sev-

---

[14] R. J. Barro and X. Sala-i-Martin, *Economic Growth* (Cambridge: MIT Press, 1992).

Table 2: Regional convergence in selected
periods

Period	ß	t value
1980–95	0.009510	5.026860
1980–87	0.001615	1.079498
1987–92	0.014207	10.21923
1992–95	-0.00334	-2.316057

Source: Padoan, *Employment and Growth in
European Monetary Union.*

eral devaluations of currencies participating in the exchange-rate agreements, the
opposite seems to have occurred, that is, divergence among regional growth rates.

The results reported above should not be overemphasized; however they should
be taken as additional evidence of the effect of monetary integration on output convergence, hence of partial endogeneity of another of the criteria suggested by the
optimum currency area literature, increasing similarity among regions and thus decreasing exposure to asymmetrical shocks.

Specialization

Changes in industry specialization across the European Union over the past two
decades clearly reflect both the effects of the implementation of the Single Market
project and of monetary integration. In a report prepared for the EC Commission,
Midelfart-Knarvik, Overman, Redding, and Venables show that industrial specialization in EU countries decreases from 1970 to 1980 and increases from 1980–83 to
1994–97, especially in small countries. More specifically high-return to scale, high-
skill, and high-tech industries are increasingly located in core regions, pointing to
the growing importance of economic geography factors in determining location,
whereas skill-intensive industries are more widespread and also show higher rates
of growth. To the extent that national specialization increases risks of asymmetric
shocks, it carries negative consequences for the sustainability of EMU.[15] However
other evidence shows that specialization in the European Union increases at the regional rather than national level.[16]

Increasing regional specialization has a number of implications for the functioning of EMU. Institutional differences among national labor markets become less

[15] K. Midelfart-Knarvik, H. Overman, S. Redding, and A. Venables, "The Location of European Industry" (Report prepared for the Directorate General for Economic and Financial Affairs, European
Commission, 2000).
[16] R. Paci and F. Pigliaru, "European Regional Growth: Do Sectors Matter?" in J. Adams and F.
Pigliaru, eds., *Economic Growth and Change: National and Regional Patterns of Convergence and Divergence* (Cheltenham, U.K.: Edward Elgar, 2000); B. Verspagen, "European Regional Clubs: Do they exist
and where are they heading?" in Adams and Pigliaru, *Economic Growth and Change;* Padoan, *Employment and Growth in European Monetary Union,* chap. 8 and references therein.

important whereas regional policies appear to be an essential tool for the performance of economic and monetary union. *Employment and Growth in European Monetary Union* offers a description, based on cluster analysis, of different regional specialization patterns and their relationship with unemployment. This work finds a positive relationship between specialization in advanced manufacturing sectors and employment. Regions with a relative intensity of advanced service sectors, that is, sectors closely integrated with industry, are associated with low unemployment. The opposite occurs in regions with a high intensity of traditional services and commerce. During the period between 1981 and 1991, which covers most of the period of the EMS, regional specialization increases.

Financial Market Pressures

EMU is changing the European financial landscape and has the potential to continue to do so in the future, both in terms of performance and of pressure on policy makers. Danthine, Giavazzi, and Von Thadden show that several important changes in European financial markets have emerged since the introduction of the euro. A corporate euro bond market has developed to the point at which issues in 1999 exceeded issues in the dollar market. Portfolios are increasingly being allocated along pan-European lines rather than on a country-by-country basis. The banking industry is undergoing rapid transformation through mergers and acquisitions. Other direct effects of EMU include standardization and transparency in pricing, the shrinking of the exchange market, the elimination of currency risk, the elimination of currency-related regulations, and the homogenization of the public bond market and bank refinancing procedures. Indirect effects include lower costs of cross-country transactions, increasing depth and liquidity of European financial markets, better diversification possibilities, decreasing importance of the home-bias effect in investment. In addition, the emerging euro financial market has prompted new pressures on policy makers to harmonize legislation, taxation, and standards. The establishment of TARGET and EURO1, the settlement systems for large transactions of the European System of Central Banks and the European Banking Association respectively, and the implementation in 1999 of the EU Directive 97/5/EC of January 1997 on cross-border credit transfers are some visible examples.[17] Kraus provides additional evidence that investment in the euro area increasingly follows sectoral rather than national criteria, indicating a gradual elimination of country risk.[18]

One relevant implication of the process of financial integration will be an increasing convergence in national monetary policy transmission mechanisms, thus making the management of supranational monetary policy more effective.

[17] J. Danthine, F. Giavazzi, and E. von Thadden, "European Financial Markets after EMU: A First Assessment," *CEPR Discussion Paper* 2413 (2000).
[18] T. Kraus, "The Impact of EMU on the Structure of European Equity Returns: An Empirical Analysis of the First 21 Months," *IMF Working Paper* WP/01/84 (2001).

Labor Markets

European labor markets have been repeatedly considered to be the major stumbling blocks for the success of EMU. Critics have long claimed that excessive rigidity in EU labor markets would simply be inconsistent with monetary union. Two aspects have to be considered here, one macroeconomic and the other microeconomic. The macroeconomic aspect concerns the relationship between the centralization of monetary policy and the wage-bargaining process. The microeconomic aspect relates to pressure on labor-market legislation arising from the loss of the exchange rate.

Macro Aspects: Labor Markets and Monetary Stability

Economic and Monetary Union rests on the fundamental principle of monetary stability, and one of the main pillars of EMU is the independence of the central bank, according to the widely held view that central bank independence is a necessary and sufficient condition for price stability.[19] This principle has been (partially) challenged on the premise that the correlation between central bank independence and inflation has to be assessed taking into account the characteristics of industrial relations and of the wage bargaining process in particular.[20] More precisely, one result of these analyses is that the higher the level of wage-bargaining coordination, the more efficient and less costly in terms of unemployment is (independent) monetary policy in curbing inflation.

Hall and Franzese advance, and test, the following three hypotheses: a) there is a negative relationship between inflation and central-bank independence (the traditional view about central bank independence and monetary stability); b) the level of wage-bargaining coordination has a direct effect on inflation irrespective of the role of central bank independence; c) in cases in which the level of wage coordination is low, central bank independence lowers the rate of inflation only at the cost of higher rates of unemployment. Taken together, these three hypotheses determine a structure of monetary independence and wage-bargaining arrangements leading to differentiated patterns of macroeconomic performance. Based on the average performance of the OECD countries during the period 1955–90, Hall and Franzese's findings are summarized in table 3.

At first glance, the implications are a source of concern. EMU introduces no incentive to increase the degree of wage-bargaining centralization to match the de-

---

[19] For a reassessment of the issue, see S. Eijffinger and J. De Haan, "The Political Economy of Central Bank Independence," *Special Paper in International Economy* 19 (Princeton: Princeton University Press, 1996).

[20] T. Iversen, "Wage Bargaining, Central Bank Independence, and the Real Effects of Money," *International Organization* 52, no. 3 (1998): 469–504; P. Hall and R. Franzese, "Mixed Signals: Central Bank Independence, Coordinated Wage Bargaining, and European Monetary Union," *International Organization* 52, no. 3 (1998): 505–35.

Table 3: Monetary policy and wage-bargaining regimes and results

	CBI low	CBI high
CWB low	high unemployment with high inflation	high unemployment with low inflation
CWB high	low unemployment with high inflation	low unemployment with low inflation

CBI = central bank independence
CWB = coordinated wage bargaining
Source: Hall and Franzese, "Mixed Signals."

gree of centralization and independence of monetary policy. As a matter of fact, the establishment of EMU and of the European Central Bank *decreases* the centralization of wage bargaining as it leaves it, in the best case, at the national level. The straightforward implication is that EMU will achieve price stability at a higher cost in terms of unemployment compared with cases in which wage-bargaining centralization was higher. In addition, according to this view, higher unemployment would be unevenly distributed among countries according to the levels of wage-bargaining centralization. Facing the same degree of central-bank independence, countries in which wage bargaining is more decentralized will suffer from higher unemployment.

By contrast, Bertola argues that wage bargaining within the euro area as a whole should be made less rather than more centralized. Given relevant differences in productivity, not only between countries but especially between regions, wage-bargaining structures should be kept at the lowest possible level (at least regionally).[21] Decentralization would also take into account the fact, addressed above, that regional specialization has been increasing over the recent past. Regional wage-bargaining structures would therefore represent a partial substitute of low labor mobility within EMU.[22] An issue to be watched closely, therefore, is to what extent monetary integration increases (or decreases) the amount of wage-bargaining centralization or, to put it differently, to what extent national trade unions across Europe coordinate wage bargaining. Some initial evidence suggests, however, that European trade unions are increasingly taking into account the EMU dimension in their bargaining strategies.[23]

Micro Aspects: The Evolution of Labor Market and Welfare State Institutions

The view just presented may be further specified, however. Another view holds that the amount of unemployment, for a given level of monetary policy independence,

[21] G. Bertola, "Labor Markets in the European Union," *EUI Working Papers* 99/24 (1999).
[22] Ibid.
[23] European Foundation for the Improvement of Living and Working Conditions, *The "Europeanisation" of Collective Bargaining* (EIROnline [http://www.eiro.eurofound.ie/], 1999).

is inversely correlated with the degree of labor-market flexibility.[24] In addition, given a supranational central bank, unemployment costs of monetary stabilization will be a function of the level of structural unemployment (i.e., the rate of unemployment not dependent on cyclical factors) which is the average of national levels of structural unemployment. In such a case, what improves the smooth operation of monetary union is an increase in the level of labor-market flexibility, itself dependent on national labor-market policies and institutions.

A comprehensive review of this issue is presented by Nickell, who studies the impact of labor-market regulations on unemployment. Drawing on labor-market data for a number of OECD countries, he finds that continental European countries exhibit different degrees of labor-market rigidities and they are generally higher than in the United Kingdom and the United States. He regresses his indicators of labor-market rigidity against total, long-term and short-term, unemployment. The unemployment rate is *positively* affected by (unrestricted) unemployment benefits, especially if associated with lack of incentives to accept jobs; lower pay rates in different sectors; a high level of union militancy *without* a high level of coordination with employers' associations in wage bargaining (which is equivalent to a *low* level of wage-bargaining centralization as discussed above); high labor-tax rates, especially if associated with high minimum wages; and a low level of workers' skills. The same analysis, however, shows that other labor-market institutions do *not* affect the rate of unemployment, such as workers' protection legislation and labor standards; unemployment benefits, if they are accompanied by appropriate job search incentives; and high union militancy rates, if associated with high levels of coordination with employers' associations in wage-setting procedures (thus confirming evidence reported in the previous section).[25]

These results are relevant to our discussion especially from one point of view. Although some labor-market institutions may affect unemployment more than others, their interaction plays a potentially important role. We can, therefore, draw some additional implications: increased "flexibility," understood as the appropriate combination of different labor-market institutions, may increase employment for a given degree of monetary-policy independence.

The Road to More Flexibility: Institutional Competition or Social Dumping?

What are the implications for the endogenous approach to EMU? The priority of a national as opposed to a European dimension in labor-market policies and the rele-

---

[24] See, for instance, Center for Economic Policy Research, *Monitoring European Integration 5: Unemployment Choices for Europe* (London: Center for Economic Policy Research, 1995); S. Nickell, "Unemployment and Labor Market Rigidities: Europe versus North America," *Journal of Economic Perspectives* 11, no. 3 (1997): 55–74.

[25] Nickell, "Unemployment and Labor Market Rigidities."

vance of the labor-market institutions for employment have led many analysts and policy makers to predict "institutional competition" or, in some cases, "social dumping" under EMU. Deeper international integration and "globalisation" increase competition between product and factor (especially labor) markets, they reason. Elimination of exchange-rate movements clearly increases such competitive pressures. To the extent that labor-market regulations affect labor costs and hence competitiveness, absent a supranational labor-market regulation, national (and subnational) regulatory bodies, often with the agreement of, or under the pressure of workers' and employers' representative bodies, can be expected to loosen labor-market regulations in order to increase competitiveness. Better competitive positions, and hence better employment opportunities, could be the result of cheaper domestic production costs and increased foreign capital inflows attracted by them. As a consequence, a "race to the bottom" might result in labor regulations. This concern has been raised especially with respect to the EU's future enlargement to Central and Eastern European countries, which typically have much lower labor costs compared with those of current EU members.[26]

How real is this possibility? As of now, evidence is still too limited to offer a final verdict. Here we can report evidence regarding the impact of international competition on employment and wage levels and evidence on the recent evolution of social institutions in Europe.

A first set of evidence looks at the effects of international competition on employment and wage levels in manufacturing sectors in the core EU countries.[27] It is useful in assessing the degree of exposure of these economies to competition from low-wage countries. Estimation results show that labor markets in continental European countries, irrespective of the manufacturing sector considered, react to international competition more through changes (decreases) in employment levels than through wage cuts. The reverse is true in the United Kingdom and the smaller Nordic countries. This can be taken as evidence of a generalized "labor market rigidity" in continental Europe.

Secondly, international competition exerts a stronger (negative) pressure on both wages and employment levels in sectors where the country exhibits a trade comparative *disadvantage*, whereas such pressure is much weaker or absent in sectors in which the country enjoys a comparative *advantage*. This implies that the widespread assertion—that international competition, which may be increased by forms of social dumping, will hurt especially unskilled labor-intensive sectors—must be qualified. (For instance, Italy, which has a comparative advantage in traditional labor-intensive sectors, does not show strong pressures on its labor markets in these sectors). One implication is the following. The role of labor-market institu-

---

[26] Central and Eastern European countries have hourly labor costs which are from one-third to one-tenth of EU average. See CEPR, *Monitoring European Integration*, table 4.4.

[27] Padoan, *Employment and Growth in European Monetary Union*. Based on a model suggested in D. Neven and C. Wyplosz, "Relative Prices and Trade Restructuring in European Industry," *CEPR Discussion Paper* 1451 (1996).

tions, which affect performance of both wage and employment levels, cannot be separated from the role of other factors (most notably, cumulated learning, scale effects, and specific knowledge), which determine the overall trade performance of a sector.

A second set of evidence looks at changing labor-market institutions. Boeri provides a detailed analysis of institutional changes in labor-market regulation and social-security legislation in Europe over the past fifteen years, a period of increasing monetary integration. His relevant findings are four. First, there is no evidence of a "race to the bottom" in social-security contributions. Quite the contrary, a "race to the top" may be identified, especially in the D-mark-zone countries (i.e., those where monetary integration has been more intense and prolonged). Second, there is some evidence of convergence in pensions schemes toward the middle range. Third, some evidence of declining generosity in unemployment benefits exists, but this trend has not been uniform and has been only marginal in the D-mark zone. Finally, there is some evidence of a diminishment of the extent of employment-protection legislation.

Finally, we cannot find any clear evidence of a tendency toward one model of European social legislation or of increased labor-market flexibility. Participation in currency agreements (the D-mark zone) does not seem to matter much for the direction and intensity of changes in social legislation. In addition, the hypothesis of social dumping (race to the bottom) is not supported, although the two Iberian countries and the Netherlands have recently introduced "major" reforms in employment-protection legislation.[28]

Interactions between Policy Areas

The evidence that we have reviewed in the previous paragraphs is mixed. In some cases, such as cyclical convergence or integrating financial markets, the evolution of the EMU area is pointing toward a strengthening euro-zone. In other cases, such as the evolution of national specialization, words of caution are in order. Evidence on the evolution of social- and labor-market institutions, in addition, does not show any clear sign that a euro-zone model is emerging. Nonetheless, over the past two decades, under the impact of the single-market and monetary integration, the EU economy has been changing in ways that facilitate adjustment. An increasing convergence toward an optimum currency area configuration, however, would represent only a necessary and not sufficient condition for a successful EMU. A convergence of national economic policies toward a coherent European model of governance is needed.

The issue of policy convergence covers two aspects. The first deals with policy spillovers (interactions), whereas the second deals with policy convergence

---

[28] T. Boeri, "Social Europe: Dramatic Visions and Real Complexity," *CEPR Discussion Paper* 2371 (2000).

strictly defined. In the case of markets, the mechanism leading to endogenous change is deeper monetary integration. In the case of policies, the driving force is centralization of monetary policy at a supranational level. Once the shift is made from several national monetary policies to a single, supranational policy and institution, other policy areas and institutions are affected and face pressures to adjust.

The interaction between policy areas is a more complex issue than can be fully explored here. Let us nonetheless consider the extent to which outcomes in one policy area influence outcomes in another.

Monetary and Fiscal Policy

Cooperation between the single monetary policy and national budget policies increases benefits in terms of improved performance. Spillovers between monetary and fiscal policy support the idea that coordination is beneficial. OECD simulations show that switching to a common monetary policy increases the effectiveness of monetary stabilization to the extent that common monetary policy is geared to average and not country-specific inflation rates.[29] However, as Bini-Smaghi and Casini stress, since the establishment of the European Central Bank (ECB), the exchange of information between monetary and fiscal policy authorities has become much weaker compared to, for instance, the EMS period, when national monetary and fiscal authorities in the ERM interacted on a permanent basis with tangible benefits for macroeconomic management.[30] The implication is that centralization of monetary policy requires a strengthening of the so-called "Euro-group" (former Euro-11).[31]

Cooperation among National Fiscal Policy Authorities

There are other reasons to favor a stronger "Euro-group." The OECD shows that losses in the stabilization power of budget policies decrease when the number of countries allowing automatic stabilizers to operate increases. This number, in turn, increases as budget flexibility is restored.[32] The extent to which budget cooperation in the Euro-group increases the speed of convergence toward a "stable budget regime" (understood as the fulfillment of the requirements of the Stability and

[29] OECD, *EMU: Facts, Challenges and Policies* (Paris: Organization for Economic Co-operation and Development, 1999).

[30] L. Bini-Smaghi and C. Casini, "Monetary and Fiscal Policy Co-operation: Institutions and Procedures in EMU," *Journal of Common Market Studies* 38, 3 (2000): 375–91.

[31] P. Jacquet and J. Pisani-Ferry, "La coordination des politiques économiques dans la zone euro: bilan et propositions, en Conseil d'Analyse Économique," *Questions Européenes* (Paris: La Documentation Française, 2000).

[32] OECD, *EMU*. On the implications of cooperation for economic policy in EMU, see M. Buti and A. Sapir, eds., *Economic Policy in EMU: A Study by the European Commission Services* (New York: Oxford University Press, 1998).

Growth Pact) is an important issue. In a low-growth situation in the core Euroland countries (notably Germany, Italy, and partly France) such as the one prevailing at the early start of EMU, fiscal-stabilization measures are harder to obtain. Budget coordination increases, if marginally, the overall growth rate, making it easier to converge to the "stable budget regime." Benefits from coordination increase if externalities can be exploited. Informal evidence suggests that these externalities are present. Within Euroland, incentives for a coordinated policy action are larger in the core countries. At the outset of EMU, for example, peripheral countries (notably Ireland, Portugal, and Spain) experienced higher growth and would have preferred a more restrictive policy stance. In this situation, the peripheral countries could tighten fiscal policy beyond the requirements of the Stability and Growth Pact, whereas others could be somewhat more relaxed within the limits the Stability and Growth Pact.

Budget Policy Composition

Once financial and monetary stabilization are obtained, attention can be shifted toward a "qualitative approach" to budget policy, and focusing on the composition of expenditure and taxation becomes more relevant. As discussed in the EC Commission document about public finances in EMU, as financial equilibrium approaches and growth resumes in Europe, the room for tax cuts increases. However, the Commission has reiterated that tax cuts are justified only when corresponding expenditure cuts are implemented, especially in light of unfunded pension liabilities.[33] Using this approach, new attention is given to the composition of taxation with an eye toward its implications for long-term growth in particular. Once attention is shifted from aggregate revenues and expenditures to their composition, the allocation function of economic policy comes to the foreground, and the interaction between the macroeconomic and the microeconomic dimensions deepens. This is becoming particularly relevant for the exploitation of the opportunities offered by information and communication technologies (ICT).[34]

Tax Policy Cooperation

A widely held view is that monetary union requires tax harmonization to operate effectively under a regime of full capital mobility. An alternative view is that tax competition is beneficial, as it stimulates policies to attract mobile capital and to enhance the efficiency of financial markets. To the extent that tax competition pro-

---

[33] Commission of the European Communities, *Public Finances in EMU* (Luxembourg: Office for Official Publications of the European Communities, May 2000).

[34] Exploiting such technology requires more efficient and flexible product markets as well as more investment and integration in innovation activities. Success in these tasks can be expected to reduce unemployment accordingly. This is the focus of the so-called Cardiff Process.

duces effects on national budgets, it may interfere with cooperation among national fiscal authorities. It is not clear to what extent an "optimal" tax regime can be designed in a monetary union. Different views and incentives are present. Core EU-12 countries have favored some form of tax harmonization. At the Feira European Council meeting in June 2000, a compromise agreement was reached under which countries will continue to set their own, different tax rates, but national authorities will exchange information to prevent tax evasion. In practice, all major continental European governments (Germany, France, and Italy) announced, in 2000, major tax cuts favoring both households and businesses. This possibly suggests that a "mixed regime" of tax harmonization and competition is emerging.[35]

These linkages between monetary unification on the one hand and other economic and structural reform on the other illustrate a more general point. The launching of monetary union and the introduction of a supranational central bank lead to a growing interconnection between macro and micro (structural) policies. This makes the issue of policy convergence much more complex than is generally assumed.

Policy Convergence

Policy convergence in EMU is really another name for a more complex and ambitious goal: a new model of EU economic governance. In discussing this point, one has to come to terms with the unique features of EMU, the coexistence of different levels of economic sovereignty—supranational, national, and local—in which the community and intergovernmental dimensions coexist.

To understand the features of the EU policy regime, it is useful to distinguish between the macro and the microeconomic domains. It is not just a question of different policy domains, however; it is rather an issue of different mechanisms and rules, that is, different, yet interacting, policy regimes. In what follows, we will look at the macroeconomic (monetary-fiscal) regime and at one specific microeconomic regime, employment policy (which is dealt with at the Community level using the so-called "Luxembourg process"), one of the few areas where some evidence of performance is available.

The stability of policy regimes is a central issue. Are regimes based on a structure of incentives that leads to mutually consistent behavior by actors involved, both policy and market agents? Are agents' behaviors consistent with monetary union specifically? These questions should be evaluated in an evolving framework.

---

[35] C. Daveri and G. Tabellini, "Unemployment, Growth, and Taxation in Industrial Countries," *CEPR Discussion Paper* 1615 (1997), argue that tax competition has led to excessive labor tax loads, which in turn may explain a large part of European unemployment. So it may be that tax competition, to the extent that it leads to excessively low taxation on capital, may lead to more labor-market competition *and thus adjustment*.

As we have discussed above, monetary union generates pressure for change both in markets and policies. So we have to consider whether the response of agents to the pressures arising from EMU supports monetary union itself.

The Macroeconomic Regime

The discussion on policy interaction in the previous section has two implications. First, the creation of a supranational institution in one policy area generates pressures for change in other policy areas, in all of which at least some degree of supranationality is introduced. This suggests that a model of pure supranational monetary policy and pure national policies in other areas is unstable. Second, to the extent that a "mixed" model of economic policy emerges, it must be based on a coherent set of policy incentives to produce consistent and stable outcomes. Policy convergence should be examined within this context. To discuss the point, it is useful to reconsider the evolution of macroeconomic policy regimes in place under the EMS, before EMU. This is because one of the main (economic) justifications for the move from the fixed exchange-rate regime to a single currency is that the former was becoming increasingly unsustainable in the presence of full capital mobility.[36]

The EMS can be described as a "weak hegemonic regime," based on asymmetric adjustment obligations between the key country, Germany, and the periphery. The main incentive for Germany's partners was the importation of monetary discipline, the exploitation of the public good of monetary stability provided by the center economy. The incentive for Germany to participate in the regime was, given domestic price stability, the support of its international competitiveness, which was gained by preventing or limiting exchange-rate devaluations in the periphery. The stability of the regime was obtained to the extent that national policies converged toward the German monetary-policy stance. The regime collapsed when, after German unification, the core country was not willing to bear the cost of supporting the weaker (more inflation-prone) economies, and the periphery was not willing to make the (deflationary) adjustment necessary to support the exchange-rate regime in light of high capital mobility. The policy regime proved to be effective as an anti-inflationary mechanism, but it produced limited, if any, policy spillovers toward other areas (especially fiscal policy). The ERM crises of 1992–93 showed that policy convergence had to extend to other areas beyond monetary and exchange-rate policy, if it were to pass the judgment of the markets. As long as it succeeded, it proved that an "intergovernmental" approach to macroeconomic policy requires leadership; its failure demonstrated that weak hegemonic leadership may be insufficient when market integration deepens beyond some critical threshold.

The decision to move forward from the EMS to EMU has led to a major change

---

[36] B. Eichengreen, *International Monetary Arrangements for the 21st Century* (Washington: Brookings Institution, 1994), argues that, once full financial integration is achieved, only two monetary regimes are sustainable, monetary union or fully flexible exchange rates. Intermediate regimes such as pegged exchange rates come under heavy pressure and are likely to eventually collapse.

in the policy regime and in the policy convergence process. Policy convergence has been witnessed with respect to both monetary and fiscal policy. More importantly, it has shifted toward a more *symmetric* configuration. The greater symmetry has in turn required two additional conditions in order to be effective: a) the move from a hegemonic leadership structure to a supranational one; b) the imposition of high entry costs (fulfillment of the Maastricht convergence conditions under the threat of exclusion) as well as high exit costs (the costs associated with the possibility of one country leaving the single currency). In this respect, monetary union can be described as a club good.[37]

The Microeconomic Regime

The Stability and Growth Pact guarantees that, once monetary convergence has been obtained, and a single monetary policy becomes feasible, national fiscal policies are managed according to common guidelines (and hence fiscal-policy convergence is also obtained). However, the sustainability of monetary union requires some movement toward the configuration of an optimum currency area. Consequently, as one cannot rely on market forces alone to produce this convergence, monetary union requires the adoption of appropriate microeconomic (structural) policies to overcome labor-and product-market rigidities. The extent of harmonization or convergence of microeconomic policies toward common standards required by EMU remains to be seen, and evidence discussed above shows little recent movement in this respect.

To accelerate policy reform, the European Union has launched three sets of consultative procedures, known as the Luxembourg, Cardiff, and Cologne processes. The Cardiff process involves the adoption of measures aimed at improving the performance of product markets. The Luxembourg process deals with employment policies. The Cologne process calls for enhanced interaction between microeconomic and macroeconomic policies. The voluntary, consultative approach taken in these processes is very much still in its infancy and, in many respects, lags behind the degree of cooperation that we observe even for budget policies.

To explore the implications of this approach, consider the case of employment polices within the Luxembourg process in more detail. Because "institutional dumping" does not seem to be taking place in the EU, as concluded above, any convergence of social policies is likely to take the form of a "race to the top." It is interesting to ask, therefore, whether the existing policy framework can support such a process.

In a nutshell, the EU employment policy framework operates as follows. Each year, every EU member state sets out its National Action Plan (NAP), which contains the policy actions it has taken to improve employment. The general philoso-

---

[37] P. C. Padoan, "Regional Agreements as Clubs, the European Case," in E. Mansfield and H. Milner, eds., *The Political Economy of Regionalism* (New York: Columbia University Press, 1997).

phy of the approach is that flexibility in European labor markets can be obtained by moving away from "passive" employment policies, such as unemployment benefits, toward "active" policies, such as welfare-to-work schemes and active learning and retraining. Within the process, however, a wide range of polices is considered, including those supporting small and medium-sized enterprises.

Policies are implemented at the national level, as only national governments have jurisdiction over such policies, and are classified according to a (long) list of "policy guidelines" established by the Commission. Those guidelines are grouped under four headings: employability (employment policies in the strict sense of the term, such as the creation of job-placement agencies), adaptability (policies aimed at adapting workers to the new market conditions, such as retraining policies), entrepreneurship (policies aimed at improving the demand side of the labor market, such as incentives for small businesses), and equal opportunity (policies aimed at increasing the employment opportunities for women).

Each year, the NAPs are presented to the Commission and are reviewed by member states through a "peer review" procedure. A final "score" is assigned to each government, indicating the degree of fulfillment of the policy guidelines and identified "best practices." Policy recommendations are then directed to each member country by the Commission and the Council.

Retaining full control of policy, national governments are not subject to any explicit obligation.[38] Failure to follow recommendations brings no punishment or threat of exclusion, as was the case prior to the creation of the monetary union. In other words, as we move away from policies in which the supranational element prevails, the strength of the convergence process weakens.

Even in areas where there is no explicit obligation to adjust, however, there are substantial incentives for national governments to change policies. Two distinct sets of incentives operate: a "competition" incentive and a "cooperation" (regime-building) incentive. The competition incentive derives from both the policy arena and from the market. A country that performs poorly in improving its employment policies would see its reputation weaken and, consequently, its leverage in the design and implementation of EU policies at large diminish. This would be particularly worrisome whenever the intergovernmental dimension is relevant. In addition, markets would punish a poor performer to the extent that inefficient policies make that country less attractive for investment, whereas good performers would presumably enjoy greater profitability and thus increased investment. The competition incentive will be increasingly relevant in a world of high capital mobility. In short, institutional competition will not go away; rather it may well produce a healthy improvement in EU economic performance, provided that it takes the form of exchange of best practices and provides content to the principle of subsidiarity.

The cooperation incentive is relevant to the extent that poor performance in any

---

[38] In some areas of course national governments must fulfill obligations emanating from Commission directives, such as those related to the prohibition of implementing state aids.

member of EMU weakens the performance and attractiveness of the euro area as a whole vis-à-vis the rest of the world. Poor policy and economic performance in any one member of the club decreases the quality of the club good (monetary union) and generates a negative externality on the other club members. This will presumably lead to strengthened peer pressure on the poor performer from the rest of the club members (and from the Commission). In this case, the supranational pressure might be more important than the intergovernmental pressure. To the extent that such an incentive-structure strengthens, therefore, policy convergence could well be the result of the interaction of inter-governmentalism and supranationalism.

Conclusions

EMU is endogenous, to some extent, and such endogeneity derives from two complementary viewpoints. As suggested by Collignon's approach to currency areas, first, benefits from monetary union increase with the degree of economic integration for a given distribution of policy preferences among countries. Second, given the degree of integration, convergence in the distribution of policy preferences is necessary for net benefits to be generated by monetary unification. Pre-EMU monetary convergence has led to deeper integration, thus increasing net benefits. This has been obtained because the process of monetary integration in Europe has produced (or rather "forced") convergence in "revealed" policy preferences. However, although observed convergence relates to preferences for financial stability, the same is not yet clear for preferences and policies for more flexible product and labor markets. It remains to be seen whether the incentives to implement policies more consistent with an optimum currency area will be effective enough to produce the necessary policy adjustments. To the extent that the convergence of economic preferences and the convergence of policy preferences are self-reinforcing, however, EMU is indeed a self-fulfilling, evolutionary mechanism.

Finally, if EMU can be considered to be a substantially endogenous process, one should ask: What are the exogenous forces that are also contributing to adjustments in markets and policies that could underpin a more viable currency union?[39] A short answer is that the exogenous forces are the same ones that drive the EU integration process at large. Three main factors are particularly important.

The first factor can be understood as a regional response to the excess demand for international public goods,[40] which in turn is the consequence of the collapse of the postwar hegemonic system. Regional agreements have been strengthened as a response to external threats. As Henning suggests, whenever the United States has behaved "aggressively" in its macroeconomic and monetary relations with Europe,

---

[39] I thank Randy Henning for raising this issue.

[40] P. C. Padoan, "Globalization, Regionalism, and the Nation State: Top Down and Bottom Up," in M. Franzini and R. Pizzuti, eds., *Globalization, Institutions, and Social Cohesion* (Berlin/Heidelberg: Springer, 2000).

European countries have increased the degree of monetary cooperation among themselves in order to stem such "aggressiveness." Periods of "benign" attitudes on the part of the American authorities saw retardation or even backsliding in European monetary integration.[41]

Henning's framework can be adapted to the EMU phase, which represents the highest degree of European monetary cooperation, and broadened. An "aggressive" U.S. attitude toward Europe would favor a European attitude of "non-cooperation" vis-à-vis the United States and perhaps would even foster an attempt to redirect abroad factors of instability inside the EU.[42] Conversely, a benign American attitude would favor adoption of a similar attitude by Europe. Such a pattern of response would constitute "tit-for-tat" behavior, which, as Axelrod shows, could lead to more cooperation by raising the costs of defection.[43]

The second exogenous factor is related to the traditional European strategy of deepening integration to support its overall performance and to close the competitiveness gap with the United States. The most notable examples are the launching of the Single Market as a response to "eurosclerosis" and the "Lisbon strategy" to make Europe the "best knowledge-based economy in the world."

The institutional response to the enlargement of the European Union to perhaps twenty-seven members represents the third exogenous factor. The Intergovernmental Conference that was concluded at Nice delivered a clear message: The way forward for EU integration is "reinforced co-operation," that is, through initiatives taken by a subset of members, a restricted club, to move further on toward deeper integration. EMU will most likely be the most relevant example of this new institutional model and, to the extent that EMU membership increases, it would both signal the success of monetary union and represent a major engine for deeper European integration in areas beyond economic and monetary union.

[41] C. R. Henning, "Systemic Conflict and Regional Monetary Integration: The Case of Europe," *International Organization* 52, no. 3 (1998): 537–74.

[42] This scenario is explored by A. Benassy, M. Benoit, and J. Pisani-Ferry, "The Euro and Exchange Rate Stability," presented at the Fondation Camille Gutt, IMF Seminar on EMU and the International Monetary System, Washington, D.C., March 17–18, 1997.

[43] R. Axelrod, *The Evolution of Co-operation* (New York: Basic Books, 1984).

CHAPTER SEVEN

State Building, the Territorialization of Money, and the Creation of the American Single Currency

Kathleen R. McNamara

The geography of money is becoming increasingly complex. Currency borders blur with globalization, and the conventional notion of "One Money, One State" is under attack by the multiplicity of national monies circulating and competing outside their home borders.[1] Some states are dollarizing their economies, surrendering their national money. Other states are choosing to merge their currencies, as in the case of the monetary union in Europe. Both choices are variants of the regionalization of money, which Cohen defines as occurring "when two or more countries formally share a single money or equivalent."[2] The list of countries that have taken on external currencies is growing beyond the traditional small entities, such as Monaco, to include larger ones, such as Ecuador and El Salvador. States and currencies, in other words, are no longer coterminous.[3]

However, we have yet to fully understand the implications of deterritorialization for state sovereignty and political authority. The adoption of outside currencies signals the delegation of monetary management to foreign central banks. To what extent does such delegation imply the loss of *political* power or legitimacy? How does deterritorialization impact national identity? Does it challenge the essence of the state? What are the ties between sovereignty and currency? To address these ques-

---

I thank Sheri Berman, Jerry Cohen, Frank Dobbin, Aaron L. Friedberg, Jeffrey Herbst, James Savage, Steven Teles, Keith E. Whittington, and the editors for helpful and thoughtful comments on earlier versions of this chapter.

[1] B. J. Cohen, *The Geography of Money* (Ithaca: Cornell University Press, 1998).

[2] See B. J. Cohen, "Monetary Governance in a World of Regional Currencies" (paper prepared for a project on Globalization and Governance, directed by M. Kahler and D. Lake, 2001), 2, and the appendix of the paper, which provides a comprehensive catalog of contemporary currency arrangements worldwide.

[3] Helleiner probes the reasons for the growing "unpopularity" of national currencies in his contribution to this volume.

tions, this chapter provides a suggestive historical analysis of the relationship between state building and monetary consolidation, with reference to the case of early
American monetary consolidation and the development of the greenback, or American paper dollar, in the Civil War era. Knowing how currency became nationalized
in this American case may help us better understand the implications of the globalization of money today.

In telling the story of the early origins of the American single currency, this chapter
highlights two key causal dynamics that shaped the transition to a single currency: (1)
the role of war and wartime economic mobilization and (2) the desire to create a single
national market to facilitate economic development. By creating a unifying political
symbol, American political leaders also sought to encourage a redrawing of the lines of
collective identity and community. The dynamics at work in currency consolidation
were thus both functional and symbolic. However, the greenback's function in helping to create an independent federal fiscal capacity with the power to raise revenues
was ultimately more important than monetary symbolism for the consolidation of internal political power in the American state. Moreover, the American case strongly
suggests that the development of the national currency should be interpreted as one
important part of a larger project of institutional development. The initial development of the U.S. single currency suggests, finally, that although the deterritorialization of money today does indeed erode political capacity, its effects are more akin to
the chipping away of sovereign authority rather than its wholesale destruction.[4]

The chapter begins by reviewing the literature on state building and its relationship to national currencies. What is state building and how does it proceed? What
role have theorists ascribed to a national currency in this political development? A
summary history of the drive toward a single currency in the United States, focused on the nineteenth century and the Civil War as a catalyst for monetary consolidation, is then provided. The final section suggests some lessons from the
American experience in light of the different relationship between money and
states today compared with that relationship in the nineteenth century.

Theoretical Approaches to State Building

State building implies the domestic centralization and internal consolidation of political power. Many writers on state building have focused on the development of
states in Western Europe, often seeking to draw out comparative observations about
the component dynamics of that process.[5] A second strand of literature, the Amer-

---

[4] At least two caveats to this historical comparison need to be kept in mind, however: first, the political meaning of national money may have changed over the past century, and second, the effects of removing currency from policy capacity may be different in a mature state from the effects of currency
adoption early in the process of state formation. These issues are taken up in the conclusion.

[5] C. Tilly, ed., *The Formation of National States in Western Europe* (Princeton: Princeton University
Press, 1975); G. Poggi, *The Development of the Modern State* (Stanford: Stanford University Press,
1978).

ican Political Development literature, has focused on the American experience.[6] Although there are important differences in the timing and social and political histories of the American and the European experience, a general description of the foundations of the modern Western state is possible. The characteristics of a modern state with a unique, distinct, independent power of rule include: the unity of state territory, bounded as much as possible by geographically defensible borders, a single currency and unified fiscal system, a single national language, often imposed over others which are sometimes "harshly suppressed," and a unified legal system.[7] All Western states in the nineteenth century pursued these basic goals "self-consciously and explicitly" and "the most significant exceptions to the principle of unity were federal states but even there the principle was embodied in a federal constitution and a federal government charged (at the very least) with the conduct of foreign relations. . . ."[8]

Scholars have attempted to offer a generalized trajectory of political development that identifies the sequence and timing of the stages of state building. Here the American and European experiences are generally agreed to have diverged. From the European experience, Huntington has proposed a three-stage model of state building.[9] First, state power is extended and centralized, and authority is rationalized throughout the nation at the same time as decentralized institutions that might contest authority are dismantled. This process is marked by internal struggles over the relative balance of power across different power centers and over the content and direction of the powers of rule.[10] Second, the bureaucracy undergoes an increasing specialization; new political functions are differentiated and specific institutions are designed to perform them. The process of state building itself is directed toward multiple foci as a differentiation of political activities is one of the hallmarks of state development. Finally, in conjunction with these new state capacities comes an increase in political participation and democratic accountability. At the same time, attention to and concerns over political legitimacy increase and efforts are made toward the maintenance of a degree of civility in public affairs, despite the inevitable and contentious power struggles.

In contrast to this stylized European model, political development in the American case is generally agreed to have occurred in a somewhat different trajectory. Most clearly, the broadening of political participation came early in the American

---

[6] W. D. Burnham, *Critical Elections and the Mainsprings of American Politics* (New York: Norton, 1970); S. Skowronek, *Building a New American State: The Expansion of National Administrative Capacities, 1877–1920* (Cambridge: Cambridge University Press, 1982); P. B. Evans, D. Rueschemeyer, and T. Skocpol, eds., *Bringing the State Back In* (Cambridge: Cambridge University Press, 1985); R. Bensel, *Yankee Leviathan: The Origins of Central State Authority in America, 1859–1877* (New York: Cambridge University Press, 1990); A. L. Friedberg, *The Shadow of the Garrison State: America's Anti-Statism and Its Cold War Strategy* (Princeton: Princeton University Press, 2000).

[7] Poggi, *The Development of the Modern State*, 93.

[8] Ibid.

[9] S. Huntington, *Political Order in Changing Societies* (New Haven: Yale University Press, 1968).

[10] Poggi, *The Development of the Modern State.*

case, preceding much of the political centralization of state building. Democratic participation came early, because foreign wars and social conflict were not decisive in shaping the state at its founding in the ways they were in Europe, which had a feudal tradition as its base of evolution.[11] Rationalization of authority and differentiation of institutions occurred much earlier and more completely in Europe than in the United States. In seventeenth-century Europe, the state itself replaced fundamental law as a source of political authority, whereas in America, the law continued to play the role of ultimate authority and arbitrator, not the central state. Sovereignty also was dispersed across institutions and society in America, not instilled in a single supreme body as in the European state.

The American experience is, therefore, considered unusual in upending the order of political development. Scholars disagree, however, over the implications of this trajectory. Huntington has argued that there is an inverse correlation between the modernization of governmental institutions and the expansion of political participation. "Political modernization in America has thus been strangely attenuated and incomplete. In institutional terms, the American polity has never been underdeveloped, but it has also never been wholly modern. In today's world, American political institutions are unique, if only because they are so antique."[12]

An entirely different view is articulated by Skowronek, however, who notes, "the absence of European state forms need not be equated with an undeveloped state." Indeed, Marx saw the more minimalist state apparatus, individualistic and society-based focus, and strong legal system of the United States as "the most perfect example of the modern state."[13] The U.S. state, in this view, has been very successful in providing the structure for advanced capitalism while balancing democratic needs in its more participatory and open political form.

What are the dynamics that push forward state building? Theorists stress that state building does not occur mechanistically but rather is a highly political and contingent process, as will be demonstrated in the narrative of the American case which follows. However, we can identify a series of historical developments which have formed the impetus for state building across many states. Theorists have specifically focused on the role of war—as summed up in Tilly's succinct phrase, "War made the state and the state made war."[14] As will be discussed further below, the requirements for effective mobilization for war have proved a comprehensive spur to the development of the modern state, as state bureaucracy increases to meet the demands of war, revenue extraction widens, and governments become involved in a wide array of activities within the economy.[15] Other theorists have emphasized, instead, the interactions between the dynamic evolution of capitalism and state

[11] Huntington, *Political Order in Changing Societies*.

[12] Ibid., 98.

[13] Skowronek, *Building a New American State*, 7.

[14] Tilly, *The Formation of National States in Western Europe*, 42.

[15] B. C. Porter, *War and the Rise of the State: The Military Foundations of Modern Politics* (New York: Free Press, 1994).

building.[16] As economic activity becomes more integrated and complex, authority must be centralized in order to stabilize and regulate markets against the volatility inherent in their growth.

Skowronek incorporates such factors in his overview summary of the factors stimulating the growth of the modern state.[17] First, crisis, whether international such as foreign wars or national such as internal unrest or strife, is an undeniable spark to state building. Class conflict is a second important dynamic. The interclass struggle between labor and capital, and the struggles among capitalists themselves, demand the increasing capacity of the state to either mediate or suppress such conflict. Finally, the state can develop in response to social complexity, "the growth and concentration of the population, the division of labor, the specialization of functions, the differentiation of social sectors, and the advance of technology."[18]

Although several general models of state building have been presented, and the sources of state building regarded as most critical have been identified, it is important to note that this does not imply the necessity of a teleological view of state development. These historical processes have been open-ended, with different states addressing their particular problems in ways which vary based on their political and historical circumstances. State building is pursued by specific individuals and groups for particular political purposes, yet it is difficult to predict which groups will produce a state, or when and where. For example, although it would seem that state building would be the natural result of a search by a national society, "that is, a geographically, linguistically, ethnically, and culturally distinctive population seeking a political guarantee and expression of its distinctiveness," in many cases no such grouping can be shown to have existed, much less to have prompted the centralization of state power.[19] Instead, the process of state building has historically been attenuated, tentative, and circuitous, with different groups using different justifications for political centralization at different times, without consensus on the desirability of an overarching and explicit design.

National Currencies and States

Monetary consolidation and the creation of a national currency has been a component part of the state building process, although few of the authors central to the state-building literature have explicitly focused on this policy area. Theorists of international political economy, in contrast, have looked at the role a national currency plays in the development of external sovereignty, that is, in the formation of a Westphalian state with exclusive territoriality. Cohen, for example, articulates the functions of a national currency in creating a powerful political symbol for unity, in

---

[16] Poggi, *The Development of the Modern State*.
[17] Skowronek *Building a New American State*, 10–12.
[18] Ibid., 11.
[19] Poggi, *The Development of the Modern State*, 98–99.

providing for seigniorage gains, in facilitating macroeconomic management, and in providing some measure of monetary insulation against external forces.[20] The emphasis of this international political-economy literature, however, has been largely on the external repercussions of currency consolidation and on interactions with actors in the international system, not on the internal political meaning of currencies. Those who have studied the effects of the globalization of currency regimes and the increasing "unpopularity" of national currencies have done much to illuminate the interplay of markets and politics, but explicit connections to the literature on state building remain to be made.[21]

If we examine the territorialization of currency from the perspective of state building, a national currency can be understood as contributing to the enforcement of domestic-level sovereignty, which performs the general tasks of consolidating state power and developing a specialized organizational and bureaucratic apparatus while addressing the political needs of actors within states, particularly in prosecuting war and furthering market integration and capitalist development.

First, a national currency contributes to the organizational and bureaucratic development of the state. Government institutions must assume responsibility for the management of the national currency. The responsibility for this task is often initially housed inside preexisting treasury or finance departments or ministries and then evolves in more differentiated ways in conjunction with a national bank system, and finally, to a modern national central bank. In so doing, policy-making capabilities and the structures needed to execute them come under purview of central authorities, moving power to the national government and providing the instruments for its effective use. This can easily be seen as congruent with the generalized theoretical model of state building outlined above.

Second, the national currency can play a key role in state building as it relates to the unification and development of the national fiscal policy-making system. The ability to run deficits and issue national public debt greatly enhances the capacities of states, and having a national paper currency unlinks the money supply from traditional metallic standards, loosening the ties on government spending. A national currency also makes it easier both to raise and organize public debt, as well as to tax more effectively. In the American case, as we shall see, nationalizing the currency enhanced the growth and efficiency of private financial markets as well, which were critical to fighting the Civil War and to postwar reconstruction.[22]

Finally, a single currency has long been a partner to the deepening and broadening of national markets. Capitalist development and state building have gone hand

[20] Cohen, *The Geography of Money*, chap. 2.

[21] The most developed literature by far is found in the following: E. Helleiner, "Historicizing Territorial Currencies: Monetary Space and the Nation-State in North America," *Political Geography* 18 (1999): 309–39; E. Helleiner, "National Currencies and National Identities," *American Behavioral Scientist* 41 (1998): 1409–36; E. Gilbert and E. Helleiner, eds., *Nation-States and Money: The Past, Present and Future of National Currencies* (New York: Routledge, 1999); and his chapter in this volume.

[22] Bensel, *Yankee Leviathan*.

in hand in history, as politicians and state representatives have sought to regulate and profit from market interactions at the same time as private actors have sought government action to stabilize an increasingly dense and deep market. As will be shown in the U.S. case, while private actors devised ways to cope with multitudes of paper and metallic currencies circulating in the antebellum period, a standardized medium of exchange, developed during the Civil War, facilitated trade and investment across the United States and achieved the important political goal of political unification.

In sum, national currencies have been important not only for their symbolic political meaning and specific functions, but also as part of a broader program of monetary consolidation and reorganization, including the enhancement of financial markets and national fiscal capacity. These dynamics will now be illustrated by an examination of the American case of state building and the greenback created in the second half of the nineteenth century.

Development of the American Single Currency

This section will review the basic history of the development of paper currency in the United States. We begin with the constitutional foundation and early years of the U.S. state formation, highlighting some of the tensions that arose over state versus federal power in the context of the establishment of a U.S. national bank. A discussion of the currency reforms that created the greenback in the throes of the Civil War follows, and some of the difficulties which arose in implementing the nineteenth-century currency-consolidation program are noted.

Two distinct moments of institutional transformation mark the history of the American experience in centralizing monetary authority. The first was the development of a national currency in the Civil War period, and the second was the consolidation of monetary control in the U.S. Federal Reserve, the American central bank established in 1913. The story of the U.S. Federal Reserve is relatively well known and has received careful study.[23] There has been less focus, however, on the steps taken toward the consolidation of monetary authority and the development of a single currency in the Civil War era. The Civil War, more than the end of British colonial rule, is viewed by some scholars as "the true foundational moment in American political development," as the administrative structures arising during the war and dominance of the Republican Party in its aftermath decisively shaped U.S. political development.[24] I therefore focus solely on this earlier period in this analysis.

---

[23] J. L. Broz, *The International Origins of the Federal Reserve System* (Ithaca: Cornell University Press, 1997); J. Livingston, *Origins of the Federal Reserve System: Money, Class, and Corporate Capitalism, 1890–1913* (Ithaca: Cornell University Press, 1986); R. C. West, *Banking Reform and the Federal Reserve, 1863–1923* (Ithaca: Cornell University Press, 1977).

[24] Bensel, *Yankee Leviathan*, 10.

Early and Antebellum Monetary History

The constitutional basis for the organization of monetary authority in the United States is straightforward.[25] The U.S. Constitution simply states that Congress has the power to coin money and regulate its value, and there is no specific legal outline for a single currency or central bank. The assumption at the founding of the United States was that a self-adjusting specie standard would be the basis for monetary governance. The roots of this decision lie in the political cleavages between those who wanted to give the federal government the capacity to borrow and hold public debts and those who wanted to limit the financial reach of the central government in favor of leaving authority in the hands of the American states.

The pre-Revolutionary American colonies had issued bills of credit which functioned as state-based paper money "not only to finance wars and fight recessions, but also to meet the demands of trading with England."[26] These bills of credit differed from greenbacks and other forms of later currency in that they were in effect circulating government bonds, and the size of the national debt was directly tied to the amount of currency in circulation. Of course, the stability of each note system was directly reliant on the credibility of the state in making good on its IOUs, which varied across time and by place. However, the relatively successful experience with the state-level paper-currency system led the Continental Congress to issue a single paper currency, the "continental," during the Revolutionary War, as the primary vehicle for financing the war. The continental, however, was plagued by inflationary spirals and diminishing confidence as the Congress repeatedly issued more paper money in the face of rapidly depleting domestic specie reserves.[27] The Articles of Confederation severely constrained the federal government in its revenue extraction powers, and by the end of the war, one of the problems which the new United States would have to deal with was a substantial debt left over from the war without much recourse for funding it.

When it came time to organize the public finances of the new American nation, a national paper currency standard was rejected and a metallic standard formed the basis of governance as outlined in the Constitution. The system was relatively automatic and self-regulating once begun, but political authority was a crucial foundation of its functioning. The government had to define the unit of account, the dollar, in terms of a weight of precious metal, such as gold. It had to also "be ready, willing, and able to convert gold bullion (bulk metal) into coined money at this ratio." In addition, the government had to assure citizens that the coined metal would be legal tender for all debts, public and private.[28]

---

[25] J. W. Hurst, *A Legal History of Money in the United States, 1774–1970* (Lincoln: University of Nebraska Press, 1973) offers an extended discussion of the constitutional foundation for federal monetary authority.

[26] J. Savage, *Balanced Budgets and American Politics* (Ithaca: Cornell University Press, 1988), 60.

[27] Ibid., 68.

[28] R. H. Timberlake, *The Origins of Central Banking in the United States* (Cambridge: Harvard University Press, 1978), 2.

State level monetary standards were also reformed, as the pre-Revolutionary bills of credit were outlawed by the Constitution at the behest of creditors and business interests and by those favoring financial and fiscal centralization.[29] This decision spurred the creation of a new state banking system with state bank currencies, which differed from bills of credit because they did not serve as bonds and were backed by gold reserves rather than promises to pay via tax obligations. A new system of finance developed in response to the Convention, one which tentatively began a nationalization of money but which in turn spurred a response from the state level as a new system of state banks developed. The critical issue of who would have power to issue money and finance deficits remained unresolved. Thus, the first step in the European model of state building, the centralization of institutional capacity, had occurred only in a very measured way, and it provoked a strong counter response on the part of the decentralized centers of power. This interactive dynamic would turn out to be decisive in shaping the next century of American national monetary politics.

The early years of the new American state followed this limited, stripped-down organization of monetary authority. The supply of gold mined determined the overall money supply, which pleased those who wanted to tie the hands of politicians in the financing of federal projects. Yet this also made economic downturns particularly difficult, as there was no recourse to cushioning their effects through a conscious expansion of the money supply. The supply of money was also augmented by the use of foreign coins, which circulated inside the U.S. as currency. Until the mid-nineteenth century, Mexican pesos, and gold coins from several other countries were used widely in the United States and were protected legally by federal legislation.[30]

The costs of the specie standard were high, however, in terms of basic logistics of storing and transferring gold. The substitution of paper monies for specie began in earnest in the late eighteenth century as part of the development of the commercial banking system, with three state banks chartered when Congress incorporated the First Bank of the United States in 1791. These banks issued paper notes to be used locally for payment, as will be explained further below.

The tensions between national political authority and local control of money were evident from the start of the attempts to regulate and standardize paper currency in the American union. Although it did mark a preliminary institutional development toward more centralized monetary authority, the First Bank was not anything close to a modern-day national central bank, nor did it oversee a national currency. To its key designer, Alexander Hamilton, its functions were not to serve as a lender of last resort or to regulate the flow of money but rather to allow for the funding of public debt to promote national growth, and, one day, to oversee the development of a single currency. As Hamilton argued in 1781, "A national debt if it

---

[29] I thank James Savage for his interpretation of this historical period.
[30] Cohen, *The Geography of Money*.

is not excessive will be to us a national blessing: it will be a powerful cement of our union."[31]

Opponents of the First Bank criticized it as usurping state interests in determining their own banking systems and setting a precedent for national power. Despite this, the First National Bank was enacted largely as per Hamilton's design, functioning as a fairly large-scale creditor and debtor of the government and setting the terms of its currency transactions with private banks with an eye to the overall need for credit restraint or ease.[32] Although it undertook its responsibilities adequately, when it came time for renewal of the Bank's charter in 1810, the political strength of those against an overly centralized monetary authority and the desire of the state banks to take over government deposits doomed its Congressional renewal.

After a period of state-level control over banking, a Second National Bank was established in 1816, but it too struck only a temporary and precarious balance between federal power and state sovereignty. In part, the Bank's founding was spearheaded by members of Congress who were concerned with strengthening the union and its national capacities in the wake of the War of 1812.[33] The war with Britain had occurred at a time when the United States was without a national bank, and the lack of fiscal and monetary control was thought to have been damaging to American efforts in prosecuting the war. These so-called "War Hawks" sought to shore up some of the weaknesses of the U.S. state, and the rechartering of the Bank was in line with their desire to solidify powers at the center, and, more urgently, to house the interest-bearing government debt incurred in the war. The crisis brought on by war strengthened the case of the War Hawks for more powers at the center and weakened the opposing claims by states.

There is disagreement among historians over the degree to which the Second Bank actually centralized powers and functioned as a proto-national central bank. Timberlake depicts the Second Bank as primarily concerned with rationalizing the flow of monies throughout the state-banking system and offering some level of external discipline on state activities.[34] While its charter outlined the Bank's responsibilities in terms of acting as a commercial bank and helping in the fiscal affairs of the government, it did not assign responsibility for the provision of a sound and uniform currency. However, other historians have emphasized the centralizing and federalist nature of the Bank, arguing that although these efforts were unsuccessful, its policies aimed at eventually creating a monetary union with a national currency standard.[35]

---

[31] D. Higginbotham, *The War of American Independence* (Bloomington, Ind.: Indiana University Press, 1977), 294, quoted in Savage, *Balanced Budgets and American Politics*, 70.

[32] Timberlake, *The Origins of Central Banking in the United States*, 10.

[33] B. Hammond, *Banks and Politics in America* (Princeton: Princeton University Press, 1957).

[34] Timberlake, *The Origins of Central Banking*; R. H. Timberlake, *Monetary Policy in the United States: An Intellectual and Institutional History* (Chicago: University of Chicago Press, 1993).

[35] Arthur Fraas, "The Second Bank of the United States: An Instrument for an Interregional Monetary Union," *Journal of Economic History* 34 (1974): 447–63; Hammond, *Banks and Politics in America;* R. C. H. Catterall, *The Second Bank of the United States* (Chicago: University of Chicago Press, 1902);

With the inauguration of the Jackson administration in 1828, a series of congressional inquiries into the renewal of the Second National Bank began. The central issue for many was whether Congress could and should exercise powers not enumerated in the Constitution and thus potentially reserved for the states. Some political leaders viewed as unacceptable the chartering of a national corporation and the establishment of an institution with the capacity to significantly consolidate economic powers at the federal level. After years of congressional dialogues—often heated ones—over the bank and its fate, the Second National Bank's charter ended without renewal in 1836.

Despite the lack of a national bank, the American economy developed and modernized in the period before the Civil War; unsurprisingly, however, its monetary system was highly decentralized and often chaotic. Sheridan describes the antebellum period using the distinction between "inside" and "outside" money.[36] The federal government issued specie money, gold and silver coins, which were used as "outside money" to settle accounts. But a variety of paper currencies not created by the federal government circulated as "inside monies" (that is, internal to individual states). Basically, inside money was an IOU from a bank to pay outside money. These bank notes were the most common form of money circulating in the antebellum United States, as finances were managed primarily by state banks during the period until the Civil War–era reforms.[37] In fact, Helleiner states that before the Civil War, approximately 7000 different kinds of bank notes were in circulation and, to further complicate matters, probably fifty percent of those in circulation were counterfeit. "To cope with this chaos, merchants were forced to consult monthly bank note 'detectors' which informed them of the relative value of each note."[38] State governments were charged with overseeing these local banks after the demise of the Second National Bank. A large variation existed in the extent and effectiveness to which they did so, however.

To further the confusion, the local bank notes also were traded across state borders, and these paper currencies would rise or fall in value based on the assessment of the credibility of the commitment to exchange the note for outside money, much like national exchange rates today. While some state bank systems were sound, such as those of New York and Louisiana, "others, particularly those along the Western frontier, were unstable and poorly managed. Since bank notes were often of uncertain value, they were heavily discounted by eastern banks."[39] So the actual value, in practice, of a bank dollar often varied from the supposed one-to-one link with the U.S. dollar. Because bank notes were risky as a store of value unless there was some

W. B. Smith, *Economic Aspects of the Second Bank of the United States* (Cambridge: Harvard University Press, 1953).

[36] J. Sheridan, "The Deja Vu of EMU: Considerations for Europe from Nineteenth Century America," *Journal of Economic Issues* 30 (1996): 1143–61.

[37] G. Ritter, *Goldbugs and Greenbacks: The Antimonopoly Tradition and the Politics of Finance in America* (New York: Cambridge University Press, 1997), 66.

[38] Helleiner, "Historicizing Territorial Currencies," 320.

[39] Ritter, *Goldbugs and Greenbacks*, 66.

credibility on the part of the banks to pay out an equivalence in specie money, financial intermediaries would test the willingness of the banks to redeem notes, and by the mid-1860s, clearinghouses were set up in major cities to facilitate this process. In sum, monetary authority was fragmented, decentralized, and marked by important political and regional divisions.

The Civil War and Monetary Consolidation

A national American paper currency became a reality only with the onset of the Civil War. On one hand, it is peculiar that an important and strongly centralizing step such as currency unification would be taken at a moment of such political disunity as the Civil War. On the other hand, the single currency can be seen as an instrument that arose in response to crisis as political leaders in the North struggled to meet the compelling threat to the security and political unity of the union presented by Southern succession. The single currency, based on a paper standard not tied to metal, promised a way to increase revenues and deal with the practical financing needs of war fighting, promote a stronger American identity, and improve the chances of lasting political union by building an integrated national market bolstered by a new national dollar. A look at the institutional dynamics behind this development allows us to understand the nature of the struggle and the trajectory of political power from the states to the federal level as monetary consolidation occurred.

Bensel has persuasively articulated how the balance was tipped toward state building in this period by showing the links between the nationalization of the currency, war mobilization, and a strengthening of the state. He argues that Northern Republicans undertook the financing of the war by carrying out a set of policies to consolidate and rationalize the monetary system and to increase state capacity.[40]

First, Northern Republicans created a national bank system that abolished the locally chartered banks and effectively nationalized the currency. This underlined the primacy of the federal authority over financial flows, facilitating the collection of revenues and the control of the monetary system. This action decisively shifted the weight of the monetary system toward the federal authorities at a time of great sectional pressures to further decentralize.

Second, the Union permanently placed a large part of the national debt with finance capitalists through the nationalized banking system. The federal government did this by forcing private banks that issued newly standardized and recognized "national bank" notes to hold government bonds and "thus created an instant market for these bonds which could finance its spending requirements."[41]

Finally, the Northern Republicans abandoned the domestic specie or gold standard and conferred legal-tender status on greenbacks, the new dollar paper cur-

---

[40] Bensel, *Yankee Leviathan*, 14.
[41] Helleiner, "Historicizing Territorial Currencies," 325.

rency issued in the winter of 1861–62. In part, the immediate decision to halt specie convertibility was prompted by the pressure on gold reserves from the new federal bond market.[42] This unlinking of the paper currency from specie gave the Union government much more policy flexibility to pursue the financing of the war. Direct revenue extraction was limited, as there was no system of personal income taxes before the war; instead, the federal government relied largely on customs duties. Printing money was one way of financing, in addition to raising funds through federal bonds. As the currency did not need to be matched by gold or silver reserves, it gave much more potential leeway to governments, provided they could maintain some credibility over the worth of the paper currency.

The legislation at the center of these Civil War era changes was the 1863 National Bank Act. This law made those state banks issuing notes into "national banks," regulated by the federal government, issuing similar notes and required to accept other national bank notes at par value. Ritter explains the system as follows:

> Congress sought to create a uniform national currency guaranteed by public credit and limited in overall volume. Each new national bank would deposit federal bonds with the Treasury Department. The banks were permitted to issue currency notes worth up to 90 percent of the value of the bonds. Should a bank fail, the Treasury would redeem its bonds to settle the notes. Otherwise, the banks received the interest that accrued on the bonds.[43]

These policy moves strengthened the position of the state in the economy: they also forged important new links between the state and powerful private actors. Substituting greenbacks for gold-redeemable bank notes "effectively nationalized the payment clauses of private and public contracts in the northern economy and tied these agreements to the future financial policy of the central state. (For example, an inflationary expansion of the money supply would diminish the value of the principal owed by all debtors)."[44] The explosion of government bonds served to create a client group and social base of support for the federal government by establishing an enduring interest in the welfare of the state, as Union policies strongly encouraged banks to invest and hold debt.

Several other key legislative acts sought to promote further monetary, and thus political, consolidation. To further reinforce the usage of national, not local, bank notes, Congress in 1864 passed legislation putting a 10 percent tax on state bank notes, which hastened the state note decline. The 1870 National Bank Currency Act promoted the expansion in national bank notes, particularly to the South and West to integrate those states more into national markets.[45] Federal authorities also aggressively pursued counterfeits. Although far from complete, the 1860s moved

---

[42] Bensel, *Yankee Leviathan*, 249.
[43] Ritter, *Goldbugs and Greenbacks*, 67.
[44] Bensel, *Yankee Leviathan*, 162.
[45] Ritter, *Goldbugs and Greenbacks*, 68.

the United States toward a much higher degree of homogeneity in paper currency than in the previous decades, when thousands of different bank notes and foreign currencies were circulating, creating transaction costs that acted as a barrier to the creation of a true single market.[46]

In addition, the greenback itself was a vehicle for promoting a more homogenous, unified, and collective vision of the American state. Treasury officials carefully chose nationalist imagery for National Bank notes in 1863 to promote unity at a time of great strife. "The symbolic shift here was dramatic. The notes issued by private banks before 1863 had also been elaborately decorated, but the images had been overwhelmingly of local landmarks, personalities and historical events."[47]

Although the nationalized monetary system engineered during the Civil War represented a transformation in the nature of federal control over money, it had many flaws, and in no way put to rest the continuing struggle with the states over monetary centralization. The lack of a central bank, not established until the Federal Reserve System in 1913, meant that the greenback system was subject to crises and panics, and to stabilize the financial system the only government recourse was to operate through the markets. Market interventions were carried out in the Treasury department, which was not viewed as terribly competent.[48] State banks, which went into decline after the taxes levied on them in 1864, began to recover, and by 1900, state banks were once again more numerous than national banks, reflecting the deficiencies of the system. In addition, "Southerners and Westerners complained that poor note distribution and high interest rates left their regions with little currency and few credit services. Farmers complained that the banks were not oriented to the needs of agriculture, and businessmen complained that the pyramid-reserve structure (PRS) made the economy vulnerable to financial panics."[49] Regional disparities were exacerbated in the National Banking reorganization. Instead of truly integrating national markets, capital flows remained skewed to the East because of the lack of financial networks in the South and West. Yet potent political forces that opposed both increased state banking and greater government control defended the maintenance of the system, despite its flaws.

The era of the pure greenback standard ended with the resumption of the gold standard on January 2, 1879. Paper dollars became gold-backed, or redeemable into gold; one greenback dollar was equal to the bullion in one gold dollar. Specie, or gold coins, had continued to be used for foreign exchange and for certain federal transactions, and national bank notes were still in circulation; but the United States had a national currency, now backed by gold.[50] This link to gold once again placed constraints on the ability of the government to run its own monetary policies and proved to be the source of fierce political battles over the next several decades. De-

---

[46] Helleiner, "Historicizing Territorial Currencies," 321.

[47] Ibid., 329.

[48] Bensel, *Yankee Leviathan*.

[49] Ritter, *Goldbugs and Greenbacks*, 67.

[50] See Ritter, *Goldbugs and Greenbacks*, for an insightful analysis of the political and social meaning of debates between supporters of gold and advocates of greenbacks.

spite the limitations being tied to gold placed on the federal government, the centralizing and state building processes set in motion with the nationalization of the U.S. currency persisted as social coalitions organized themselves around a new set of integrated financial markets at the federal level. While the Civil War "ratcheted up" the institutionalization of the federal state, it was not immune to "rollbacks" produced by the long-standing and pervasive anti-federalist ideas and structures still dominant as the pressing necessities of the Civil War faded.[51]

This overview of the history of U.S. monetary organization indicates that far from springing to life as a single political entity with a single currency, the U.S. state experienced a series of transformations in the nature of governance, both monetary and political, throughout its first century of existence. One such transformation, the creation of greenbacks, occurred as an act of political power by the Northern Union republicans and was extended to the Southern secessionist states only after their defeat in war. The South had developed their own monetary system during the war, outlawing greenbacks in 1864 and issuing vast quantities of their own paper currency. The Southern financial system was devastated after the Civil War and did not influence postwar development, which made Northern policies of mobilization crucial to the monetary system during reconstruction.

The Civil War–era reforms had given the American state a single currency and an emergent political control over money, but these reforms did not end the debate. Instead, they ushered in a new era of deep political divisions over monetary organization. The degree of federal control and the extent of government involvement in money and finance, the distributional effects of the gold standard, and the structure of the national banking system were central to these ongoing debates. A long evolution in the political development of the American state, punctuated by key points of transformation such as the Civil War, was necessary to produce the single currency, unified market, and developed federal United States we see today.

Dynamics of State Building in the American Case

The tug-of-war between those seeking to centralize policy capacities and political authority in the center and those seeking to keep sovereignty at the state level was significantly influenced by two critical factors: war and market integration. The following section briefly reviews the dynamics of those factors that spurred movement toward a single currency.

The Role of War

As noted earlier, war has featured prominently in the work of scholars of comparative political development. Hintze states baldly: "All state organization was origi-

---

[51] Friedberg, *The Shadow of the Garrison State*, 30–31.

nally military organization, organization for war."[52] Building up the capacity to fight a successful war required a great deal from a populace and its central political authorities, taxes being the first necessity to provide the financial basis for the prosecution of war. This organizational capacity inevitably "produced arrangements which could deliver resources to the government for other purposes. (Thus almost all the major European taxes began as "extraordinary levies" earmarked for particular wars and became routine sources of governmental revenues)."[53] The prosecution of war promoted territorial consolidation, institutional centralization, and the differentiation of the instruments of government, and strengthened the position of the state as the monopolist in the use of coercion.

The importance of war in state building is clearly demonstrated in the American move to the greenback, illustrating the reciprocal nature of this relationship. The greenback was an instrument to help the North prosecute the war and increase its authority within the U.S. political economy. The stakes were extremely high: the divisions within the Union went beyond the North–South divide, and the Union faced a choice between either repressing and coercing the South to stay in or having a number of secessionist regions take leave. Disintegration into a very loose confederation would have been the result. As Bensel writes, ". . . the choice for the North posed by southern secession was never between one nation and two but between one nation and many."[54] The dollar was, therefore, created at time of disunity to save the United States from disintegration, and the centrifugal forces that the North feared would be unleashed if the South was allowed to succeed. At the time, the central U.S. government was extremely weak, centered on "a very few functions such as the collection of customs duties and delivery of the mail."[55] The U.S. Army, the most developed arm of the government, was led by a General who loudly favored secession, and key posts were held by those strongly sympathetic to the South and disloyal to Lincoln. Mobilization for the war was therefore a central concern for Lincoln's administration, and the Northern war effort was dependent on active financial markets and industrial production—encouraged in no small part by the creation of a newly standardized monetary system based on the greenback and decoupled from a metallic standard.

However, it would be too simple an interpretation to place all the causal force for the centralization of monetary authority on the requirements of war. The Civil War created the conditions under which Lincoln could go forward with the nationalization of currency, but the roots of the move had been established long before. The debates concerning the need for more power over financing at the center had been long-standing and had been argued fervently over the rechartering of the First and Second National Bank. Lincoln's early involvement in the Whig Party, which sup-

---

[52] O. Hintze, *The Historical Essays of Otto Hintze*, F. Gilbert, ed. (New York: Oxford University Press, 1975), 181.

[53] Tilly, *The Formation of National States in Europe*, 42.

[54] Bensel, *Yankee Leviathan*, 62.

[55] Ibid., 85.

ported a more federalist view of the economy and the government's place in it, suggests that the evolution toward a single currency and system of debt financing was likely, regardless of the pressures of war. The transformation of the United States from agrarian to industrial economy was also pushing political leaders to develop the American economic infrastructure.

A Single Market

The second major factor that precipitated the gradual consolidation of monetary authority in the American case was the desire to create a unified, single market. As Tilly has noted ". . . a powerful reciprocal relationship between the expansion of capitalism and the growth of state power developed, despite the frequent efforts of capitalists themselves to fight off state power."[56] Indeed, the forces of the capitalist mode of production permeated the nineteenth-century Western state development, pushing toward certain organizational outcomes while making others less likely. However, market imperatives were still open-ended despite their force. The ways in which each nation balanced the private nature of authority over market relationships versus the need for state regulation of market activities varied tremendously, as many of the European states took a much more active role in directing the market whereas the U.S. federal state played only a minimal role.

In the U.S. case, creating the single market was a key political goal in the post-reconstruction era, and this desire both shaped and, more surprisingly, *limited* the growth of the central U.S. state at the same time as the war provoked unprecedented state-building efforts. A single market is mostly about "negative integration," the removal of barriers to interstate trade and investment. But it does require some "positive integration," such as the single currency and the work of a judiciary in promoting the single-market rules. Indeed the courts, according to Bensel, were the most important state agency driving the emergence of national markets in the post-Reconstruction era.[57]

By making a national market the cornerstone of the political project, however, American leaders significantly limited the nature and extent of the state-building process. The development of a single currency, a single market, and a federal debt underpinned by integrated financial markets permanently changed the internal organization of U.S. national capital markets and the relationship of the central state to societal elites, particularly finance capitalists. Financial elites were "both enticed and coerced into becoming agents of Union fiscal policy and subsequently cooperating with the Treasury in marketing government debt securities and managing the circulation and value of Union currency."[58] After the war, these elites turned against the state and supported retrenchment in part because of their concerns

---

[56] Tilly, *The Formation of National States in Europe*, 30.
[57] Bensel, *Yankee Leviathan*, 15, footnote 20.
[58] Ibid., 238.

about the federal state's administrative competence, but also because they sought a more unfettered capitalism in conjunction with the resumption of a domestic gold standard. This standard promised to limit federal authority over money and impose external discipline on the economy.

A more extensive state with wealth-redistribution and social-protection policies ended up outside the U.S. market-integration project, for it had no natural constituencies among the Northern elites, only opponents. "In sum, American state formation assumed the form of a northern, industrial program in which incomplete political integration coincided with the creation of national markets and corporate consolidation."[59]

Conclusion: States and Contemporary Deterritorialization of Money

What does the story of the territorialization of one national currency, the U.S. greenback, tell us about the implications of the loosening of the bonds between states and currencies today? First, let us review the lessons learned from nineteenth century America. The historical trajectory of the U.S. case demonstrates that a single currency played a critical role in the development of the state, but also shows that its importance was linked to a set of interlocked programs, policies, and competencies. The currency had a symbolic importance in conveying political unification in the wake of the Civil War, but it may have been more important because it provided an instrumental means of financing for the federal government in a time of acute need. Establishing a national currency that was not tethered to gold or silver, for a time, enabled the federal government to prosecute the Civil War. But the repercussions of this wartime decision continued long after the U.S. linked the greenback to the gold standard after the war. The public debt assumed by the Union during that time was a breakthrough in governance, as the federal government had never before taken on such a responsibility, feared by leaders like Jefferson, Madison, and Jackson but resolutely sought by Hamilton. The single American currency also began to create a nationalized system of financial markets. This created a new class of monied elites invested in the welfare of the broader national economy but also wary of too much growth of the federal government. The point is that the single currency's potency as an instrument of state building had as much to do with its institutional and political repercussions and fiscal effects as it did with the specific act of creating the greenback itself.

The basic lesson that a single currency is fundamentally important to political development continues to apply today. There are nonetheless important differences between the past and the contemporary world, which might bear on the connections between currencies and states. Most centrally, the nineteenth-century currency project was built on a foundation that did not include activist monetary pol-

[59] Ibid., 17.

icy but rather was constructed on fiscal and financial capacity and centralization. Therefore, national money did not have the same demands and expectations of macroeconomic management and control over the economy more broadly as it does today. The Keynesian revolution of the twentieth century raised the stakes for monetary sovereignty, which made national currencies even more important for state building and the exercise of political authority through the manipulation of the money supply.

Conversely, in the late twentieth and early twenty-first centuries, disillusionment with fiscal and monetary activism has contributed to the deterritorialization of currencies—a point also underscored in Helleiner's contribution to this volume. Loosening the ties of sovereign money today impinges more directly on the capacity of states to manage their finances and the macroeconomy more than the creation of national currencies bolstered this capacity in the nineteenth century. The dismantling of the national currency of a mature state might well also have political and institutional repercussions that are different from the initial adoption of a single money. The stage of the historical trajectory may matter: once formed, political capacity and legitimate authority may persist in the broader institutional environment even as the specific instrument, the national currency, is lost. This historical institutionalist insight raises an important empirical question for future research on currency deterritorialization. Scholars would do well to assess, in specific cases of deterritorialization, the degree to which the currency itself is critical to the exercise of sovereign authority and its relationship to the web of related state institutions.

Let us now consider the implications of these lessons for political development in the wake of currency unification. The European Union is, of course, the most visible case of a new supranational currency arising in conjunction with deterritorialization of the ancien régime of national currencies. Does EMU imply state building at the EU level and a movement of power away from member states? As in the U.S. case during the nineteenth century, fierce battles are being fought over the degree to which the euro will contribute to the consolidation of political authority in the European Union. The American case suggests that, although the euro will have important institutional effects, the development of fiscal responsibility and debt financing would have more potent state-building effects. As currently designed, an independent fiscal capability for the EU institutions is prohibited. The EU member states understand as clearly as did the United States that the ability to extract revenue forms the central basis for political capacity. The EU must make do with funds provided by member states, capped as a small percentage of EU GDP, and cannot run deficits or issue public debt.

Yet the advent of the euro and the establishment of the European Central Bank are bound to have repercussions in the financial and even fiscal fields. Even absent a fiscal capacity, the development of the European-level monetary institution will create a relationship between financial interests and the ECB that, be it adversarial or congenial, will begin to change the political dynamics and the balance of authority in Europe. Any such evolution of fiscal authority toward Brussels, as some analysts believe is likely in the long run, would signal a critical transfer of power and conformity to historical models of state building.

In sum, the political decision to create a single currency in Europe is a shift in a policy-making capacity that has the potential to transform the institutional environment from one of sub-unit political control to a much more collectively governed arena, just as in the American case. The euro, like the greenback dollar, will have profound consequences for the shaping of political union, but the trajectory of change is far from clear. There are reasons to believe that the creation of the single currency could be a precursor for further political consolidation at the center of the EU, but the U.S. case also suggests some of the contradictions and limits to such growth which will have to be overcome before we will see a unified European state.

The American state-building project also might suggest some broad perspectives on other contemporary deterritorialization cases. The deterritorialization of the dollar has proved to be positive for U.S. authorities in the sense that they continue to condone its extensive use outside U.S. borders and its status as the premier global currency. Establishing the ability to print paper money in which investors had confidence was one of the chief goals of the creators of the greenback. Since the United States closed the gold window in 1973, it would appear that the U.S. is reaping the benefits of this position. As long as investors continue to view the dollar as a safe haven, the power of the American state would seem to be enhanced, not diminished, by its internationalization. Should investors turn against the dollar, however, dollarization places new constraints on the federal government and would be a serious constraint on its national power.

On the other end of the scale, the example of Ecuador surrendering its national currency, the *sucre*, to adopt the dollar internally seems to challenge the state-building model. While the Europeans are giving up their currency within a relatively symmetrical power structure of monetary organization at the EU level, Ecuadorian monetary policy is completely subordinate to American policy. As its own economic policy institutions appear to have failed Ecuador, this surrender of sovereignty is understandable. If dollarization enables Ecuador's leaders to raise national revenue and finance the government budget more successfully, it will restore some measure of authority and capacity to the Ecuadorian state.

Much more work remains to be done on the linkages between state building and the territorialization and organization of national money. A national currency does not define by itself the essence of the state; it is one function alone of state capacity. When the greenback was created in 1861, the development of the U.S. into a unified federal state was by no means a foregone conclusion. However, the creation of the greenback was tightly linked to a set of institutional innovations that collectively moved the American state one important step along the developmental path from a very loosely organized political system toward a more developed, although still distinctively decentralized, modern state. Further research on the historical development and consolidation of the polity *within* particular states may well help us better understand today's multiple, overlapping, and evolving lines of contemporary authority *among* states in the international political economy.

CHAPTER EIGHT

Why Are Territorial Currencies Becoming Unpopular?

Eric Helleiner

Astriking trend in recent years has been the growing unpopularity of what Cohen calls "territorial currencies"; that is, currencies which are exclusive and homogeneous within the territorial borders of a nation-state.[1] One manifestation of this trend is the new enthusiasm for currency unions. Such enthusiasm is, of course, most pronounced in Europe, where eleven members of the European Union agreed to eliminate their national currencies in favor of a supranational currency. But it also has spread to other regions. In North America, an active and high-level debate broke out for the first time in 1999–2000 on the subject of a common currency for the members of NAFTA.[2] Prominent calls for a common currency were also suddenly heard in 1997–98 among the South American member countries of the trade grouping Mercosur.[3] Although the prospects are much more remote, there have also been some calls for a common currency in the East Asian region, particularly in the wake of the 1997–98 financial crisis.[4] Also worthy of note has been the way in which some nationalist movements today that are seeking to

For their helpful comments, I am very grateful to Tom Willett, Peter Kenen, and the editors of this volume. I would also like to thank the Social Sciences and Humanities Research Council of Canada for helping to fund some of the research underlying this paper.

[1] B. J. Cohen, *The Geography of Money* (Ithaca: Cornell University Press, 1998).

[2] In Canada during 1999, the issue assumed a prominent place in public-policy debates, and Senate hearings were held on the issue. In Mexico, the issue was widely debated and in mid-2000, the newly elected President Vicente Fox argued a common currency was a strong possibility in the medium-term future.

[3] Argentine President Carlos Menem promoted the common-currency idea in late 1997. The proposal was also supported in a detailed study by Fabia Giambiagi, manager of the Macroeconomic Bank of Economic Development of Brazil, which suggested the currency could be in place within fifteen years. See F. Giambiagi, "Una Propuesta de Unificacion Monetaria Para Los Paises Del Mercosur," published at www.cefir.org.uy/docs/dt25/04giambi.htm, 1998.

[4] L. Lucas, "Asian Monetary Union Is Mooted," *Financial Times* (31 December, 1998): x.

create new independent states in these regions—such as those in Quebec or Scotland—are strong supporters of these supranational currency proposals. Their position signals an interesting departure from traditional nationalist movements that have understood the creation of a new territorial currency as an integral part of their project of building a nation–state.

A second manifestation of the unpopularity of territorial currencies today is the growing acceptance of the use of foreign currencies within national territories. This trend first took off back in the 1960s when the British government began to encourage the rapid growth of the inter-bank market in dollar deposits in London. Foreign-currency deposits had existed in earlier periods, but the rapid growth of this "eurocurrency market" in London was quite unprecedented. More recently, foreign-currency deposits—again usually U.S. dollars—have also become very widespread in many countries across Latin America, Africa, the Middle East, and ex-Eastern-bloc countries. In these instances, the phenomenon has not been restricted to an inter-bank market but has also involved many domestic citizens holding such accounts. In some cases, "dollarization" has even extended to widespread use of the dollar as a medium of exchange.[5] Again, this phenomenon is not new: individuals in countries with high inflation or political uncertainty in the past have often lost "trust" in the national currency and have turned to foreign currency. But novel today has been the long endurance of "currency substitution" in many countries and the degree to which this trend has received official endorsement and even encouragement in many poorer countries. Dollarization in Latin America, for example, began to accelerate in the 1970s after their governments deliberately relaxed restrictions on foreign-currency use as part of broader monetary and financial reforms.[6] By the 1990s, many poorer governments had gone so far as to extend central-bank guarantees to foreign-currency bank deposits, to create clearing and payments systems for domestic transactions in foreign currency, and to give foreign currencies full legal-tender status.[7]

An even more dramatic step was recently taken by Ecuador and El Salvador when they each chose to abolish their national currencies and to adopt the U.S. dollar in 2000 and 2001, respectively. Again, this choice was not unprecedented among independent countries: Panama and Liberia have long used the U.S. dollar as their currency. But they did not abandon an existing national currency, and their policies were always seen as anomalous ones, linked to their close dependence on the United States. The choices of Ecuador and El Salvador also may not be isolated ones. In early 1999, the former Argentine President, Carlos Menem, suggested that

    [5] B. J. Cohen, *The Geography of Money*.

    [6] S. Edwards, "Dollarization in Latin America," in Nissan Liviatan, ed., *Proceedings of a Conference on Currency Substitution and Currency Boards* (Washington: World Bank, 1993).

    [7] See, for example, D. Brand, *Currency Substitution in Developing Countries* (Munich: Weltforum Verlag, 1993); M. Savastano, "Dollarization in Latin America," in P. Mizen and E. Penecost, eds., *The Macroeconomics of International Currencies* (Cheltenham, U.K.: Edward Elgar, 1996); R. Sahay and C. Vegh, "Dollarization in Transition Economies: Evidence and Policy Implications," *IMF Working Paper*, no. 96 (Washington: IMF, 1995).

his country move to "full dollarization." Similar proposals are being debated prominently in other countries such as Costa Rica, Guatemala, and Mexico.[8] The United States Congress has also held prominent hearings on the question of whether the United States should be encouraging this practice.[9]

One final sign of dissatisfaction with territorial currencies has been the growing interest in the possibility of privately-issued electronic currencies emerging in the near future.[10] Information technologies have already begun to be used to create monetary devices carrying electronic representations of prepaid value, such as stored value cards (or "electronic purses") and software products that can be used to make payments across computer networks (sometimes referred to as "digital cash"). In contrast to credit or debit cards, these devices do not access a bank account or credit line but rather represent general liabilities of the issuer. For this reason, some analysts are excited by the possibility that these new forms of money could be used to break the state's monopoly over currency. They argue that anyone could potentially issue these new forms of money and that private issuers might choose to issue money in an entirely new private currency.[11]

Particularly enthusiastic about this possibility are "free bankers" who have long advocated the replacement of the state's monopoly of currency with a system of competing privately-issued forms of money. Although support for free banking was considerable in economic liberal circles during the nineteenth century, it has had few adherents during most of the twentieth century. Since the mid-1970s, however, it has experienced a notable revival. Hayek's 1978 work *The Denationalisation of Money* played a central role in this process. While nineteenth-century free bankers had assumed privately-issued forms of money would be convertible into a common gold standard, Hayek went further in this work to argue that market forces should also determine the standard of value itself. His ideas have attracted a growing number of supporters, many of whom have reinterpreted the history of nineteenth-century free-banking experiences in a more positive light than conventional histories had portrayed them.[12] Many of these modern free bankers see the emergence of

[8] K. Schuler, *Basics of Dollarization*, Joint Economic Committee Staff Report (Washington: U.S. Senate, 2000).

[9] U.S. Senate, *Hearing on Official Dollarization in Emerging-Market Countries*, Senate Committee on Banking, Housing, and Urban Affairs, Subcommittee on Economic Affairs and Subcommittee on International Trade and Finance (15 July, 1999).

[10] A quite different manifestation of the unpopularity of national currencies has come from the emergence of the "local currency movement." Since the early 1980s, hundreds of subnational currencies have been created in countries from Australia and Sweden to Japan and Canada. These currencies serve as a means of exchange within a clearly defined local community network and are not convertible into the national currency or any other currency. These currencies will not be discussed here; for a discussion, see E. Helleiner, "Think Globally, Transact Locally: Green Political Economy and the Local Currency Movement," *Global Society* 14, no. 1 (2000): 35–51.

[11] For example: S. Kobrin, "Electronic Cash and the End of National Markets," *Foreign Policy* 107 (1997), and B. J. Cohen, "Electronic Money: New Day or False Dawn?" *Review of International Political Economy* 8 (2001): 197–225. For a more skeptical view, see E. Helleiner, "Electronic Money: A Challenge to the Sovereign State?" *Journal of International Affairs* 51, no. 2 (1998): 387–409.

[12] For example, L. White, *Free Banking in Britain: Theory, Experience, and Debate, 1800–1845* (Cambridge: Cambridge University Press, 1984); H. Rockoff, "Lessons from the American Experience with

"electronic money" as the tool with which they can finally challenge directly the state's control over money.[13]

It is clear, then, that we live in an era when serious questions are being raised about the future of territorial currencies. The trend should not be overstated. Each of the challenges described above has its opponents, and their continued support for territorial currencies is often very strong and influential. Support for territorial currencies also varies considerably in different regions of the world. The creation of new territorial currencies has, for example, recently been a key goal of the new countries emerging from the breakup of the USSR, Czechoslovakia, and Yugoslavia. In each of these instances, new national currencies have been created as a central component of the process of creating new nation-states. Still, the fact that territorial currencies are being challenged in so many different ways and in so many different contexts does suggest that their growing unpopularity is more than simply a region-specific trend. Indeed, I argue in this chapter that it reflects some broader developments that can be systematically analyzed, even if the responses to these developments vary in their form and intensity considerably from region to region.

What are the sources of the growing unpopularity of territorial currencies today? In this chapter, I suggest that one way to begin to develop a more general analysis of this phenomenon is to recall the reasons why territorial currencies were initially created. I have shown elsewhere that these monetary structures were first created in most parts of the world during the nineteenth and early twentieth centuries with four goals in mind: (1) to bolster national markets; (2) to provide a tool for national monetary management; (3) to augment the state's revenue base; and (4) to strengthen national identities.[14] If territorial currencies were created for these reasons, to what extent can their growing unpopularity today be attributed to disillusionment with these goals? I argue below that disillusionment with these goals—particularly those relating to national markets and monetary management—is indeed driving many monetary transformations today. I suggest that this sentiment, in turn, is linked to a broader reconsideration of the proper economic role of the

---

Free Banking," in F. Capie and G. Wood, eds., *Unregulated Banking* (London: Macmillan, 1991). Hayek's ideas are outlined in F. Hayek, *The Denationalisation of Money—The Argument Refined*, 3d ed. (London: Institute for Economic Affairs, 1990).

[13] See, for example, many of the articles in J. Dorn, ed., *The Future of Money in the Information Age* (Washington: Cato Institute, 1997).

[14] E. Helleiner, "National Currencies and National Identities," *American Behavioral Scientist* 41, no. 10 (1998): 1409–36; E. Helleiner, "Historicizing National Currencies," *Political Geography* 18 (1999): 309–39; E. Gilbert and E. Helleiner, "Introduction: Nation-States and Money," in E. Gilbert and E. Helleiner, eds., *Nation-States and Money: The Past, Present, and Future of National Currencies* (London: Routledge, 1999). See also McNamara's chapter in this volume. In his analysis of the reasons why states may prefer territorial currencies in the modern age, Cohen, in *The Geography of Money*, adds one important motivation that I have not mentioned: the fact that this monetary structure can insulate the state from external coercion. Although there were some historical instances where this concern did play a role in prompting policymakers to create territorial currencies (see J. Kirshner, *Currency and Coercion* [Princeton: Princeton University Press, 1995], chap. 4), it was a much less common motivation than the four I have cited here.

nation-state in an age when "neoliberal" ideas have triumphed and international economic integration is intensifying.

Reducing International Transaction Costs

One of the key reasons that territorial currencies were initially created was to facilitate the emergence of nationally coherent markets. Pre-national monetary systems were often quite heterogeneous, with various kinds of money circulating simultaneously within the territory of a state. By constructing an exclusive and homogeneous national currency, transaction costs associated with intra-national trade were eliminated. Policymakers also sometimes used territorial currencies as a tool to discourage economic transactions with the outside world by making these currencies inconvertible.

Today, however, intensifying international economic integration has led to growing disenchantment with the constraints and limitations of national markets, a sentiment that has, in turn, extended to the territorial currencies that complement these markets. The motivations for supporting the initial growth of the eurocurrency market in London during the late 1950s and 1960s provide an early example of this. This monetary innovation initially derived much of its support from internationally-oriented economic interests who sought to create an "offshore" or "transnational" economic space in which to operate free from the kinds of national capital controls which had become popular during the post-1945 years. In Britain, crucial support came from key financiers in the City of London, backed by British officials, who saw how this monetary innovation could allow them to rebuild the City's traditional cosmopolitan orientation in face of the national capital controls designed to defend the British national currency. American banks and multinational firms, again supported by U.S. officials, also saw the eurocurrency markets as a way for their transnational activities to remain unencumbered by U.S. capital controls that were imposed in 1963.[15]

More recently, as capital controls have been eliminated in many countries, some supporters of international economic integration have promoted supranational currencies or "full dollarization" as another tool to eliminate international transaction costs. Their goals are, in fact, reminiscent of the mid-nineteenth century, a period also characterized by a dramatic growth of international economic integration driven by liberal economic policies and rapid technological changes. Then as now, a flurry of proposals for currency unions were presented for the same reason; indeed, the proposals in that era were much more ambitious, with an international conference held in 1867 to discuss the creation of a "universal currency" that could circulate in all countries.[16] In the mid-nineteenth century, the international monetary

---

[15] E. Helleiner, *States and the Reemergence of Global Finance* (Ithaca: Cornell University Press, 1994), chap. 4.

[16] See, for example, M. Perlman, "In Search of Monetary Union," *Journal of European Economic History* 22, no. 2 (1993): 313–32. This initiative garnered a remarkable degree of support from international businesses and economic liberals across the world from Europe to Asia and the Americas. In the end, however, it could not find enough support in leading countries such as Britain and the United

transaction costs that most concerned supporters of currency unions were those associated with exchanging national currencies and comparing prices across countries. Both concerns are also highlighted by supporters of currency unions today.[17] But much more prominent today than in the mid–nineteenth century is the desire to eliminate exchange-rate instability in today's atmosphere of very high capital mobility.

Indeed, it is no coincidence that discussions of monetary unions and full dollarization have accelerated in the wake of dramatic currency crises during the 1990s. As financial capital has become increasingly mobile, governments have found it increasingly difficult to maintain a credible fixed exchange rate or even a well-managed floating rate. Countries that have let their currency float freely have also often experienced significant short-term exchange-rate misalignments which have been quite costly for open economies. In these contexts, the idea of creating an irrevocably fixed exchange rate through a currency union or full dollarization has become increasingly attractive to many of those seeking to promote international economic integration. Supporters of a common currency in Europe and North America, for example, have argued that exchange-rate instability is undermining the project of accelerating regional economic integration. Many Latin American supporters of full dollarization also argue that exchange rate risks vis-à-vis the dollar must be eliminated in an effort to encourage foreign investment, stop flight capital, and eliminate the possibility of disruptive speculative attacks against the national currency. One of the most prominent advocates of this monetary reform, Ricardo Hausmann, has also called attention to the need to eliminate uncertainty in international debt repayments, many of which are denominated in U.S. dollars in Latin American countries. He notes that unexpected devaluations can cause major domestic financial crises as firms face a mismatch between their dollar-denomination debts and their local currency-denominated revenue.[18]

Those familiar with nineteenth- and early twentieth-century monetary history may be surprised by the idea that exchange rate-related international transaction costs can be eliminated only by abandoning a national currency. After all, the goal of reducing this kind of transaction cost was also prominent in the integrated world economy of that era, but it was achieved simply by ensuring that all national currencies were tied to a common standard, gold. To the extent that the credibility of

---

States, but two more limited European currency unions—the Scandinavian Monetary Union and the Latin Monetary Union—were created.

[17] In making the case for currency union, the European Commission, for example, has argued that the elimination of costs associated with actual currency conversions will bolster Europe's GDP by as much as 0.5 percent. See European Commission, "One Market, One Money," *European Economy* 44 (1990).

[18] Indeed, Hausmann notes that in many poorer countries most long-term domestic loans are also denominated in dollars because expectations of future inflation and currency depreciation have prevented the development of debt markets denominated in local currencies. See R. Hausmann, "Should There Be Five Currencies or One Hundred and Five," *Foreign Policy* 116 (Fall 1999): 65–79. In this context, a devaluation can cause financial difficulties for borrowers of these loans too. This provides a key reason for Hausmann to advocate full dollarization: it might promote financial stability and economic development by encouraging the growth of indigenous capital markets.

the peg to gold might be questioned, countries ensured that their national currencies were managed by independent central banks devoted to this goal or even currency boards. Even in the context of colonial monetary relations, exchange-rate uncertainty between the colonizing and colonized country was not usually eliminated through a monetary union or the adoption of the colonizing country's currency, but rather by establishing a distinct colonial currency managed by a currency board.

Why are countries today not considering similar mechanisms to guarantee the credibility of their exchange-rate peg? In a case such as the European Union, the answer is linked to the fact that monetary union is being sought for other reasons as well. In countries considering the adoption of the U.S. dollar, however, the question is an important one. There has in fact been a dramatic increase over the past decade in the use of independent central banks and currency boards across the world partly for this reason. But many countries have found that these structures still did not do enough to establish credibility. In Argentina, for example, Menem's sudden interest in full dollarization stemmed from the fact that international financiers still charged an exchange-rate risk premium on loans to Argentina during times of large external shocks despite the existence of a currency board since 1991. Unlike in colonial times, independent countries with currency boards today face the difficulty of convincing the markets that a change in local government will not simply eliminate the currency board. Full dollarization is seen by Menem and others as a way to eliminate this credibility problem.[19] As Larry Summers has noted, "the presumed irrevocability of dollarization" is its appeal.[20]

One final point needs to be made about the relationship between international economic integration and the growing interest in alternatives to territorial currencies: the growing support for privately-issued e-currencies is also linked partly to a desire to reduce international transaction costs. In this case, the goal is to reduce transaction costs in one of the most rapidly growing sectors of the global economy: e-commerce. The growth of e-commerce has provoked interest in more efficient electronic-exchange media to facilitate transactions in this new sector. A key feature of e-commerce transactions is that they take place in a kind of "cyberspace" which does not respect traditional sovereign borders of nation-states. It is not surprising, then, that participants in this commerce would be searching for a kind of currency that is less tied to the sovereign nation-state. In Kobrin's words, the growing interest in privately-issued "state-less" e-currencies is linked to the fact that e-commerce is ushering in "the end of national markets."[21]

[19] R. Hausmann and A. Powell, "Dollarization: Issues of Implementation," *IADB Working Paper* (1999).

[20] L. Summers, "Rules, Real Exchange Rates and Monetary Discipline," in N. Liviathan, ed., *Proceedings of a Conference on Currency Substitution and Currency Boards* (Washington: International Monetary Fund, 1993).

[21] Kobrin, "Electronic Cash and the End of National Markets."

Disillusionment with Activist National Monetary Management

Historically, support for territorial currencies stemmed from their ability not just to bolster national markets but also to provide the state with a tool for national monetary management. During the pre-1914 period, this goal was a relatively modest one because of the dominance of economic liberal ideas. Policymakers simply sought to ensure that new kinds of money emerging in that era—especially bank notes—would be managed in a fashion that closely resembled the automatic market principles by which old kinds of "commodity money" had been regulated. The monopolization of the note issue in this period, in particular, was frequently driven by the desire to manage its supply in accordance with the requirements of the gold standard. As the electoral franchise was widened and left-of-center political parties grew in influence during the inter-war period, the macroeconomic rationale for state control became more ambitious. In the wake of the Great Depression, governments across the world began to manage national currencies in much more active ways to promote national objectives, particularly the reduction of unemployment and the promotion of rapid industrial development. This new ambitious objective then provided a key rationale for creating fully-fledged territorial currencies in countries that had not yet done so.

The growing unpopularity of territorial currencies today is often closely linked to disillusionment with the kinds of activist national monetary policies that became popular during and after the 1930s. This sentiment has emerged partly out of the experiences of inflation which often accompanied those policies. Equally important has been the success of the rational expectations revolution in the discipline of economics over the last two decades. It undermined a key idea that had sustained support for activist monetary policies: the Keynesian notion that there was a long-term trade-off between inflation and unemployment. By highlighting how experiences of inflation over time will encourage people to adjust their expectations, this new economic analysis suggested that activist monetary management would simply result in stagflation. To break inflationary expectations, it was argued that authorities would have to re-establish their credibility and reputation for producing stable money by a strong commitment to price stability. The need for this kind of credibility and reputation has also been reinforced by the enormous growth of international capital markets. The fear of the discipline these markets can apply against inflationary countries has encouraged a dramatic change of macroeconomic views.[22]

Out of these circumstances, a "neoliberal" consensus has emerged amongst policymakers that monetary policy has no long-term impact on real output and employment, and that the maintenance of price stability should be the primary objective of monetary policy. This disillusionment with activist monetary policies has also sometimes extended to the use of the exchange rate to foster macroeconomic

[22] D. Andrews and T. D. Willett, "Financial Interdependence and the State," *International Organization* 51, no. 3 (1998): 479–511; S. Maxfield, *Gatekeepers of Growth: The IPE of Central Banking in Developing Countries* (Princeton: Princeton University Press, 1997).

adjustments. Most policymakers and economists defend the use of floating exchanges as a tool to foster macroeconomic adjustments in a context where wages and prices are slow to adjust, or as a mechanism providing some autonomy to national policymakers seeking to pursue the goal of price stability. But others have questioned whether exchange-rate adjustments have any lasting effect on the real economy. A devaluation, they argue, may simply produce inflation, if domestic citizens anticipate and react to its consequences.

The growing disillusionment with activist monetary management has played an important role in encouraging alternatives to territorial currencies to be considered. By eliminating a key macroeconomic rationale for wanting a territorial currency in the first place, it has made policymakers less resistant to the idea of giving these monetary structures up. In Europe, the shift from Keynesian to neoliberal monetary ideas was a key precondition for the move to monetary union; indeed, many policymakers saw currency union as a better way to achieve price stability than maintaining a national currency because the union appeared to allow them to "import" the Bundesbank's anti-inflationary monetary policy.[23] Many advocates of monetary union in other regions, such as North America, also subscribe to the new monetary orthodoxy and argue that there is little to be lost in a macroeconomic sense from the abandonment of a national currency.[24]

This shift in macroeconomic ideology has also been enormously important in putting the idea of dollarization and common currencies on the agenda in poorer countries. Many of these countries created territorial currencies for the first time only in the early post-1945 years, and a key reason was their belief that activist monetary policy had a key role to play in promoting domestic economic development.[25] Today, it is much harder to find prominent policymakers in the developing world advocating that view. More common is the idea that growth is best fostered by maintaining price stability as the prime objective of monetary policy because this will encourage foreign investment, reduce the likelihood of balance-of-payments crises, and create a more stable macroeconomic environment for business activity.[26] Given the volatility of exchange rates in these regions, advocates of full dollarization also argue that exchange rates are not able to perform a useful adjustment function or provide autonomy for a country to pursue an independent monetary policy.[27] Not surprisingly, these new views have made policymakers much less resistant to the idea of adopting a common currency or the U.S. dollar than they would have been in the early post-war years.

[23] K. McNamara, *The Currency of Ideas* (Ithaca: Cornell University Press, 1998).

[24] T. Courchene and R. Harris, *From Fixing to Monetary Union: Options for North American Currency Integration* (Toronto: C. D. Howe Institute, 1999).

[25] E. Helleiner, "The Southern Side of Embedded Liberalism: Power and Ideology in Postwar Monetary Reforms," in J. Kirshner, ed., *Power, Ideology, and Conflict: The Political Foundations of Twenty-First-Century Money* (Ithaca, N.Y.: Cornell University Press, forthcoming).

[26] For example, Schuler, *Basics of Dollarization*.

[27] R. Hausmann, M. Gavin, C. Pages-Serra, and E. Stein, "Financial Turmoil and the Choice of Exchange Rate Regime," *IADB Working Paper* (1999).

The changed thinking about monetary policy has not just made policymakers less resistant to alternatives to territorial currencies. It also encouraged them to see the abandonment of territorial currencies in a positive light as a key way to insulate money from the arbitrary interference by politicians. Hayek's advocacy of the "denationalization of money" represents the most radical view of this kind. For most of his academic career, Hayek was an advocate of the gold standard. The suspension of gold convertibility of the dollar in the early 1970s, however, demonstrated to him how difficult it had become to "protect money from politics" in the traditional way when the principal commitment of governments in an age of mass democracy had become activist monetary management aimed at domestic monetary objectives.[28] The inflation of the following years did little to calm his fears about the dangers of the new world of universal fiat money, and it prompted Hayek to re-evaluate his thinking about the merits of territorial currencies. If the gold standard could not be reintroduced as a means of preventing politicians from manipulating territorial currencies, he wondered whether monetary discipline could better be achieved by eliminating territorial currencies altogether. If people were given "choice in currency" (either between government-issued currencies or between privately-issued currencies), Hayek argued that they would choose the most stable currency. Currency competition would thus discipline governments, forcing them to maintain the value of money they issued and restrain spending. In an age of mass democratic politics in which politicians were beholden to what Hayek called "special interests," he believed, the nation was no longer a community which could be trusted to manage money according to his ideals.[29] In the terms of Rodrik's political "trilemma," mentioned in this book's introduction, Hayek sought to resolve the tension between deep international economic integration, mass politics, and autonomous national decision making by eliminating the latter.

Written in the 1970s, Hayek's concerns about the way in which modern governments inevitably produce inflation now seem somewhat dated. Many countries have, after all, embraced neoliberal monetary goals over the past two decades without abandoning territorial currencies. They have simply come to manage their territorial currencies in a more orthodox fashion or introduced currency boards in which discretionary monetary management is impossible. In these instances, Hayek's objective of "removing money from the realm of politics" has in fact been achieved but in a way that is compatible with the maintenance of a territorial currency. But in countries where fears exist that orthodox monetary policies may be more difficult to introduce or sustain, support for alternatives to territorial currencies has often emerged for the reason Hayek stated.

In those emerging-market and developing countries that have experienced very high rates of inflation, the circulation of foreign currencies has often been seen as

---

[28] Quotation from Hayek, *The Denationalization of Money*, 16.

[29] For Hayek, the denationalization of money also had particular appeal because of his scepticism about the value of any kind of government planning. Thus, he attacked not just Keynesians but also monetarists for believing that even conservative monetary planning was desirable.

desirable because it helps discipline national macroeconomic policymakers and societal groups. This connection was evident in the 1970s among Latin American policymakers who first encouraged dollarization by relaxing rules concerning foreign currency deposits. Although this move was often designed simply to curb flight capital, it also was frequently introduced as part of dramatic "neoliberal" economic reforms of the time. In the face of populist pressures and the dramatic political upheavals of the period, these neoliberal reforms were designed to radically shift the institutional context by encouraging market forms of discipline that would restore business confidence and promote neoliberal outcomes.[30] In the monetary sector, neoliberal reformers sought to replace activist monetary policies with a passive monetary policy that was determined by changes to the balance of payments. For this reason, some saw little reason to maintain the integrity of the territorial currencies. Indeed, in Chile in the late 1970s, Diaz-Alejandro notes that some reformers "dreamed of doing away with the national currency altogether, but feared the military might not wish to go that far."[31] More recently, a decision by Argentina in 1991 to allow dollars to be used as legal tender was designed to send a signal to the population about the seriousness of the government's intent to reestablish the "trustworthiness" of the national currency by subjecting state monetary managers to the "competition" provided by a more "credible" foreign currency.[32] In Ecuador, too, "full dollarization" was introduced only after a period of hyperinflation and it was designed to restore monetary stability by removing control of monetary management from domestic politicians altogether.

In Europe, some support for EMU has also had a similar motivation, particularly in economic liberal circles: abandoning the national currency in favour of the euro will prevent national policymakers from pursuing Keynesian macroeconomic policies.[33] The goal of "locking in" neoliberal reforms has also been made explicit by some supporters of North American monetary union. In Canada, one of the more prominent advocates of a common currency, Herb Grubel, told the Canadian Senate: "I would like to have an institution that protects me against the future, when another generation of economists is rediscovering Keynesianism, or whatever threats there might be in the future."[34]

Some neoliberals in both regions have also seen the abandonment of national currencies as a way to force domestic deregulatory policies that might have been difficult otherwise to promote politically. In Europe, the elimination of exchange-

[30] A. Foxley, *Latin American Experiments in Neoconservative Economic Policy* (Berkeley: University of California, 1993); A. Canitrot, "Discipline as the Central Objective of Economic Policy: An Essay on the Economic Programme of the Argentine Government Since 1976," *World Development* 8 (1980): 913–28.

[31] C. Diaz-Alejandro, "Good-bye Financial Repression, Hello Financial Crash," in Andresandro Velasco, ed., *Trade, Development and the World Economy: Selected Essays of Carlos Diaz-Alejandro* (Oxford: Basil Blackwell, 1988).

[32] F. de la Balze, *Remaking the Argentine Economy* (New York: Council of Foreign Relations, 1995).

[33] McNamara, *The Currency of Ideas.*

[34] Government of Canada, *Proceedings of the Standing Senate Committee on Banking, Trade and Commerce, Issue 48—Evidence*, 25 March 1999.

rate adjustments is seen as a tool to fostering more flexible domestic wages; in the European Commission's words, the euro will bring "increased labour market discipline," as devaluations can no longer be used to offset higher wage demands from workers.[35] In Canada, the elimination of the devaluation option is seen as a move that will force manufacturers to bolster productivity and workers to moderate wage demands.[36] On the same grounds, Hayek also strongly rejected the argument that territorial currencies should be managed actively to compensate for inflexible domestic wages and prices: "such an adaptation of the quantity of money to the rigidity of some prices and particularly wages would greatly extend the range of such rigidities and must therefore, in the long run, entirely destroy the functioning of the market." He continued: "Depriving government of the power of thus counteracting the effects of monopolistically enforced increases in wages and prices by increasing the quantity of money would place the responsibility for the full use of resources back to where it belongs: where the causally effective decisions are taken—the monopolists who negotiate the wages or prices."[37]

It is not just those opposed to activist national macroeconomic policies who back these alternatives to territorial currencies. Support has also come from traditional advocates of activist macroeconomic management who have concluded that the nation–state's capacity to pursue this kind of management in an age of global financial integration has been curtailed. One response to this situation has been to embrace partial dollarization as a way of signaling to the markets that national macroeconomic trends will be disciplined by currency competition. Another more ambitious response has been to support the delegation of power to a supranational authority such as the European central bank, which might be able to challenge the markets more effectively and insulate countries from their effects.[38]

Constraining the Fiscal Resources of the State?

In addition to bolstering national markets and creating the capacity to conduct national monetary policy, a third objective that drove the creation of territorial currencies during the nineteenth and early twentieth centuries was the desire to strengthen the fiscal resources of the state. The seigniorage gains to be realised by monopolizing the currency were attractive as a means to help finance the expanding fiscal needs of the state, particularly in the context of the emergence of mass warfare (as McNamara's chapter in this volume highlights in the U.S. case).[39] If the

---

[35] European Commission, "One Market, One Money," 47. See also Padoan's essay in this volume.

[36] Courchene and Harris, *From Fixing to Monetary Union*.

[37] Hayek, *The Denationalization of Money*, 96, 98.

[38] A. Verdun, "Does European Economic and Monetary Integration Limit Policy-Making Autonomy?" (paper presented to the annual conference of the International Studies Association, San Diego, 1996).

[39] More broadly, the creation of a single homogenous currency also greatly reduced the transaction costs associated with the administration of taxation and the running of modern bureaucracy associated

fiscal priorities of the state played this important role generating support for territorial currencies, are those rejecting territorial currencies today driven by an opposite goal: that of restricting the fiscal resources of the state?

To be sure, some advocates of the abandonment of territorial currencies hope this move will constrain the state's ability to finance large budget deficits through money creation. This motivation is apparent among some supporters of monetary unions in Europe and North America and is also evident among many of those pushing for full dollarization in many poorer countries of the world. Many supporters of privately-issued e-currencies also see this as one of the central reasons to pursue this monetary reform.[40]

What explains these new fiscal priorities? Some analysts point to the changing military-security context as one factor. David Glasner notes that currency monopolies were particularly useful in the past for financing unexpected, short-term and small-scale wars when other sources of quick finance were difficult to find. Their importance has diminished today, he argues, because changes in military technology (e.g., nuclear weapons) and the advent of large standing armies now require constant, much heavier expenditures in peacetime.[41] In the European context, Goodhart speculates in a similar vein that the EU countries may have been more willing to give up national seigniorage privileges because of the lack of prospect of war between them.[42]

Although these factors may play some role, a more important explanation can be found in a development we have seen already: the growing dominance of neoliberal economic ideas around the world today. Those who celebrate the fact that currency unions will diminish the state's ability to finance fiscal deficits are usually advocates of the neoliberal goal of reducing the economic size and role of the state more generally. Support for privately-issued e-currencies also comes primarily from neoliberal thinkers who see this as part of a broader project of attacking "big government."[43]

The role of these new fiscal goals in undermining support for territorial currencies should not be overstated. As Glasner acknowledges, one reason is that the enhanced tax collection and borrowing powers of contemporary states have greatly reduced the fiscal significance of currency monopoly. For most countries, seigniorage revenue is only a small share of the country's GDP, usually below 1 percent.[44]

---

with the nation-state. For this reason, initiatives to consolidate the currency often took place at the same time as modern accounting, taxation, and financing systems were introduced into government.

[40] See for example Dorn, *The Future of Money in the Information Age;* Hayek, *The Denationalization of Money.*

[41] D. Glasner, *Free Banking and Monetary Reform* (Cambridge: Cambridge University Press, 1989), 45–50, 205; D. Glasner, "An Evolutionary Theory of the State Monopoly over Money," in K. Dowd and R. Timberlake, eds., *Money and the Nation-State* (London: Transaction, 1998).

[42] C. Goodhart, "The Political Economy of Monetary Union," in P. Kenen, ed., *Understanding Interdependence* (Princeton: Princeton University Press, 1995).

[43] For example, Dorn, *The Future of Money in the Information Age.*

[44] Hausmann, "Should There be Five Currencies or One Hundred and Five?"; Fischer notes that in 1988, it was higher in some unusual cases such as Peru (6 percent), Jordan (8 percent), China (6 percent), Turkey (4 percent), Greece (3.8 percent). S. Fischer, "Seigniorage and Official Dollarization," in N. Liviathan, ed., *Proceedings of a Conference on Currency Substitution and Currency Boards* (Washington: World Bank), 8.

From the standpoint of policymakers, the more relevant statistic may be its share of government revenue, but this figure is still not large. When Israel launched its well-known and successful de-dollarization program in 1985, for example, one rationale mentioned was that of recapturing seigniorage. But as Bruno notes, this was hardly a major consideration since seigniorage revenue had been only approximately 4 percent of government revenue even in the period of high inflation. He notes that this figure was also true for high-inflation countries such as Argentina and Mexico.[45] These figures could be somewhat higher if one included the indirect fiscal effects of inflation that result from income tax "bracket creep," or the devaluation of government debt (in cases where the debt was issued at an interest rate that did not anticipate inflation).[46] But Friedman and Schwartz highlight how these two inflation effects are diminishing in many countries as indexation of income taxes is introduced and as financial markets become better at anticipating inflation.[47]

The diminishing fiscal significance of territorial currencies may thus help to explain why challenges to territorial currencies are less likely to be resisted on fiscal grounds than in the past.[48] For countries experiencing dollarization, or considering abandoning their national currency, the costs of forgoing seigniorage revenue have often been raised as a possible objection, but the issue rarely seems to be the decisive one influencing policy decisions one way or the other. Indeed, supporters of these initiatives are often able to argue easily that this loss will be clearly offset by other economic gains to be realised by their proposals.[49] The European Commission, for example, argued that the loss of seigniorage revenue generated by inflation in poorer EU countries will be more than offset by lower inflation premiums on these countries' borrowing in the new euro zone.[50]

Supporters of these initiatives have also noted that seigniorage revenue could still be found in alternative ways in the absence of a national currency. The new European Central Bank, for example, will divide its profits among its shareholders that are the national central banks of the participating countries. In advocating the adoption of the dollar in Latin American countries, Hausmann and Powell also highlight that countries could still generate some seigniorage revenue in a fully dollarized economy through the use of non-remunerated reserve requirements on cer-

[45] M. Bruno, "Overview of chapters 2 and 3," in M. De Cecco and A. Giovannini, eds., *A European Central Bank?* (Cambridge: Cambridge University Press, 1989). A former Minister of Finance from El Salvador, Manuel Hinds, also recently noted that in some Latin American countries, seigniorage can even be negative since the central bank is paying banks a higher rate of interest for their reserve deposits than it is receiving for its reserves backing these deposits and other currency. U.S. Senate, *Hearing on Official Dollarization in Emerging-Market Countries*, 1998.

[46] S. Fischer, "Modern Central Banking," in F. Capie, C. Goodhart, S. Fischer, and N. Schnadt, *The Future of Central Banking* (Cambridge: Cambridge University Press, 1994), 286.

[47] M. Friedman and A. Schwartz, "Has Government Any Role in Money?" *Journal of Monetary Economics* 17 (1986): 37–62.

[48] Similarly, David Glasner notes that fiscal considerations did not inhibit the growth of the eurodollar markets since states encouraging its growth on their territory were not undermining their own seigniorage but rather that of another state. Glasner, *Free Banking and Monetary Reform*.

[49] Schuler, *Basics of Dollarization*.

[50] European Commission, "One Market, One Money."

tain deposits (the "seigniorage" would be the interest earned on the reserves).[51] More prominent has been the suggestion that the United States might agree to share seigniorage as a way of reducing opposition to the adoption of the dollar. Larry Summers, before he became U.S. Treasury Secretary, had in fact proposed this as early as 1993,[52] and a bill was introduced into Congress in November 1999 to support this notion.

Efforts to Transcend National Identities?

In addition to objectives relating to transaction costs, monetary policy, and fiscal concerns, contemporary challenges to territorial currencies may also reflect some new ideas concerning political identities. Economists usually restrict their analyses of national currencies to their economic purposes. But territorial currencies were also created for a more political-cultural reason in the nineteenth and early twentieth centuries: they were seen to strengthen national identities.[53] In a symbolic sense, territorial currencies came to be seen as one of the key attributes of the sovereignty of a modern nation-state in that era. Policymakers also recognized that coins and notes could act as important carriers of nationalist imagery aimed at constructing a sense of collective tradition and memory (see McNamara's essay in this volume). By reducing transaction costs within a nation, territorial currencies were also seen to play a role similar to that of a national language: they would create a sense of unity by facilitating "communication" among members of the nation. As a tool of national macroeconomic management, territorial currencies have also been associated with a sense of national collective purpose. Finally, because trust plays such a large role in the use and acceptance of modern forms of money, territorial currencies were often seen as encouraging identification with the nation-state on a deeper psychological level.

To what extent is the growing unpopularity of territorial currencies indicative of a desire to transcend national identities? The creation of a supranational currency in Europe presents an interesting case to examine. It is clear that some of the motivation for creating EMU stems from a view that it will promote a greater sense of European political unity. As one group of scholars put it, EMU has "acquired symbolic meaning as a cornerstone of European political unification" and it is driven partly by political forces committed to a more "Europeanized" form of identity.[54] More concretely, enthusiasts for European integration also hope that EMU will encourage spillover effects—particularly the need for stronger federal fiscal arrangements—that foster further European political integration.[55] In addition, many Eu-

[51] Hausmann and Powell, *Dollarization*, 8.

[52] Summers, *Rules, Real Exchange Rates and Monetary Discipline*, 32.

[53] Helleiner, "National Currencies and National Identities."

[54] D. Engelmann, H.-J. Knopf, K. Roscher, and T. Risse, "Identity Politics in the EU: The Case of Economic and Monetary Union," in P. Minkinen and H. Patomaki, eds., *The Politics of Economic and Monetary Union* (Boston: Kluwer Academic Publishers, 1997), 105.

[55] See Kenen's chapter in this volume.

ropeans have seen EMU as an initiative that could bolster Europe's collective identity on the global stage.

Although those with a more "Europeanized" identity may be key supporters of this initiative, they have been quite hesitant to use the new currency in a symbolic sense to promote a collective sense of identity. It would be difficult to argue, for example, that the imagery on the euro has been designed in a way that is meant to foster a strong sense of common European identity. Although the face of the coins has a common image of a map of the EU and the stars of the EU flag, each Member State has been allowed to continue to decorate the obverse side with its own motifs and the various states have chosen traditional nationalist images for those motifs. The banknotes are also quite timid in their invocation of a new European identity. On their front side are images of windows and gateways, while the back side of each denomination has a map of Europe and an image of a different bridge. The official EU website suggests that the former is meant to be "a metaphor for communication among the people of Europe and between Europe and the world" and the latter are "symbols of the spirit of openness and cooperation in the EU."[56] But nowhere do we find images of a common history, landscape, or culture of the kind that are found on most national banknotes.[57] In the words of one journalist, "[t]he currency looks as if it has been designed for a "Star Trek" episode about some culturally denuded land on Mars—not for the home of Socrates, Charlemagne, Martin Luther, Notre Dame, the Uffizi, Bach, Beethoven, and Mozart."[58]

The quite limited use of imagery on the new euros to cultivate a common European identity undoubtedly reflects the limited extent to which political support exists for such a conception of identity within the EU. There is much stronger support among Europeans for the EU as a community that offers certain political rights and economic benefits than there is for the EU conceived as a unified, organic people with a common cultural identity that replaces the nation. For this reason, EMU supporters appear much more comfortable discussing how the euro will promote "one market" than its role in cultivating a sense of "one people." While opponents have seized on the idea that the euro might "dilute" national identities,[59] supporters have generally downplayed this potential. In a 1995 publication discussing the introduction of the euro, for example, the European Commission acknowledged briefly "for some people, the change will feel almost like a change of identity," but it felt compelled to add quickly that "[n]ational identity is not in peril, however."[60]

---

[56] Commission of the European Communities, "Euro—Coins-Notes," European Commission public information web page [http://europa.eu.int/euro/html], 2000.

[57] The EU website attempts to suggest that "[t]he designs are symbolic for Europe's architectural heritage" but it quickly goes on to say that "[t]hey do not represent any existing monuments." It also notes that graphic symbol for the euro "was inspired by the Greek letter *epsilon*, in reference to the cradle of European civilisation and to the first letter of the word 'Europe.' "

[58] F. Zakaria, "Money for Mars," *Newsweek*, 11 January 1999.

[59] Quotation from Helleiner, "National Currencies and National Identities," 1409.

[60] European Commission, *Green Paper: On the Practical Arrangements for the Introduction of the Single Currency* (Brussels: European Commission, 1995), 48–49.

This kind of defensiveness is also apparent among supporters of monetary unions and dollarization in other regions. In North America, supporters of monetary union are quick to acknowledge the nationalist opposition they anticipate to their proposals, leading some to stress that each country could retain nationalist images on one side of the new common coins and notes.[61] Similarly, advocates of the adoption of the dollar in Latin America have wondered aloud whether that the U.S. might help reduce nationalist objections to their proposals by replacing images of past U.S. Presidents on U.S. dollars with that of Columbus, or even allowing dollars printed for use in Latin America to carry the images of people such as the Mexican revolutionary Emiliano Zapata.[62]

Many supporters of monetary unions or dollarization have tried to deflect nationalist opposition by suggesting that these monetary reforms will not in fact dilute national identities. In countries that have experienced high levels of inflation or currency instability, the argument is sometimes made that the national currency is a liability rather than a source of national pride and unity. In Argentina, for example, Menem has argued that his country's national identity would be strengthened by adopting such a hard currency as the U.S. dollar: "It is stupid when we affirm that this is an attack against sovereignty. . . . Real sovereignty is the one that gives the people the possibility of having more security in their economic affairs."[63] Similarly, an American advocate of full dollarization told the U.S. Congress that the use of the dollar should not be seen in foreign countries as "an act of political submission" but rather as "an act of economic liberation" permitting citizens to "build a better economic future for their families."[64] Many nationalists in the poorer EU countries also seem quite happy to abandon their currencies in favor of a more stable common currency for this reason.

Another common argument is that the abandonment of a territorial currency will not undermine national identities because monetary sovereignty is a thing of the past. No longer should the abandonment of a national currency be seen to undermine popular sovereignty since "the people" appear to have little desire to actively manage money anyway. Even if people still had this wish, nationalists are asked to recognize that global financial markets have already rendered monetary sovereignty a hollow shell (a point disputed by many economists). These have long been common arguments of Quebec nationalists supporting their case that they do not need a territorial currency upon achieving independence.[65] The European

---

[61] Courchene and Harris, *From Fixing to Monetary Union*.

[62] For the first suggestion, see Hausmann et al., "Financial Turmoil and the Choice of Exchange Rate Regime," 19. The second is Guillermo Calvo's idea, reported in A. Oppenheimer, "Zapata Dollar in 2010?" *Miami Herald*, 25 January 1999. Schuler, *Basics of Dollarization*, 16, suggests that countries with strong concerns about national identity might retain national coins, as Liberia and Panama have done.

[63] Quoted in J. Nudler: "No vamos a ser menos soberanos," *Pagina* 12 (Argentina daily newspaper), 24 January 1999. (I am grateful for the translation to Laura Chrabolowsky.)

[64] J. Shelton, "Prepared Testimony of Dr. Judy Shelton," in U.S. Senate, *Hearing on Official Dollarization in Emerging-Market Countries*.

[65] See, for example, R. Levesque, *My Quebec* (Toronto: Methuen, 1979).

Commission has highlighted the latter point prominently: "For some, the transition to the single currency means a loss of national monetary sovereignty. But how much autonomy do monetary policies really have today in Europe? With capital moving freely between interdependent economies, an autonomous monetary policy is no longer a credible policy option. Members will only lose a prerogative, which in practice they cannot use."[66] Indeed, many EMU supporters noted that, by pooling their resources, members of a monetary union might be able to regain a degree of the sovereignty that had been lost to global markets. The way in which national currencies are being challenged around the world is also invoked as a sign that territorial currencies need not any longer be considered as key part of the sovereignty of a nation-state. In North America, supporters of monetary union frequently cite the European example to make this point. As Thomas Courchene in Canada put it: "the euro is also signaling that in a progressively integrated global economy, currency arrangements are emerging as one of those supranational or international public goods, an international public good that will be fully consistent with the 21st century notion of what national sovereignty will be all about."[67]

What is interesting about these various arguments is that they explicitly reject the idea that the abandonment of territorial currencies is intended to challenge national identities. This marks an interesting contrast to the nineteenth-century period. In that era, monetary reforms were explicitly linked to political projects designed to alter political identities. This was true not just of the nation-builders who created territorial currencies but also of liberal advocates of the universal currency during the 1860s. Walter Bagehot, for example, argued in favor of this proposal in 1869 on the following grounds:

> [if England were to introduce the universal currency] all Englishmen would lose some of the exceptional national feeling which retards their progress, which makes them look at others as strange, which makes them think us singular too. If civilization could make all men of one money, it would do much to make them think they were of one blood.[68]

Today, with the partial exception of the EU case, the goal of using monetary reforms to alter political identities in these ways is much less prominent.

Conclusion

The widespread nature of the challenges to territorial currencies is one of the more interesting phenomena in the contemporary world. Perhaps because these challenges are so uneven geographically and heterogeneous in form in the contempo-

---

[66] European Commission, *Green Paper*.

[67] Government of Canada, *Proceedings of the Standing Senate Committee on Banking, Trade and Commerce*, 9.

[68] Quoted in Perlman, "In Search of Monetary Union," 318.

rary age, scholars have not devoted much attention to the development of a general analysis of the causes of this phenomenon. This chapter begins such an analysis by reviewing the four goals that drove the initial creation of territorial currencies during the nineteenth and early twentieth centuries: (1) the bolstering of national markets by altering transaction costs; (2) the provision of a tool for national monetary management; (3) the widening of the state's revenue base; and (4) the strengthening of national identities. I have suggested that an examination of the question of whether policymakers are turning their backs on these goals may help us to explain why territorial currencies are becoming unpopular.

My conclusions can be quickly summarized. Growing disenchantment with the first two goals is playing a significant role in encouraging challenges to territorial currencies today. Concerning the first, deepening international economic integration has led many to question the limitations of national markets. Although territorial currencies eliminated *intra*-national transaction costs, many policymakers are now more concerned to reduce the *inter*-national transaction costs associated with the existence of distinct territorial currencies, particularly those costs associated with exchange-rate instability. Concerning the second goal, disillusionment with the kind of activist national monetary policies that became prominent after the 1930s has also been important in reducing support for territorial currencies; indeed, some policymakers have employed alternative monetary structures to prevent states from pursuing such policies. This new disillusionment reflects both the growing power of global financial markets and the emergence of a "neoliberal" consensus that monetary policy has no long-term impact on real output and employment. In these two ways, the growing unpopularity of territorial currencies can be seen to be associated with broader reconsideration of the proper economic role of the nation-state generated by the triumph of "neoliberal" economic ideas and intensifying international economic integration.

What, then, about the role of fiscal stabilization and political identities, the other two motivations that drove the original creation of territorial currencies? Has disenchantment with them also played a role in encouraging challenges to territorial currencies today? I have argued that they are less significant. Revenue goals have played a role in some instances; some of the contemporary enthusiasm for currency unions, dollarization or private e-currencies stems from a "neoliberal" desire to curtail the size of the state and the ability of governments to finance deficits through money creation. To the limited extent that fiscal goals are important, then, they seem to fit my general thesis that challenges to territorial currencies stem from a reconsideration of the proper economic role of the nation-state in the contemporary age. New conceptions of political identities have also played some role in generating support for a supranational currency in Europe. But their significance should not be overstated there and, in most other parts of the world, policymakers are usually bending over backward to explain that alternatives to territorial currencies are *not* designed to undermine national identities. In contrast to the nineteenth century, monetary reformers are driven primarily in the current age by political-economic goals rather than political-cultural ones relating to national identities.

My analysis is not designed to provide a comprehensive explanation of the growing unpopularity of territorial currencies. To explain the different ways that territorial currencies are being challenged and the different intensities of these challenges in each country, we would need to move away from this general level of explanation to examine regional and country–specific variations in the factors cited above. By explaining some general reasons why territorial currencies are becoming unpopular, however, I have attempted to provide insights that guide that kind of specific research. I also hope to remind researchers of the ways in which the diverse challenges to territorial currencies share some common causes in the current era.

CHAPTER NINE

Bounded Rationality and the World Political Economy

John S. Odell

The world's monetary system, like the rest of its political economy, is driven by bounded rationality, yet many scholars still sidestep key implications of this forty-year-old idea. Accumulating evidence shows the costs of this neglect, even granting that other perspectives have been productive. This chapter assesses the theoretical underpinnings of our knowledge about these subjects from an unconventional perspective.

I argue that greater use of the bounded-rationality premise in research would improve our knowledge empirically, theoretically, and practically. Political economy knowledge would be better empirically if we paid more attention to how economic policy decisions are actually made. Theoretically, a new constructivism rebuilt upon a bounded-rationality microfoundation would be more complete and better able to account for change. Taking a fresh look at classical rational choice as well as constructivism from this perspective might help us transcend another great debate about international relations theory, this time between these two.[1] Sounder knowledge of decision making would also make our studies more useful in the practical world. These arguments apply to studies of political economy in general, including monetary and financial relations in particular. They point to rich opportunities for scholars to break new ground.

My purpose is to increase interest in the bounded-rationality perspective rather than to oppose others. Other premises have been productive, and they too should

I am grateful for comments on an earlier draft by this book's editors, other members of this project, and Hayward Alker, Michael Barnett, Benjamin J. Cohen, Daniel Drezner, Matthew Evangelista, Joanne Gowa, Peter Katzenstein, Robert Keohane, Todd Sandler, Wesley Widmaier, Thomas Willett, and participants at a panel at the American Political Science Association 2000 convention. None of these friends is responsible for remaining weaknesses.

[1] A 1998 survey found debates between rationalism and constructivism becoming prominent. P. J. Katzenstein, R. O. Keohane, and S. D. Krasner, "*International Organization* and the Study of World Politics," *International Organization* 52 (1998): 645–86.

continue to bear fruit. A scholarly division of labor is natural and inevitable. What we actually have, however, is more than a division of labor. Sometimes scholars too, like the actors they study, fall into reliance on conventions, rules of thumb, and biases in their professional work. Certain types of writings cease to be assigned as readings in graduate courses, for instance, so that out-of-fashion approaches are systematically overlooked rather than rejected because of careful scrutiny. This essay may not convince today's purest adherents to either unbounded rationality or postmodern epistemology to change their spots. But many students and other scholars are not committed irrevocably to polar positions. Some looking for fertile terrain for innovative contributions might well find such territory here.

The first section of this chapter recalls the original definition of bounded rationality. The second examines exemplars from social-science literature to see how much or little bounded rationality has penetrated into the most influential research programs and to suggest the potential losses from neglect. I try to select from the best and most influential exemplars and disproportionately from international monetary relations in keeping with this book's theme. The final sections propose concrete forms of bounded rationality investments that scholars could consider and they speculate about payoffs that could be realized.

Simon's Innovation

The bounded rationality premise stands between two better-known positions—unbounded utility maximization and anti-rationality. The most popular meaning of "rational choice" is a particular package of assumptions that are not all necessary and not shared by all rationalists. The dominant perspective assumes not only that the primary theoretical unit is the individual but also that this actor has coherent stable preferences, given a priori in a utility function. Most assume that the set of alternative courses of action is also given a priori. With respect to the consequences of alternatives, sometimes it is assumed they are known with certainty, and other times the chooser knows the probability distribution of possible outcome values. Crucially, the dominant variant assumes the decision maker will optimize. She will choose, among the alternatives available, exactly that one that is expected to yield the greatest possible utility, given costs and other constraints. The agent is assumed to be able to compute which alternative will be optimal. Many applications also assume that subjective beliefs and nonmaterial values can be safely ignored. This set of premises has spawned much influential research.

Other social scientists and humanists reject all rationalisms. Freudians were perhaps the most extreme advocates for that position, but they faded from international studies years ago.[2] More recently, post-modernists, anthropologists, and oth-

---

[2] As related non-Freudian exceptions, P. A. Kowert and M. G. Hermann, "Who Takes Risks? Daring and Caution in Foreign Policy Making," *Journal of Conflict Resolution* 41 (1997): 611–37, and E. Adler, *The Power of Ideology: The Quest for Technological Autonomy in Argentina and Brazil* (Berkeley: University of California Press, 1987), explore the effects of emotions and personality types, respectively, in bargaining.

ers have resisted individual rationality as a basis on which to build social theory. Some international relations constructivists are anti-rationalists, whereas others are looking for middle paths. Constructivists too have been adding to our understanding, though not much in the monetary sphere so far.

Bounded rationality, in Herbert Simon's words, means a variant of "rational choice that takes into account the cognitive limitations of the decision maker—limitations of both knowledge and computational capacity."[3] Here too the fundamental theoretical unit is the individual. In the financial sector this could be a banker, investor, industrial worker, legislator, or political executive. The actor is rational in the broad sense that he or she "wishes to attain goals and uses his or her mind as well as possible to that end."[4] But the postulate of rational choice is modified to fit voluminous empirical findings about systematic limits of the human mind.[5] Prospect theory is the thread of this literature that political scientists know best, but it is only one thread. Rather than consider all conceivable alternative courses of action, the bounded-rational actor conducts a limited search for a few alternative courses, often following standard operating procedures or incremental adaptation. She makes use of subjective beliefs, social norms, and cognitive shortcuts. Instead of optimizing, which is well beyond her computational capacity, she "satisfices," in Simon's early version. She chooses "an alternative that meets or exceeds specified criteria, but that is not guaranteed to be either unique or in any sense the best."[6] Nor are effective preferences necessarily stable and exogenous. They are influenced by the way issues are framed, for example, and can change under the influence of advocacy and negotiation.

Note that Simon's bounded rationality assumes two types of bounds—not only limits on knowledge or information, which are increasingly acknowledged, but also limits on the capacity to compute optima. Bentley MacLeod illustrates this second limit by pondering the task of getting dressed in the morning. Suppose a man must choose among shirts of different colors, slacks of different colors, jackets, and so on. If he had ten shirts, ten pairs of pants, ten jackets, ten ties, six pairs of socks, and four pairs of shoes to consider, and if he spent half a second considering each possible combination, "it would take forty hours to get dressed. Hence, the algorithm of studying every possible combination and then deciding what to wear is simply not feasible."[7] The game of chess has a finite number of alternative possible sequences of play, but this number is "comparable to the number of molecules in

---

[3] H. A. Simon, *Models of Bounded Rationality, Volume 3: Empirically Grounded Economic Reason* (Cambridge, Mass.: MIT Press, 1997), 291.

[4] Ibid., 293. Also see Simon's seminal 1955 article "A Behavioral Model of Rational Choice," as in *Models of Bounded Rationality, Volume 2: Behavioral Economics and Business Organization* (Cambridge, Mass.: MIT Press, 1982), 239–58.

[5] For introductions and references to these many findings, see M. A. Neale and M. H. Bazerman, *Cognition and Rationality in Negotiation* (New York: Free Press, 1991); J. S. Levy, "Prospect Theory, Rational Choice, and International Relations," *International Studies Quarterly* 41 (1997): 87–112; M. Rabin, "Psychology and Economics," *Journal of Economic Literature* 36 (1998): 11–46.

[6] Simon, *Models of Bounded Rationality, Volume 3*, 295.

[7] W. B. MacLeod, "Complexity, Bounded Rationality, and Heuristic Search" (Department of Economics, University of Southern California [www.rcf.usc.edu/~wmacleod], 1999), 6.

the universe."[8] Simon concludes, "If the game of chess, limited to its 64 squares and six kinds of pieces, is beyond exact computation, then we may expect the same of almost any real-world problem. . . ."[9] Yet the conclusions from many economics and international political economy (IPE) models are valid only on the heroic assumption that people *are* capable of optimizing.

Modes of rational decision other than full deliberation and maximization have been theorized and observed. Individuals make broadly rational decisions by adapting incrementally to changes in the environment, by emulating others who have succeeded, by obeying tradition or authority (e.g., *Consumer Reports*), and by habit, trial and error, unmotivated search, and hunches. In fact, economist Richard Day claims that "optimizing is neither the most often used nor necessarily the most effective" of these modes in economic decisions.[10] It is possible to be "too rational," if even two hours are required to optimize one's apparel every morning. Other modes of choice may yield optimal or near-optimal results at far less deliberation cost.[11] Various formal models representing modes other than optimization have been proposed and studied.[12]

Bounded-rationality research is methodologically diverse. This literature has used verbal theories, case studies, mathematical models and algorithms, simulations, experiments, and surveys. But in order to avoid common misunderstandings, let me underline two things that bounded rationality is not. Thinking of individuals as the elementary conceptual units does not necessarily mean treating them like atoms isolated from social influence or ignoring the importance of institutions. Although many economics and IPE works regarded as rationalist do make these additional simplifying assumptions, doing so is not inherent in the individualist premise. After all, parts of sociology and most of social psychology work from the individual as the fundamental unit, and social influence is what these disciplines are all about. A major attraction of the bounded-rationality perspective is precisely that it dovetails individualist ideas with cultural and organizational ideas. The content of the bounds on a given individual's rationality, and the ideas she takes for granted, may well be supplied by the surrounding society with its organizations and socialization process. Bounded rationalists are not obliged to ignore socially constructed facts, central banks, trade unions, states, or other collectives, nor must

[8] H. A. Simon and J. Schaeffer, "The Game of Chess," in R. J. Aumann and S. Hart, eds., *Handbook of Game Theory* (Amsterdam: Elsevier, 1992), 2.

[9] H. A. Simon, "Variants of Human Behavior," *Annual Review of Psychology* 41 (1990), 6.

[10] R. H. Day, "Bounded Rationality and the Coevolution of Market and State," in R. H. Day, G. Eliasson, and C. Wihlborg, eds., *The Markets for Innovation, Ownership and Control* (Amsterdam: North-Holland, 1993), 66.

[11] M. Pingle and R. H. Day, "Modes of Economizing Behavior: Experimental Evidence," *Journal of Economic Behavior and Organization* 29 (1996): 191–209.

[12] See J. Conlisk, "Why Bounded Rationality?" *Journal of Economic Literature* 34 (1996): 669–700. R. H. Day and E. H. Tinney, "How to Co-operate in Business without Really Trying: A Learning Model of Decentralized Decision Making," *Journal of Political Economy* 76 (1968): 583–600, is one early example. J. Bendor, "A Model of Muddling Through," *American Political Science Review* 89 (1995): 819–40, explores Lindblom's insights using formal models.

these be regarded as less important than individual-level properties. What is required for a coherent and convincing argument that emphasizes collectivities and is based on bounded rationality is that the theory and the evidence must somehow represent the individuals as well as the collectivities. Examples will follow.

Nor does bounded rationality mean that individuals or nations seek only material goals. Rationalist scholarship has often been criticized on these grounds too, but again it is important to recognize the difference between core premises and auxiliary assumptions that are not inherent.[13] Bounded rationality as a decision-making assumption is wholly consistent with goals such as maintaining an identity, a reputation with an audience, conformity to social expectations, or consistency with ideological principles. It would not be inconsistent, for example, to study Japanese monetary policy and experience by assuming individual bounded rationality and looking for social conformity as an influence on savings behavior, the value of the yen, and Japanese institutions. Nor would it be inconsistent to account for the creation of Europe's new monetary union by assuming bounded rationality and tracing a shared elite ideology as an influence on this decision.

Costs of Neglecting Limits on Rationality

Many scholars of the world political economy, including its monetary and financial affairs, avoid the bounded rationality premise. These scholars certainly produce valuable knowledge, but avoiding bounded rationality has costs. Systematic acknowledgment of the limits on rationality can generate valuable contributions missed by other frameworks. Factions in economics and political science recognize these shortfalls and are moving toward bounded rationality, and toward one another. Consider them in turn.

Economics: Mainstream and Minority

In economics, classic unbounded rationality still plays the dominant role by far. Becker argues that not only economic behavior but "all human behavior can be viewed as involving participants who maximize their utility from a stable set of preferences."[14] Not all the economics majority goes this far, but they have conventionally invoked Milton Friedman's 1953 methodological argument: even though most people and firms actually are not classically rational, it will be productive scientifically to assume they act as if they are. This dominant approach certainly has been productive of much useful scientific output.

---

[13] E. Adler, "Seizing the Middle Ground: Constructivism in World Politics," *European Journal of International Relations* 3 (1997): 319–63 is one example of overlooking the distinction between rationalist and materialist.

[14] G. S. Becker, *The Economic Approach to Human Behavior* (Chicago: University of Chicago Press, 1976), 14.

In international monetary economics, a nuanced example is Benjamin Cohen's *Organizing the World's Money*, situated at the global level of analysis. Others had advanced proposals for reform of the international monetary system, but governments had avoided most of these schemes. Cohen treated this prescriptive problem "as one of joint maximization of two objectives," efficiency and consistency.[15] His study went beyond politically naïve proposals by building in sovereign states' political goals in addition to economic welfare and by recognizing that some states have more power than others. Consequently his plan did not attempt to integrate the system as tightly as would a gold standard or a world central bank; Cohen aimed instead for "optimum disintegration."[16] His recommended compromise regime added different ingredients to hit different sub-goals, aiming to minimize conflicts among governments rather than to eliminate them completely. But although this book adds political goals to the economic ones, the apparatus of optimization is clear and explicit throughout. The need for compromise arises from inconsistent objectives held by fully rational sovereign actors, not from cognitive biases. Thus the plan was not designed to deal with financial pathologies that might arise from decision makers' incomplete searches, herd behavior, or cultural biases.[17]

In contrast, a growing minority in economics has been challenging the dominant position that has been influential in political science as well as economics. The challengers have now accumulated a mass of evidence showing that people act systematically as if they are not classically rational, at least under some conditions. A multitude of careful studies has documented that individuals faced with choices often do not choose the alternative that orthodox theory predicts. These findings can be grouped into three sets.[18]

The first set challenges less central postulates, outside rationality proper. They show that people care about values other than short-term material self-interest, even in their economic behavior. We have social goals; we reciprocate cooperation and exploitation in business even when an alternative course would be more profitable; we are disproportionately averse to losses.[19] These findings do not threaten the postulate that individuals make choices through a classically rational decision process.

A second set of findings strikes closer to the heartland. These studies show that when attempting to optimize, people make what look (at least to orthodox theory)

[15] B. J. Cohen, *Organizing the World's Money: The Political Economy of International Monetary Relations* (New York: Basic Books, 1977), 271.

[16] Ibid., 283.

[17] Although the book discusses the familiar problems of confidence in international reserve currency and of overshooting by flexible exchange rates, these phenomena are not understood through bounded rationality or psychological lenses, and in this too the book is representative. In *The Geography of Money* (Ithaca: Cornell University Press, 1998), 137, however, Cohen takes a step toward bounded rationality when he adds "mimesis," a psychological tendency to imitate past behavior, as one factor accounting for inertia in the popularity of an international currency.

[18] Rabin, "Psychology and Economics."

[19] Ibid. This section relies heavily on this fine review article and Conlisk, "Why Bounded Rationality?" which provide direct references to this literature.

like systematic, not random, reasoning errors. Unable to carry out the full compu-
tations assumed by classic rationalism, even when getting dressed in the morning,
we regularly substitute mental shortcuts that imply predictable biases. To take one
example, when placing a value on an alternative, people do not conduct a complete
search and integrate multiple value dimensions with varying weights. Instead we
anchor our valuation on one analogue that happens to be psychologically salient
and make adjustments from there. Thus realtors put a value on a house for sale by
taking the asking price as a convenient starting point.[20] We also infer too much from
small samples, as in the notion of the basketball player with the "hot hand."[21] We
adapt incrementally and satisfice.

In finance, money illusion on the part of workers or others is not surprising to a
bounded rationalist. Unimpeachable evidence that even central bankers are people
too came recently from Alan Blinder, academic economist who served as Vice Chair
of the Federal Reserve during the mid-1990s. Speaking after his return to Princeton, he reported decision-making heuristics and problems he observed inside the
Federal Reserve. He was troubled by a "psychological" reluctance to wait patiently
for the lagged effects of past actions to be felt. His colleagues tended to "take the
economy's temperature" at each meeting and make new changes each time it was
off target. This widespread heuristic for maintaining flexibility "reflects a complete
misunderstanding of the dynamic programming way of thinking." He reported a
"truly serious" problem—abroad as well as in the United States—of central
bankers following the markets too closely. "I often witnessed central bankers sorely
tempted to deliver the policy that the markets expected or demanded" in the short
term. This cognitive shortcut is a problem, he said, "because I believe that markets
tend to get hyper-excited by almost any stimulus, sometimes succumb to fads and
fancies and are often short-sighted." For Blinder the very purpose of a central bank
is to take a long view.[22]

While reporting this second set of findings, it is appropriate to note that academic economists did take steps during the 1970s to make their theories more realistic by introducing certain departures from complete information. Allowing one
player in a signaling game to have private information that the other lacks, theorists
could account for some behavior patterns that otherwise seemed inexplicable, such

[20] G. B. Northcraft and M. A. Neale, "Amateurs, Experts, and Real Estate: An Anchoring-and-Ad-
justment Perspective on Property Pricing Decisions," *Organizational Behavior and Human Decision Processes* 39 (1987): 84–97. Further, R. M. Liebert, W. P. Smith, J. H. Hill, and M. Keiffer, "The Effects of
Information and Magnitude of Initial Offer on Interpersonal Negotiation," *Journal of Experimental Social Psychology* 4 (1968): 431–41, shows that sellers tend to let buyers' initial bids anchor the final agreement. Willett's public-choice approach (this volume) also emphasizes biases as influences on the IMF's
behavior.

[21] Rabin, "Psychology and Economics."

[22] A. S. Blinder, "Distinguished Lecture on Economics in Government: What Central Bankers
Could Learn from Academics—and Vice Versa," *Journal of Economic Perspectives* 11 (1997): 4, 5, 8–10,
15. Blinder also criticized academic economists for making some assumptions for mathematical conven-
ience and for barking up the wrong tree in their concentration on the danger of time-inconsistent monetary policymaking.

as the decisions of both a union and a management to accept the onset of a costly strike that someone was going to lose. In this way mainstream economics began to recognize the first of Simon's two bounds on rationality (limits on information), and this line of modeling has been fruitful. Still, these models represent information in a highly stylized way that falls far short of incorporating documented knowledge biases. What is more, most of these theories still assume people optimize perfectly given the information they have. Rationality is still unbounded in this second fundamental sense.

Theorists have been tempted to save optimization by blaming behavioral anomalies on bad information in the hands of perfect optimizers, rather than to model other decision rules such as satisficing. This is a modeler's choice rather than a necessary postulate of rationalism. Without denying the importance of information, economist John Conlisk observes this convention.

> When I walked into a post while watching a bird, my family called it a dumb move. Among economists, however, I could have claimed that, given the spatial distribution of lamp posts, the expected utility of bird watching exceeded the expected disutility of a collision. Ex ante, the post probably was not there, and it is entirely rational to collide with an ex post post. This example illustrates the confounding of rationality issues with information issues. Am I dumb to walk into a post or merely a rational victim of imperfect information? . . .
>
> It is curious that such similar economic issues, costly deliberation and costly information collection, have been treated so differently in standard economics, one avoided and the other embraced. In practice, the difference in treatment has required that anything resembling imperfect deliberation be passed off as imperfect information. . . . [23]

Another response—attempting to add deliberation cost as one more cost in an optimization model—quickly confronts a conundrum. Suppose the actor making a financial choice tries to minimize her deliberation cost; in other words, she attempts to economize on economizing.[24] Now she has two tasks, the original decision and deciding how much to deliberate in making the original decision. How will she make the second decision? It too will require costly deliberation. If she is to optimize there, she must undertake a third task, deliberating on how to minimize the costs of the second decision, and so on. Soon, it seems, the optimization theorist falls into an infinite regress with no escape, other than some resort to intuition or bounded rationality.[25] Another defense by the economics majority has been that experience and learning will tend to correct such biases. This has been found to be so only under certain conditions. Under common conditions, learning is selective and tends to reinforce

---

[23] Conlisk, "Why Bounded Rationality?"

[24] R. H. Day and M. A. Pingle, "Economizing Economizing," in R. Frantz, H. Singh, and J. Gerber, eds., *Behavioral Decision Making: Handbook of Behavioral Economics* (Greenwich, Conn.: JAI Press, 1991), 509–22.

[25] Conlisk, "Why Bounded Rationality?" 687.

biases.[26] Still another defense is that in business, those who do not optimize fail to survive. Yet research has documented common conditions under which suboptimizers—firms and individuals—do survive.[27]

Most serious of all is evidence, from a third set of studies, casting doubt on the assumption that people have consistent, stable, exogenous preferences to be optimized in the first place, even on purely economic issues. Many Americans demonstrate a tendency to prefer short-term gratification that is plainly inconsistent with their own long-term preferences, for instance by saving less money than they believe they should. We also fail to take optimal account of "internalities," the effects a current choice can have on the utility of later choices.[28]

Some preferences seem to be unstable and to vary with the institutional setting. Lottery winners underestimate how quickly and fully their reference points will adjust upward after receiving their windfalls, and they end up less happy than they themselves had expected to be. Much laboratory and survey evidence shows that changing the way options are framed can change what a person prefers.[29] To take a financial illustration, economist Richard Thaler finds that the number of options on a 401(k) menu can affect the employees' selections. Those with a choice of a stock fund and a bond fund tend to invest half in each. Those with a choice of three stock funds and one bond fund are likely to sprinkle an equal amount of their savings in each, and thus put 75 percent of the total in stocks.[30] Is the preference for equities exogenous?[31]

The possibility that preferences vary according to framing (by the institutional setting, advertising or "spin") seems even greater when we move from choices by investors to governments' economic policy choices—say over whether to comply with an IMF adjustment program—that can be framed in terms of such values as national independence and retribution for past exploitation.

In addition, observers of financial markets have often noted herd behavior, suggesting that decision makers' judgments and preferences can be changed by influences other than market fundamentals that dominate mainstream models. Historians have documented dozens of financial manias and panics. Stock market swings up and down are notoriously difficult for modelers to predict or explain. Evidence consistent with the herding hypothesis has been reported for less-experienced se-

---

[26] L. Babcock and G. Loewenstein, "Explaining Bargaining Impasse: The Role of Self-Serving Biases," *Journal of Economic Perspectives* 11 (1997): 109–26.

[27] Conlisk, "Why Bounded Rationality?" 684.

[28] Rabin, "Psychology and Economics."

[29] D. Kahneman, J. Knetch, and R. Thaler, "Experimental Tests of the Endowment Effect and Coase Theorem," *Journal of Political Economy* 98 (1990): 1325–48, and earlier works cited there.

[30] R. Lowenstein, "Exuberance Is Rational, or at Least Human," *New York Times Magazine* (11 February 2001), 70.

[31] J. G. March, "Bounded Rationality, Ambiguity, and the Engineering of Choice," *Bell Journal of Economics* 9 (1978): 587–608, points out that rational choice also entails a guess about what one's future preferences will be and calls for theorizing about preference processing—how we decide how ambitious to be, how much sin to permit, and how much rationality to practice.

curities analysts and mutual-fund managers, who seem to follow the herd into popular earnings forecasts and stocks, respectively.[32]

Soon after the Mexican government devalued the peso in December 1994 and investors suddenly fled the country, the herd also pulled back from other Latin American markets whose prospects had not changed suddenly. This was sneeringly dubbed the "tequila effect." Evidently some decision makers classified certain countries into a single "Latin American" category regardless of their payments balances, fiscal deficits, and international reserves.[33] Meanwhile the herd was moving massively into southeast and east Asian emerging markets. Was each of those investment decisions based on exhaustive search, deliberation, and optimization, or was there some follow-the-leader going on?

In 1997 quite a few more people walked into posts. A new financial crisis began in Thailand and spread quickly to larger countries. "To judge from most market indicators of risk, private creditors and rating agencies were asleep prior to the outbreak of the Thai crisis."[34] Was inadequate information the only reason for the sudden, unexpected capital flight that followed? Financial contagion can spread partly because of material links such as trade and competitive devaluation, but hypotheses from bounded rationality also represent promising research opportunities.

In sum, the accumulating evidence looks to a minority in the economics profession like an elephant in the living room—more than ample testimony to the costs of neglecting to investigate how bounded-rational agents operate, and the macroeconomic implications. Herbert Simon has been joined by Ronald Coase, Kenneth Arrow, Richard Day, Douglass North, Oliver Williamson, and Ariel Rubinstein, each in his own way. Public choice scholars discuss "rational ignorance"; elsewhere in this volume, Thomas Willett suggests a broader approach to public-choice analysis reflecting such concerns.[35] The economics of transaction costs as a generator of economic organization is well known. Williamson derives economic institutions from the assumptions that human beings need to economize on rationality and that they are prone to opportunism. Some scholars have been formally modeling alternative choice processes and their implications. Recently such prestigious U.S. economics departments as those at MIT and Harvard have begun to recognize the im-

[32] H. Hong, J. D. Kubik, and A. Solomon, "Security Analysts' Career Concerns and Herding of Earnings Forecasts," *Rand Journal of Economics* 31 (1999): 121–44; J. Chevalier and G. Ellison, "Career Concerns of Mutual Fund Managers," *Quarterly Journal of Economics* 114 (1999): 389–432.

[33] A quantitative study of twenty-four emerging markets from 1989 to 1998 found evidence that bank lending decisions within a region are contagious, especially during a crisis. "If two countries shared common bankers, financial pressure was significantly transmitted between them—regardless of their distinct fundamentals." Wendy Dobson and Gary Clyde Hufbauer, *World Capital Markets: Challenge to the G-10* (Washington: Institute for International Economics, 2001), 50.

[34] J. Goldstein, *Ideas, Interests, and American Trade Policy* (Ithaca: Cornell University Press, 1993), 19.

[35] See also T. D. Willett, "International Financial Markets as Sources of Crises or Discipline: The Too Much Too Late Hypothesis," *Princeton Essays in International Economics* 218 (Princeton: International Economics Section, Department of Economics, Princeton University, 2000).

portance of behavioral economics with their faculty-hiring decisions. Some young rising stars have been trained in psychology as well as in economics.[36]

Conlisk reviews much of this expanding work. He recommends the postulates that human cognition is a scarce resource and that deliberation has costs. Bounded-rational actors will use a rule of thumb whenever a classically rational computation would cost more than it is worth. In many situations it could be a mistake to correct errors of the size produced by alternative-decision modes. Rationality may be a matter of degree depending on the conditions, and it may be partly endogenous.[37]

Unbounded Rationality in IPE

Like most economists, IPE analysts in political science have shown impressive resistance to the bounded-rationality literature and its implications. This IPE majority contrasts sharply with political-science specialists on war and peace, many of whom read cognitive psychology during the 1950s and 1960s, explored decision making, biases, misperceptions, and organizational routines, and reported careful evidence of their importance in international relations.[38] IPE scholarship, strongly influenced by mainstream economics after a lag, rarely discusses such things and rarely examines evidence about individual decision makers. Most IPE works are silent regarding the individual decision process they assume to be operating. Some detective work is therefore needed to identify these theoretical premises. My evidence comes from a selective look at influential exemplars rather than from a comprehensive survey. Here too we find some significant departures as well as opportunities for further innovation.

Frieden is one representative who assumes unbounded rationality when explaining U.S. monetary policy from the 1860s through the 1980s. Frieden argues here that when the U.S. economy was more open, monetary policy pitted producers of tradeable goods against those of nontradeables, and domestic conflict over the exchange rate was intense. Tradeables producers preferred a weak dollar and producers of nontradeables favored a strong one. When the U.S. economy was much less open (1935–1970), monetary politics were quite subdued. In Frieden's world too, it seems that all expressed policy preferences are exact reflections of producers' and consumers' market positions. No boundaries on rationality are noted and no sys-

[36] L. Uchitelle, "Following the Money, but also the Mind," *New York Times*, 11 February 2001, section 3, 1.

[37] Conlisk, "Why Bounded Rationality?"

[38] G. Allison and P. Zelikow, *Essence of Decision: Explaining the Cuban Missile Crisis*, 2d ed. (New York: Longman, 1999); O. R. Holsti, *Crisis, Escalation, War* (Montreal and London: McGill-Queen's University Press, 1972); J. D. Steinbruner, *The Cybernetic Theory of Decision: New Dimensions of Political Analysis* (Princeton: Princeton University Press, 1974); B. C. Cohen and S. A. Harris, "Foreign Policy," in F. I. Greenstein and N. W. Polsby, eds., *Handbook of Political Science* (Reading, Mass.: Addison-Wesley, 1975), 381–437; R. Jervis, *Perception and Misperception in International Politics* (Princeton: Princeton University Press, 1976); and D. Larson, *Origins of Containment: A Psychological Explanation* (Princeton: Princeton University Press, 1985), provide many additional references.

tematic deviations from optimal behavior appear. Evidently farmers, corporate managers, and workers understand the effect of exchange rates on their welfare, their thinking is free of judgment biases, and their preferences are immune from framing or persuasion. No data on the preferences or behavior of individuals are offered, however; this chapter was intended only to provide a brief historical survey.[39]

This simple argument is insightful, but its validity and relative importance can be known only after thorough empirical research. To appreciate the potential loss from stopping here, consider a study that did collect individual-level data on managers' preferences and how they are formed. This work concentrated on preferences not for monetary but for trade policy, where analysts commonly use the same assumption that an industry's policy preferences can be deduced from what it makes. Firms facing import competition will favor protection and vice versa. Bauer, Pool, and Dexter surveyed a sample of U.S. businessmen (no respondents were women) in 1954 and 1962.[40] They did find a correlation between political behavior and objective self-interest (as rated by an expert panel) but also found that this simple hypothesis failed to account for significant data. Other factors independently changed who wrote to Congress on behalf of higher or lower tariffs. Among men with an interest in protection, those whose ideologies were internationalist were less likely to write than isolationists. (Ideology was not correlated with trade interest.) Respondents who had traveled abroad tended to formulate their views "with an eye to the self-interest of the United States rather than to the self-interest of a single product."[41] The prospect of gaining a new market apparently had less impact than the prospect of losing an existing share of a market.[42]

Case studies of pressure group activity also underscore the scope for the political process to frame policy preferences and tip the policy choice. The National Coal Association worked hard to reduce fuel oil imports in 1953 and 1955. "But it was by no means clear that the self-interest of the small oil companies and particularly of the railroads lay in combining with the coal industry in opposing oil imports."[43] The railroads did transport coal, "the backbone of their prosperity," and in that way stood to benefit from restrictions on competing fuel oil. Yet the railroads were also converting their own engines from coal to diesel, and thus stood to benefit in another way from oil imports and lower prices. The coal association was the first to approach the railroads, however, asking them to sign a statement favoring the quota bill. The railroads went on record as unified in support of the protectionist side.

The evidence at the individual level showed, however, that railroad executives did

[39] J. A. Frieden, "Economic Integration and the Politics of Monetary Policy in the United States," in R. O. Keohane and H. V. Milner, eds., *Internationalization and Domestic Politics* (Cambridge: Cambridge University Press, 1996).

[40] R. A. Bauer, I. De Sola Pool, and L. Anthony Dexter, *American Business and Public Policy* (New York: Atherton Press, 1972).

[41] Ibid., 225.

[42] Ibid., 139–40.

[43] Ibid., 373.

not have a deep commitment to this position. They had not engaged in full deliberation and classic optimization.

> In effect, they had done a favor for a customer. One wonders what would have happened if, before the National Coal Association took the initiative, an exporters' association had approached the same railroads to ask them to present testimony for expanded foreign trade. They might conceivably have testified on the opposite side and in doing so have been equally convinced that they were acting rationally for their self-interest. . . . It is our best guess that the railroads could equally easily have been organized on the opposing side.[44]

Without denying that objective interests make a difference, authors like these dispute the adequacy of this simple idea.

> The theory of self-interest as a complete and all-embracing explanation of behavior breaks down when we realize that self-interest is itself a set of mental images and convictions. Whose self-interest does a man see it as his role to serve—his own as a physical individual, that of the corporation for which he works, or that of some other unit? . . . Over what period of time is he seeking a maximum—the short or the long term? What values does he pursue—solely money, or also respect and other values? The role businessmen played, the communications that impinged on them, their ideology—all influenced their definitions and perceptions of their self-interest.[45]

Research built on a bounded-rationality foundation, then, can go further to illuminate empirically how the objective and the subjective are combined. In addition to "interests," this study found shared (rather than idiosyncratic) attitudes. These variable biases helped channel behavior, and they imply predictions of future behavior that could be disconfirmed, rather than offering just a post hoc interpretation of a single case. One prediction, for example, is that among managers facing import competition, those with an internationalist ideology and those who have traveled abroad will be less likely to seek protection from Congress than those with an isolationist ideology. This hybrid theory is more valid than one limited to the purely objective components or one limited to the purely subjective ones. The evidence reported by Bauer, Pool, and Dexter is also more compelling than broad-brush interpretations that discuss policy ideas but present no evidence about ideas from the individual level.

It would seem likely that business managers and workers are if anything less alert to the consequences of international monetary policy than to those of trade policy. One hypothesis would be that monetary policy's public good properties and long lags make it even more sensitive to framing.

---

[44] Ibid., 370, 374.
[45] Ibid., 226.

Departures by Political Science Rationalists

Other political science scholars have been making concessions and contributions in the direction of bounded rationality, though these moves often are incomplete and not conceptualized in these terms. To begin with the smallest departures, some influential IPE studies are based primarily on unbounded rationality but allow subjective beliefs to enter through the back door as a marginal qualification without much empirical attention. Gilpin seems based primarily on unbounded rationality.[46] To be sure, Gilpin complains repeatedly that liberal economics is insufficient for understanding a liberal world economy. He adds emphasis on the political structure underlying market transactions and on historical change in structures. Still, at the foundation Gilpin too approves and adopts liberal theory's stress on "the important role of self-interest and the seemingly universal desire to maximize gains as driving forces in the evolution of the world economy."[47] The author acknowledges that ideologies and religious passions also drive people from time to time. But these qualifications have clearly secondary status in the Gilpin hierarchy. They never seem to outweigh the universal generalization that a liberal world economy needs a hegemonic power. Gilpin remains doubtful that a liberal order can hold together very well without a liberal hegemon committed to defending that order, no matter how popular liberal ideas may be.[48]

In contrast, international-relations-game theorists have departed from unbounded rationality to a greater degree, at least in Simon's first sense, by applying models of incomplete information, signaling, and credibility to military-security affairs.[49] Most of these studies lack evidence about actors' beliefs, however; they support their arguments indirectly with proxy variables and inferences. Moreover, the results, like those in the economics mainstream, still depend on the heroic assumption that people optimize fixed preferences perfectly rather than using a more realistic mode of reasoned choice. And most important for present purposes, curiously there has been almost no effort to apply incomplete information models from economics to political-economic phenomena such as bargaining over exchange rates or trade.[50]

Such bargaining models presumably could improve over IPE optimization mod-

[46] R. Gilpin, *The Political Economy of International Relations* (Princeton: Princeton University Press, 1987).

[47] Ibid., 81.

[48] Ibid., 91, 365.

[49] E.g., J. D. Fearon, "Domestic Political Audiences and the Escalation of International Disputes," *American Political Science Review* 88 (1994): 577–92; J. D. Fearon, "Signaling versus the Balance of Power and Interests: An Empirical Test of a Crisis Bargaining Model," *Journal of Conflict Resolution* 38 (1994): 236–69; B. Bueno de Mesquita, J. D. Morrow, and E. R. Zorick, "Capabilities, Perception, and Escalation," *American Political Science Review* 91 (1997): 15–27, and works cited there.

[50] Exceptions are: K. Iida, "Analytic Uncertainty and International Cooperation: Theory and Application to International Economic Policy Coordination," *International Studies Quarterly* 37 (1993): 431–57; K. Iida, "International Cooperation in Exchange Rate Management: Coordination of U.S. and

els that assume complete information. But stopping with incomplete information as it is usually modeled would also have costs. Many negotiation experiments support the expectation that bounded-rationality-based research would improve on our understanding of international economic bargaining too. Experimenters often give two subjects sets of instructions establishing fictional interests and have them negotiate with each other. In repeated trials each player A has the same interests as every other player A and likewise for the B players. A key finding is that the negotiated outcomes typically scatter widely over the utility space, even though interests were identical in each pair.[51] Obviously something else is at work.

Bounded rationality reminds us of biases that are different from "private information." Several documented biases tend to influence or impede negotiated settlements. One bias is a systematically greater tendency on the part of those who have invested in a course of action to remain committed to that course after it has generated negative consequences (compared with those who have the same information but have not invested), out of reluctance to admit error or concern for reputation with some audience.[52] Another is partisan bias. The partisan also tends systematically to overestimate the value of her own alternative to agreement, compared with the average judgment of neutral subjects with the same information.[53] Think of trade negotiators for the European Union and the U.S. facing off over bananas. This overestimation can shrink or eliminate the zone of agreement, which can cause the negotiators to walk away from a deal that would benefit each (in a neutral's eyes). The partisan, absent any debiasing mechanisms, also tends to use a self-serving standard of fairness, believing it to be impartial, and then interprets aggressive behavior of the other as an effort to gain unfair advantage.[54] Neglecting insights such as these prevents us from accounting fully for outcomes in international financial, investment, environmental, and trade negotiations.

A departure explicitly in the direction of bounded rationality came in Keohane's *After Hegemony*.[55] This seminal book introduced the notion of transaction costs into the explanation of international economic institutions. Assuming first that states are classically rational egoists, Keohane's theory says that states create regimes because regimes will supply information that otherwise will not be available.[56] By reducing uncertainty and raising the costs of deception and irresponsibility, the regime makes it more likely that states will agree to cooperate further.

Japanese Intervention, 1977–1990," *International Interactions* 20 (1995): 279–96; K. Iida, "Involuntary Defection in 2–Level Games," *Public Choice* 89 (1996): 283–303.

[51] J. K. Sebenius, "Challenging Conventional Explanations of International Cooperation: Negotiation Analysis and the Case of Epistemic Communities," *International Organization* 46 (1995): 323–66.

[52] B. M. Staw, "Knee-Deep in the Big Muddy: A Study in Escalating Commitment to a Chosen Course of Action," *Organizational Behavior and Human Performance* 16 (1976): 58.

[53] D. Lax and J. Sebenius, *The Manager as Negotiator* (New York: Free Press, 1986).

[54] Babcock and Loewenstein, "Explaining Bargaining Impasse."

[55] R. O. Keohane, *After Hegemony: Cooperation and Discord in the World Political Economy* (Princeton: Princeton University Press, 1984).

[56] Ibid., chapters 5 and 6.

Here the actor still optimizes, only after adding transaction costs to the other costs already recognized. Of course, the assumed computation becomes even more formidable if the chooser must estimate transaction costs and compensate for imperfect information in addition to completing all the other steps.

Chapter 7 of *After Hegemony* goes further, relaxing the assumptions of optimization and egoistic utility as well. Keohane adds the theoretical argument that if actual rationality is bounded à la Simon, states will be even more likely to form regimes than if they are classically rational.[57] The book's subsequent empirical application does not make much explicit reference to limited rationality. It focuses on the hegemony theory of stability and shows that regime cooperation persists after hegemony, with regimes facilitating agreements. Apart from one reference to the OECD countries' "severely bounded rationality" during the first oil crisis, there are few references and little evidence on decision-making modes. Nevertheless, to my eye this interpretation of the International Energy Agency and the second oil crisis seems broadly consistent with some combination of trial and error, imitation, and satisficing, with the Agency helping by providing information. Although this book did not apply these propositions about international governance to the monetary sphere in detail, such an extension would be consistent with its principles.[58]

Ideas and IPE

A different body of literature has focused attention squarely on ideas and ideologies as shapers of policy behavior. This literature moves further toward the bounded-rationality approach, though usually without explicitly considering this theoretical micro-foundation. These studies acknowledge that states and firms act in response to their interests but make the simple point that peoples' ideas shape how they per-

---

[57] This argument seems debatable. It says that if actors do not use full optimization and substitute rules of thumb, the alternative to a regime will always seem less attractive; hence the likelihood of regime formation goes up. "The rules of thumb will not yield better, and will generally yield worse, results (apart from decision-making costs) than classically rational action." Rules of thumb may yield worse results in the sense of being less optimal for the chooser. But several suboptimal rules of thumb with different content are conceivable. What if the rule of thumb says "most international organizations will be dominated by our enemies and will intervene in our domestic affairs; stay out in most cases"? It would seem that bounds on rationality could bias substantive choice either against or in favor of regime formation.

[58] A subsequent school of thought has further explored the use of transaction costs to understand international institutions and national policies; see B. V. Yarbrough and R. M. Yarbrough, *Cooperation and Governance in International Trade* (Princeton: Princeton University Press, 1992); H. Spruyt, "Institutional Selection in International Relations: State Anarchy as Order," *International Organization* 48 (1994): 527–58; David Lake, *Entangling Relations* (Princeton: Princeton University Press, 1999). But this school is not always clear whether it assumes optimization or some other choice mode and almost never has studied the operation of bounded rationality in individual decision making empirically. A. Lupia, M. D. McCubbins, and S. L. Popkin, eds., *Elements of Reason: Cognition, Choice, and the Bounds of Rationality* (Cambridge: Cambridge University Press, 2000) develop a different set of departures.

ceive their interests. Interests and ideas cannot be separated, and the former alone are insufficient.[59]

Ideas and Foreign Policy, edited by Judith Goldstein and Robert Keohane, has been an influential exemplar. This volume discusses ideas ranging from the specific, such as shared expert beliefs in the 1940s about the need for a new organization of the international monetary system, to Stalinist ideas about how to organize a national economy, to grand ideas like state sovereignty and the belief that colonialism is illegitimate. The book identifies three types of relevant ideas and suggests three distinct causal pathways through which ideas can affect foreign policy, all of which are valuable advances.[60]

The ideas literature has improved IPE theory and understanding. Yet *Ideas and Foreign Policy* also notes the daunting methodological obstacles in the way of achieving rigorous results in this murky area and characterizes its effort as only exploratory. As one of the most ambitious and careful efforts yet attempted, it can also highlight important needs for further work. Although ideas are defined as beliefs held by individuals, no attempt is made to spell out any theory at the individual level to show how individuals make decisions using these or other ideas. The resulting theory therefore misses key micro-links that are essential for clarifying how the material and the subjective merge and change. If both matter, then some scholars need to confront how these factors combine and influence one another under different conditions.

Nor do essays of this type usually provide evidence showing that any individual held the ideas in question or that these ideas were primary in shaping that individual's behavior. These essays are empirical, but they give only pieces of evidence, and often different pieces come from different individuals and documents. This broad-brush method leaves the main claim vulnerable to skepticism from those who insist on more precise evidence. Scholars building theory understandably want to concentrate on shared rather than idiosyncratic beliefs. But the claim that a belief or meaning is shared also must be supported with evidence. Doing so rig-

---

[59] The tradition of studies emphasizing ideas in international monetary and economic relations includes: C. P. Kindleberger, "The Rise of Free Trade in Western Europe, 1820–1875," *Journal of Economic History* 35 (1975): 20–55; E. B. Haas, M. P. Williams, and D. Babai, *Scientists and World Order: The Uses of Technical Knowledge in International Organizations* (Berkeley: University of California Press, 1977); J. S. Odell, *U.S. International Monetary Policy: Markets, Power, and Ideas as Sources of Change* (Princeton: Princeton University Press, 1982); Adler, *The Power of Ideology;* P. A. Hall, "Conclusion: The Politics of Keynesian Ideas," in Peter A. Hall, ed., *The Political Power of Economic Ideas: Keynesianism Across Nations* (Princeton: Princeton University Press, 1989), 361–91; P. M. Haas, "Special Issue: Knowledge, Power, and International Policy Coordination," *International Organization* 46 (1992): 1–390; J. Goldstein, *Ideas, Interests, and American Trade Policy;* N. Woods, "Economic Ideas and International Relations: Beyond Rational Neglect," *International Studies Quarterly* 39 (1995): 161–80; K. R. McNamara, *The Currency of Ideas: Monetary Politics in the European Union* (Ithaca: Cornell University Press, 1998).

[60] J. Goldstein and R. O. Keohane, *Ideas and Foreign Policy: Beliefs, Institutions and Political Change* (Ithaca: Cornell University Press, 1993).

orously is even more demanding than showing that a single individual holds the belief.

Goldstein and Keohane also differentiate their arguments from others that apply cognitive psychology. "We are interested in the impact of particular beliefs, not on the relationship between beliefs and objective reality (however defined and determined)."[61] The former issue—the content and impact of beliefs—is certainly a legitimate, interesting research question.[62] The latter issue—misperception— had been a dominant concern when students of security turned to psychology. But misperception as such is only a first cut at what bounded rationality and cognitive psychology are about. Consider one additional line of research. If human rationality is limited by rules of thumb and other systematic biases, then those heuristics and biases are also ideas whose content might explain behavior in predictable ways.

Constructivist Perspectives on Ideas

Self-described constructivist scholarship since the 1980s has also added to our understanding of how international interactions can shape states' perceptions of their interests and even their identities and has improved our appreciation of the formation and impact of international norms. These studies have so far mostly concerned themselves with the political-security realm of world politics and not the monetary, but their principles do not seem to rule out such applications in the future.[63] The growing constructivist movement is important enough that it should be addressed here as well.

Many constructivist works have been framed as challenges to rationalism, but on reflection many of their key points may be entirely consistent with rationality of the bounded variety. This is so despite the fact that many of today's constructivists reject or avoid the individual unit of analysis.[64] Following George Herbert Mead, Erving Goffman, and socialization research, they assume that individuals in society adopt roles and behave as they do because they believe others expect them to behave that way, rather than because the individual has made decisions weighing the costs and benefits of all the alternatives. Institutions like families, schools, religious organizations, governments, and mass media accomplish socialization to these roles and shared beliefs. Social norms of appropriate behavior then guide action and

---

[61] Ibid., 7.

[62] The content of beliefs was also my emphasis when studying policy ideas in U.S. monetary policy. Odell, *U.S. International Monetary Policy*.

[63] Money is a prototypical social fact. V. A. Zelizer, *The Social Meaning of Money: Pin Money, Paychecks, Poor Relief, and Other Currencies* (Princeton: Princeton University Press, 1997), is suggestive. M. Marcussen, *Ideas and Elites: The Social Construction of Economic and Monetary Union* (Aalborg, Denmark: Aalborg University Press, 2000), provides a constructivist account of the origins of EMU. I discovered it too late to include it in my review of the literature.

[64] J. T. Checkel, "The Constructivist Turn in International Relations Theory," *World Politics* 50 (1998): 324–48, makes a related point.

even help constitute the individual's sense of "who I am." Some analysts contend that much human behavior does not result from conscious individual decisions or choices in any meaningful sense. The most powerful categories are collective.[65]

Constructivists working in international relations are divided further along epistemological lines.[66] Those who reject neo-positivism will not find this essay appealing, since it speaks in that voice.[67] It is probably impossible to merge inconsistent epistemologies into a single synthesis. I do have hope of convincing some constructivists on the near side of the epistemological crevasse, those who adhere to what I call neo- or pragmatic positivist standards of knowledge, including those who fear that methodological individualism is hostile to their arguments.[68]

Norms in International Relations: The Struggle Against Apartheid, by Audie Klotz, is one of the few constructivist applications to international relations that has focused on political economy at least in part, to my knowledge.[69] It also seems to be one of the stronger recent efforts. Klotz cites the case of financial and other sanctions against apartheid South Africa to support her arguments that international norms can play crucial roles in constituting identities and interests, and that sanctions can work by providing incentives to comply with international norms. Klotz's study can illustrate both accomplishments and opportunities for further work. While earlier claims by interpretivists had been abstract, Klotz takes up the challenge of making them into explanations and supporting them with evidence. Furthermore, the author compares multiple campaigns to delegitimize the Pretoria regime in other nations and diverse international organizations. She finds that activists' success varied with the decision-making process and dominant discourse in those settings. She claims that an international norm of racial equality came into existence around 1960, and that this norm later redefined U.S. interests (explaining U.S. economic sanctions imposed in 1986) and socialized the Republic of South Africa, reforming its domestic institutions accordingly. She complains that conventional neorealist and regime theories cannot explain this case, especially because their thinking is restricted to material costs and benefits and ignores the power of norms.

Initially this book rejects the individual level of analysis and thus appears to re-

---

[65] Actually sociologists of culture more recently have been shifting away from the "oversocialized view" of culture as a latent variable that individuals enact unproblematically and toward an idea of culture as fragmented across groups and as a "toolkit" of resources that can be put to strategic use. P. DiMaggio, "Culture and Cognition," *Annual Reviews: Sociology* 23 (1997): 263–87.

[66] Adler, "Seizing the Middle Ground"; J. G. Ruggie, "What Makes the World Hang Together? Neo-utilitarianism and the Social Constructivist Challenge," *International Organization* 52 (1998): 855–85.

[67] My appeal is based on neo-positivism, not positivism in the sense of positions prominent in the nineteenth and early twentieth centuries. Hardly any practicing IPE scholar today insists on the extreme injunctions of the Vienna school. Some epistemological critiques regularly confuse debate by failing to acknowledge this distinction.

[68] Indeed, those who build on sociological institutionalism recognize that this approach began with the insights of March and Simon.

[69] A. Klotz, *Norms in International Relations: The Struggle against Apartheid* (Ithaca: Cornell University Press, 1995).

ject all rational choice as a theoretical foundation. It does not express adherence to bounded rationality.

> Examining decision-making processes through individual motivation and cognition alone ignores the commonality of shared norms underlying dominant ideas or knowledge. While any individual holds a unique, subjective conception of "reality," through social interaction individual ideologies develop into shared, intersubjective, community conceptions of normality and deviance. . . . Norms . . . are crucial in defining and shaping reactions to the world they interpret. Consequently, these intersubjective understandings—the standards by which behavior is judged—are also essential in setting the boundaries of political struggle or cooperation.[70]

I believe this position is common among constructivist analysts. But the quoted complaint seems to miss the mark. In the first place, the theoretical assumption that the individual is the fundamental actor does not restrict examination to evidence from individual decision making alone. Evidence from organizations and other units can be added without violating this assumption, although doing so without providing theoretical microfoundations that link the levels will seem incomplete. Second, recognizing that individuals share beliefs or that some cultural elements have a lasting supra-individual character is also consistent with this premise and with research on decision making. Nothing prevents a study of individual decision making from investigating whether the individual shared the hypothesized normative belief, or whether the supra-individual script or ideology shaped this individual's behavior. Although published studies in international relations and economics may not have combined elements in this way, this is not because methodological individualism inherently rules out such combinations.

Careful inquiries might of course reveal the contrary too—the deviant individual who made a significant political difference. This book's allergy to individual decision making proves to be a particular handicap when it comes to British policy. Klotz reports, although she downplays the observation, that Prime Minister Thatcher's personal beliefs and positions, at odds with those of British business leaders and even her Foreign Minister, were essential to Britain's resistance to the international norm in the 1980s.[71]

The British example raises a third general question. What proportion of the individuals in a society actually shares a norm at any given time? How many adhere to rival norms that might encourage behavior contrary to the first norm? These questions become especially important when attempting to observe an alleged change in the norms adhered to, as this book does. It seems to assume that norms and changes therein can be identified without observing individuals' beliefs or actions, or by some unspecified process of sampling individuals' statements or actions. Its claims are supported by evidence from social discourse such as arguments made by un-

[70] Ibid., 33–34. This section, like others, is not meant to be a comprehensive review of this book.
[71] Ibid., chap. 7.

named individuals on behalf of UN resolutions condemning South Africa. This type of evidence is worthwhile and seems convincing as far as it goes. But such indicators are not the most precise and convincing possible evidence for norms' operation and normative change.

The main arguments of constructivists like Klotz, if they are valid, must operate at the individual level. How else could actions by anti-apartheid activists have delegitimized the white Pretoria regime and bolstered the legitimacy of the ANC, unless many individuals in the world changed their minds or adopted the corresponding beliefs, including individuals who control organizations such as legislatures and the media? By definition the legitimacy of an object is a belief or understanding held in common by individuals. (The object in another study of legitimization could be globalization or IMF intervention in policymaking.) Yet this book does not present any survey or sustained case study, for instance, showing that any person changed behavior—or how any person changed behavior—because of arguments citing this norm. Naturally no single book does everything that could be done. But one of the more advanced offerings in the genre reveals opportunities for future scholarship that might generate even more convincing results.

As long as constructivists shy away from the individual, they will be missing a critical link.[72] On this age-old issue, constructivist pioneer John Ruggie responds as follows:

> It is, of course, true, physiologically speaking, that only individuals can have ideas or beliefs. But the reverse proposition, that all beliefs are individual beliefs or are reducible to individual beliefs, does not follow. Social constructivism . . . [also deals with social facts that] rest on what Searle calls 'collective intentionality.' . . . [I]ntentionality remains in individual heads. But within those individual heads it exists in the form of "we intend" and "I intend only as part of our intending."[73]

This type of we-belief is an interesting addition that indeed has been overlooked by many mainstream IR studies. We are indebted to constructivists for calling attention to it. But in his effort to go further, to show that neo-utilitarian thinking is philosophically incapable of dealing with it, I believe Ruggie too ends up conceding the field. Granted, these beliefs cannot be reduced to individual beliefs in the sense of beliefs that ignore all we-feeling. But Ruggie acknowledges that we-beliefs themselves remain in individual heads. The collectively shared belief *can* be faithfully re-

---

[72] A possible counter-argument might be that bureaucratic routines could account for state behavior, and that a state can be said to have adopted a norm if a bureaucracy changes its decision rules accordingly, whether or not individuals in the state agree with the norms. Investigating organizational behavior is surely worthwhile too, but I doubt it will be sufficient to displace individual-level theory and evidence. Agencies do not change routines unless individuals inside or above the agencies decide to do so. Case studies show that such decisions are often reached through debate among individuals within the organization. And top leaders in international relations commonly face uncertain situations that are not covered exactly by existing routines.

[73] Ruggie, "What Makes the World Hang Together?" 869–70, citing J. Searle, *The Construction of Social Reality* (New York: Free Press, 1995).

duced to—in the sense of represented by—its counterpart in the individual head without abandoning the intersubjective source of the meaning. Scholarship has not done this very much. But there is no inherent reason why shared beliefs or intentions could not be conceived theoretically and studied empirically as properties of individuals as well as of groups, within a neo-positivist epistemology.[74]

A Meeting of Minds?

I believe the accumulated evidence is now sufficient to show that knowledge of the world political economy, including its monetary and financial systems, would advance if the interested factions within each scholarly community paid more direct attention over the next decade to Simon's innovation and its implications. The bounded rationality premise could be the foundation for generating a new, more unified and more valid body of IPE knowledge bridging gaps between today's classic rationalists, idea analysts, and constructivists. Consider four concrete research innovations that could move us in that direction.

First, at a minimum all studies—whether using bounded rationality or not—could make explicit which individual decision process is assumed to be operating and check the analysis for consistency with this premise. Those who favor some variant of rational choice could make explicit which elements they accept and which they reject. Do individuals optimize (face zero deliberation costs), or satisfice, or follow some other alternative procedure? Do they have full information and common knowledge or are they subject to biases? We should avoid confusing deliberation problems with information problems. Are preferences fixed or subject to manipulation? Those who favor a variant of constructivism could at least make explicit which assumption their theory makes about individual decision making. They could heed sociological institutionalist Paul DiMaggio when he urges that, "before the study of lived culture can become a cumulative enterprise, scholars must clarify the cognitive presuppositions behind their theories of what culture does and what people do with it, and the fundamental concepts and units of analysis."[75] Those dissatisfied with today's packages labeled "rational choice" and "constructivism" could consider whether they must reject the entire package or only

---

[74] Actually the latter pages of *Norms in International Relations*, and most clearly the last few, indicate that its arguments, at least some of them, are consistent with rational choice after all. Chapters on U.S., British, and Zimbabwean policy toward South Africa add social values like reputation to the utility function, in effect. Klotz argues that when these governments imposed sanctions on South Africa, they acted rationally to promote their objectives, defined more broadly than material self-interest. Sanctions work by raising the reputation costs of status quo policies in the target country. On page 166, Klotz refers in passing to "the overstated dichotomy between interpretation and rationality." On page 169 Klotz declares, "Rationalist perspectives help us understand that Pan-Africanists calculated the costs and benefits of advocating racial equality" when they opposed apartheid. Clarifying these fundamental decision-making assumptions at the outset might create a stronger interpretation throughout.

[75] DiMaggio, "Culture and Cognition," 263.

particular elements. Making these premises explicit may be valuable to our collective enterprise even in studies located at the global level of analysis and even when no evidence of individuals' beliefs is reported. It is difficult, in fact, to think of any convincing argument for ignoring the assumptions we are making.

Second, some formal modelers could try to develop models of decision processes other than optimization and explore their implications with simulations and empirical research. Such models are available from the Simon tradition, the minority in economics, and the artificial-intelligence tradition.[76] For instance, work by Simon, Bendor, and others on administrative decision making might be adapted to explain central banks. Competition is still much weaker here than on the optimization side of the field.

Third, constructivists could deepen their theory by basing any concept of a collective idea explicitly on the individual-level bounded-rationality foundation. They could begin with Ruggie's acknowledgment that all ideas reside in individual minds, so that the spread of new ideas must also take place there. Without abandoning their commitment to supra-individual cultural elements, they could accept that the most rigorous empirical support means providing evidence at the individual, in addition to the collective, level. They could better show how different societies and organizations teach different intersubjective understandings to individuals and provide domain-specific boundaries to their rationality.

Constructivists could also better explain changes in norms and identities, with clearer theories and better evidence. Bounded rationality and cognitive psychology offer concepts such as emulation of the successful and herding that might help show how new shared understandings spread in popularity at the expense of older ones.[77] Finnemore and Sikkink argue that "instrumental rationality and strategic action play a significant role in highly politicized social construction of norms, preferences, identities, and common knowledge by norm entrepreneurs in world politics." Put differently, social construction is partly strategic. They conclude that "recent theoretical work in rational choice and empirical work on norm entrepreneurs make it abundantly clear that this fault line [between constructivist and rationalist arguments] is untenable both empirically and theoretically."[78]

Fourth, scholars working in diverse theoretical schools could invest in empiri-

[76] V. Hudson, ed., *Artificial Intelligence and International Politics* (Boulder, Colo.: Westview Press, 1991); Bendor, "A Model of Muddling Through"; H. R. Alker, *Rediscoveries and Reformulations* (Cambridge: Cambridge University Press, 1996); P. S. Albin, *Barriers and Bounds to Rationality* (Princeton: Princeton University Press, 1998); G. Duffy, B. K. Frederking, and S. A. Tucker, "Language Games: Dialogical Analysis of INF Negotiations," *International Studies Quarterly* 42 (1998): 271–94.

[77] DiMaggio, "Culture and Cognition" summarizes alternative cognitively based models of how specific mental structures aggregate to more general and shared constructs like ideologies, models of how cultures change, and models of how schemata are transposed from one content domain to another.

[78] M. Finnemore and K. Sikkink, "International Norm Dynamics and Political Change," *International Organization* 52 (1998): 909–11. For another perspective on norm transmission see F. Schimmelfennig, "International Socialization in the New Europe: Rational Action in an Institutionalized Environment," *European Journal of International Relations* 6, no. 1 (2000): 109–39.

cal research on monetary and economic decision making, to improve theories about it as well as to address particular policy problems. Those interested primarily in supra-individual meanings or committed to broad-brush empirical methods could at least add brief case studies that document the alleged causal links operating in the decisions of one or more individuals. A broad-brush interpretation of the financial crises of 1997 and 1998 could add a case study of one Asian monetary-policymaker. A study that added such a brief individual study confirming claims stated at the collective level would be more convincing than the study without it.

To go beyond the minimum, empirical research could delve more thoroughly into selected cases of economic policymaking, sometimes by applying hypotheses established in the psychological laboratory along with materialist hypotheses, to economic decisions in the field. The literature on security policy provides many suggestive analogues. A familiar finding from cognitive psychology is that strong predispositions make individuals more sensitive to incoming information that supports their priors than to discordant information and that we tend to interpret the latter so as to preserve our prior commitments. Holsti documented that this generalization applied to U.S. Secretary of State John F. Dulles. Dulles brought with him a strong negative predisposition toward the Soviet Union, and it deeply colored how he processed new information while in office. Dulles tended to interpret an increase in friendly Soviet behavior in a way that would not require a shift in his policy stand by attributing such moves to momentary Soviet weakness rather than as feelers worth investigating. Departures from classic optimization were systematic, not random. Does anyone doubt that financial policymakers have similarly general predispositions, such as opposing government intervention in markets, or that these biases have varied over history and across countries? Is there any good reason to doubt that these biases channel information processing and hence decisions on economic and monetary policies too, in ways that are missed by unbounded rationality?[79]

Fresh empirical research need not be limited to single case studies. One alternative is the method of difference or comparative case study. One illustrative investigation finds that Mexico gained less in one than in a second trade negotiation, even though several significant features remained constant. This difference in outcomes is explained by less-effective Mexican efforts in the first case to counter their own judgment biases. Using still other methods, students of the possible deterritorialization of money could conduct surveys in countries like Argentina to learn how corporate treasurers and households decide which currencies to hold.

[79] O. R. Holsti, "Cognitive Dynamics and Images of the Enemy: Dulles and Russia," in D. J. Finlay, O. R. Holsti, and R. R. Fagen, eds., *Enemies in Politics* (Chicago: Rand McNally, 1967). J. G. Stein and L. W. Pauly, eds., *Choosing to Cooperate: How States Avoid Loss* (Baltimore: Johns Hopkins University Press, 1992) explore how framing affects more recent decisions including trade affairs. Their case studies find evidence of orthodox utility maximization as well as relative gains maximization and loss avoidance.

Payoffs

Greater collective investment in bounded-rationality research would make sense only if doing so would generate significant gains. I believe three types of payoff—theoretical, empirical, and practical—would be realized over several years. First, looking at a problem through a less-conventional lens can be a fruitful way to generate fresh theoretical insights. In addition, if most studies made their decision-making assumptions explicit, we would see more readily the reasons for inconsistent findings. We would recognize more easily which studies are accumulating into clusters of consistent knowledge and see the true fault lines more clearly. Moreover, today's theoretical fragmentation would be reduced. We might dispense with one wasteful battle of "isms." I believe choosing between rationalism and constructivism is neither necessary nor advisable. Eventually the two, each modified and re-developed upon this common foundation, might even be replaced by a single theoretical family. Along the way, former rationalist theories would be broadened, and former constructivist theories would be deepened theoretically and better equipped to explain change.

A second payoff would come in greater empirical validity of the new theory. Successors to classical rationalists would shrink the elephant, accounting better for important behavior that plainly does not fit material optimization and preferences that shift, without abandoning rational choice altogether. Successor constructivists would support sharper accounts of organizational and norm influence and change by adding compelling evidence at the individual level, without displacing other kinds of evidence, which would persuade a wider audience.

Individual-level research and case studies sometimes evoke fears that the product will be limited to post hoc interpretations of selected cases and will not lead to theory or predictions. Although each of these concerns may be true of some case studies, neither is inherent in the method or in bounded rationality theory. Case studies are fruitful ways to generate new hypotheses.[80] The evidence in the Dulles study was not limited to a single decision. Bounded rationality studies can investigate more than one case and make theoretical contributions, including predictions that could in principle be disconfirmed.

A third problem with the status quo is that the practical world pays little attention to political-science IPE scholarship. In their 1998 survey, Katzenstein, Keohane and Krasner regretfully noted the shortage of IPE findings that had been applied directly to policy.[81] One reason for this shortfall, among many, may be that so little IPE research has tackled the process of decision making directly, even though practitioners are up to their necks in decision making. Documenting—partly at the individual level—how past monetary and economic-policy decisions went awry

---

[80] Think of C. P. Kindleberger's influential *The World in Depression, 1929–1939* (Berkeley: University of California Press, 1973).

[81] Katzenstein, Keohane, and Krasner, "*International Organization* and the Study of World Politics," 684.

would bring findings down from the global level to the level at which lessons will be applied if at all.

Information about two types of heuristics and biases would be useful to practitioners: biases at home that need offsetting and biases abroad that could constitute either opportunities or obstacles to strategies based on the assumption of unbounded rationality. It is difficult to know what moves will be effective—say toward achieving liberal financial reforms or adding labor rights to the WTO—without knowledge of the biases that operate and persuasive tactics that work in the countries concerned. Insensitivity toward actual public attitudes may explain why elites were surprised by the social backlash against globalization. Or suppose we had a body of solid evidence on how investors, governments, and the IMF actually make decisions during financial crises.[82] There have been far more calls for better information than for better processing of available information, which is not surprising, considering the priors of the economics majority. Evidence on the concrete biases and shortcuts with which players interpret information during crises could lead, for instance, to changes in our own organizations that would bring offsetting information and biases into the process. This might be at least as useful to private-sector players as to public officials.

The most fundamental practical implication is that if rationality is indeed unbounded, the only thing that can be done to improve the world is to restructure incentives in light of fixed preferences. The implied set of possibilities is not trivial. But if rationality is limited, of course there is much greater scope for influencing people's values as well as their behavior, whether by education, advertising, political persuasion, mass media, cross-cultural exchange, negotiation, the use of symbols, or creative leadership. The future legitimacy of the globalizing world economy will surely depend on such subjective contestation as well as on objective incentives, for better or worse.

But gains are only half the story. What of the costs of a major bounded-rationality research effort? Surely they would be substantial, and alternative research investments can be conceived, in an ideal world. The actual world, though, is constrained and biased in many ways. Computing the optimal distribution of research effort for the next decade is well beyond my own limited rationality. Let's follow an educated hunch and give it a try.

[82] The chapter in this volume by Willett is relevant here.

CHAPTER TEN

Webs of Governance and the Privatization of Transnational Regulation

Philip G. Cerny

As noted in the first chapter of this book, the study of international political economy is usually seen as a dialectic between economic logic and political necessity. Economic logic, "the logic of the market system"—as Robert Gilpin writes in his chapter—"is to expand geographically and to incorporate more and more aspects of a society within the price mechanism, thus making domestic matters subject to forces external to the society." The alternative to market logic is the logic of authority or "the authoritative allocation of values," which is at the core of the political system.[1] That logic has generally been translated, whether in domestic political science or international relations, into a logic of the state. This chapter argues, in contrast, that although the state has been the dominant political institution of the modern era, there are (and always have been) *other* political logics than that of the state, whether below, above, or cutting across states.

Today, in the context of globalization and increasing international interdependence, political necessity as well as economic logic have led not merely to the establishment of inter-state regimes, but, perhaps more significantly, to the emergence and expansion of decision-making processes both formal and informal, private and mixed public-private, that cut across, constrain, and jostle with states. Hybrid systems and practices of self-regulation, market authority, and private interest governance are emerging. In this context, a central focus of concern must be on how different kinds of economic activities or sectors and related political (authoritative) processes at various levels generate new, often horizontally organized, governance structures or webs of governance across borders. Finance plays a special role in this process, both as a sector in its own right and as a crossroads structure where the relationships among other sectors are worked out, because money is the universal commodity, fungible and easily measured through the price mechanism. These de-

---

[1] D. Easton, *The Political System* (New York: Knopf, 1953).

velopments are crucial to an understanding of how the world's money and the world economy more generally will be organized in the twenty-first century.

Markets and Politics

The relationship between politics and market has bedeviled political economy since it was first systematically studied in the eighteenth century. Today, when we look for modes of authority or "governance" in the contemporary international political economy, most political scientists and international relations specialists look either to states or to wider public processes and institutions involving the interaction of states as such or resembling states refashioned at, for example, a regional or global level. In contrast, classical and neoclassical economic theory emphasize the primacy of markets as the most important mode of social organization and, indeed, as the very antithesis of the kind of hierarchical, authoritative order characteristic of states in their traditional international form. In focusing on this interaction of markets and politics at an international level, International Political Economy has become an increasingly broad church, engendering a range of innovative approaches and examining how the state is being cut across by multilayered networks of influence, interests and decision-making and enmeshed in more and more complex and hybrid webs of governance.

In theory, economic markets are auction-like processes where buyers and sellers freely interact to haggle over prices, get rid of what they have, and get what they want. It should be pointed out that the market itself does not actually produce anything, in much the same way that liberal critics allege that the state does not really produce anything. The market merely *redistributes* goods, assets, services, et cetera, among different users and uses. The core issues are whether, in this process, economic markets can be self-sustaining and self-regulating or whether they are inherently unstable and failure-prone, and whether politics is something that makes markets work or that distorts them and makes them malfunction. On the one hand, the market mechanism was reified by Adam Smith into a basic tendency of human nature "to truck and to barter" and as constituting a potential "invisible hand" guiding society toward continual improvement. On the other hand, Karl Polanyi argued that economic markets as such are potentially counterproductive for society unless they are authoritatively rooted in *non*-economic social and political institutions and practices. In the absence of such foundations, they are potentially anarchical and dysfunctional—giving some groups lopsided power and wealth while condemning others to rootlessness, powerlessness, and poverty; creating conflict, instability, and social breakdown; and ultimately succumbing to the centrifugal forces of myopic self-interest and autistic antisocial behavior which they have themselves engendered, leading to self-destruction rather than self-regulation.

Economic liberals see the market as the great self-regulator. The key lies in the presence of effective competition. Should property or resources be put to inefficient uses, especially where monopolistic or cartel-like behavior is involved, then competitors will arise (especially new entrants) who will offer new or substitute products and services at a lower price and/or of better quality. Market participants (buyers and sellers) can choose from a wide variety of competing market signals using a much wider range of information than is available through other mechanisms, whether economic mechanisms like planning, social mechanisms like elite cultural hegemony, or political mechanisms like government policymaking. These market signals permit participants to make more informed and rational decisions, cumulatively leading to a more economically and socially efficient allocation of resources. The ultimate arbiters of this process will not be the wealthy owners of capital or other socio-political categories but individual consumers, who will always try to look for the best product at the lowest price.

For critics like Polanyi and John Maynard Keynes—who argue in different ways that the market, while unstable and non-self-regulating, is nevertheless also highly creative—the central political challenge of capitalism is to counteract market failure and to promote the market's creative potential through judicious regulation, steering, and redistribution. While state intervention can and does distort markets and cause market failure, the state at the same time constitutes the crucial *a priori* or *ex ante* institutional mechanism that enables markets to perform their wealth-creation and resource-allocation functions at all. For most modern capitalist political economy, indeed, the state is the only authoritative institution that can undertake these tasks with any coherence and effectiveness. But today, globalization is widely seen not only to challenge that coherence and effectiveness but also to engender alternative and hybrid processes and mechanisms—webs of governance—that are already undertaking some of these tasks in different ways.

Markets and Governance in an Age of Globalization

The traditional role of the state creates a special problem for international markets, which are neither controlled nor really controllable by states at the international level. States acting in an anarchic, self-help-driven international system simply do not have the collective hierarchical capacity to stabilize, regulate, and promote markets in the same way that individual states can at a domestic level, although they can sometimes generate international regimes that go part of the way.[2] The nineteenth-century Gold Standard was the archetype of a system in which supposedly self-regulating international financial markets, revolving around the currency needs of bankers, generated international instability and created conditions for deep and growing international *political* conflict, leading to the outbreak of the First World

---

[2] S. D. Krasner, ed., *International Regimes* (Ithaca: Cornell University Press, 1982); R. O. Keohane, *After Hegemony: Co-operation and Discord in the World Political Economy* (Princeton: Princeton University Press, 1984).

War and thence to Fascism and the Second World War.[3] Only with the emergence of liberal and social-democratic industrial welfare states—a process which accelerated in the 1930s in response to the Great Depression and that would later be embedded in the postwar settlement in the advanced industrial countries—could market, society, and politics be reconciled over the medium and long term. The result was what John Gerard Ruggie (1982) called the "embedded liberal compromise," wherein freer trade was promoted while at the same time the industrial welfare state was protected by key elements of the Bretton Woods system, including capital controls.[4]

Today, however, embedded liberalism is being undermined by the widening and deepening of transnational market mechanisms and processes taking place within a multilayered global order.[5] This process entails the development of complex governance structures with an increasingly private or mixed private-public character, rather than being organized primarily through the state or the states system. Such structures involve dimensions of all three standard "modes of coordination" or "control mechanisms" identified in organizational and economic sociology—that is, markets, hierarchies, and networks.[6] State apparatuses, in turn, are increasingly integrated into this wider structure and are less autonomous than before in relative terms vis-à-vis finance and other highly marketized and globalized economic sectors. Their primary role, therefore, shifts from one of socio-economic steering and redistribution, as it had become in the Industrial Welfare State, to one of pro-market regulation and socio-legal enforcement, especially enforcement of more internationally open market norms, practices, and outcomes—albeit with some discretion to shape marginally different roads to globalization.[7]

These emerging webs of governance are transforming our notions of political process and political space, leading to a dialectic of economic and political convergence and divergence reminiscent of certain structural characteristics of the

[3] K. Polanyi, *The Great Transformation: The Political and Economic Origins of Our Time* (New York: Rinehart, 1944).

[4] J. G. Ruggie, "Continuity and Transformation in the World Polity: Toward a Neorealist Synthesis," in R. O. Keohane, ed., *Neorealism and Its Critics* (New York: Columbia University Press, 1986), 131–57. Also, E. N. Helleiner, "When Finance Was the Servant: International Capital Movements in the Bretton Woods Order," in P. G. Cerny, ed., *Finance and World Politics: Markets, Regimes, and States in the Post-hegemonic Era* (Brookfield, Vt.: Edward Elgar, 1993), 20–48; B. J. Cohen, "Phoenix Risen: The Resurrection of Global Finance," *World Politics* 48, no. 2 (January 1996): 268–96.

[5] S. Strange, *The Retreat of the State: The Diffusion of Power in the World Economy* (Cambridge: Cambridge University Press, 1996.)

[6] G. Thompson, J. Frances, R. Levačić, and J. Mitchell, eds., *Markets, Hierarchies and Networks: The Coordination of Social Life* (Thousand Oaks, Ill.: Sage, 1991).

[7] W. Streeck, "Public Power Beyond the Nation-State: The Case of the European Community," in R. Boyer and D. Drache, eds., *States against Markets: The Limits of Globalization* (New York: Routledge, 1996), 299–315; P. G. Cerny, "Restructuring the Political Arena: Globalization and the Paradoxes of the Competition State," in R. D. Germain, ed., *Globalization and Its Critics: Perspectives from Political Economy* (London: Macmillan, 2000), 117–38.

Middle Ages but wholly new in scale, scope, and complexity, and populated by a new diversity of economic, political, and social agents. Because of the more complex, multilayered, and cross-cutting character of the political opportunity structures created through globalization, governance processes involve to a far greater extent than before the crystallization of self-organizing structures, especially transnational networks, cutting through the organizational boundaries of states and of international institutions.[8] Thus both decision-making processes and decisional outcomes involve a complex intertwining of multiple layers of market, hierarchy, and network, both public and private, within and across borders.

The main mechanism generating and shaping these webs is the transnational integration of markets across local, national, regional, and international space. In other words, underlying this process is the expansion and widening scale of market interactions beyond the boundaries of separate national economies. This global market integration takes different forms corresponding to the varying characteristics of different economic *sectors* and to the changing patterns of interaction among and cutting across those sectors.[9] Therefore markets are becoming ever more entrenched *not just as narrowly economic mechanisms* but as quasi-political governance structures in their own right deriving from the crucial systemic functions markets perform and the range of actors and transactions they encompass.

Markets are governance structures in three overlapping but analytically distinct senses. In the first place, markets are, in their most abstract economic form, a form of order beyond the authoritative world of politics but order nonetheless (the "invisible hand"). Second, they are part and parcel of the very constitution of both the modern capitalist nation-state and the modern world order, inextricably intertwined with our understanding of how states have evolved historically and what they (and state actors) "do" today. Finally, they are—in terms of, for example, organizational theory, new institutional economics, and political sociology—not merely spontaneous forms of behavior but actual institutions, historically path-dependent and embedded in social structures.

Thus at the first level, the ideal-type market is conceived by its most ideologically enthusiastic proponents as a natural phenomenon, analogous to a recasting of traditional theories of natural law. Von Hayek called it a "spontaneous order," that is, one which exists beyond man-made attempts at "organized" order—although its rules have only gradually been discovered, and only in the last couple of centuries have people and societies sought to engineer their "made orders" (i.e., socio-political orders) to fit with the eternal rules of the market—that is, tailoring society and

---

[8] R. A. W. Rhodes, "The New Governance: Governing Without Governance," *Political Studies* 44, no. 2 (September 1996): 652–57.

[9] J. Frieden, "Invested Interests: The Politics of National Economic Policies in a World of Global Finance," *International Organization* 45, no. 4 (1991): 425–52; H. Kitschelt, "Industrial Governance Structures, Innovation Strategies, and the Case of Japan: Sectoral or Cross-National Comparative Analysis?" *International Organization* 45, no. 4 (1991): 453–93; P. G. Cerny, "Globalization and the Changing Logic of Collective Action," *International Organization* 49, no. 4 (1995): 595–625.

politics consciously with the aim of creating a "grown [market] order."[10] Markets from this perspective are thus the closest human society gets to some sort of natural order, being also normatively and empirically superior to other forms (at least other worldly ones). Indeed, "market failure" results from attempts by people to impose other forms of socio-political organization on human nature, thereby distorting the naturally beneficial outcomes dictated by market forces.

At a second level, rather than merely being discovered and applied for its eternal properties, markets are socially and/or authoritatively chosen and constructed by real historical actors and social forces as a means to *other* normative ends, ends which are pursued through political society. In this case, markets are seen as having positive knock-on effects or externalities that make their construction desirable within such a wider normative context. Certain kinds of economic freedom, for example, are thought by liberals and neoliberals to lead to wider social and political freedoms, for example in terms of the spread of private property to wider groups (the notion of a "property-owning democracy") or the democratization of information through transparent market signals—both of which are often seen as leading to a greater expansion of opportunity for ordinary people—in addition to any greater economic efficiency that might (or might not) result. Furthermore, although avoiding market failure may require state intervention, the aim of such intervention is usually not only to prop up the market by counteracting failures but also actively to promote any beneficial consequences markets may have in terms of economic growth and wealth creation. The aim is not to replace it to promote other political and social aims, such as social justice, the alleviation of poverty, full employment, and so on. This conception of the positive normative value of markets formed the core of Keynesian macroeconomics and indicative planning in the mid-twentieth century as well as more conservative approaches. In other words, the preferred role of the state may be to make markets work better and thus to protect them from whatever tendencies they may possess toward instability, crisis, or negative social and political consequences. Indeed both liberal and Marxist theories of the state agree that the predominant role of politics in the modern capitalist world is to promote markets, for better or worse.

This second conceptual level, however, is often tempered implicitly or explicitly by a third—that of markets as simply one form of organizational or institutional structure among others. Market failure derives, in this view, not from the distortion of the market by the application of other organizational principles and forms but by the *mis*application of market structures and principles to inappropriate activities and institutions. Indeed, in neo-institutionalist social science generally, the main debate is centered squarely on evaluating the correct mix of organizational forms necessary to minimize inequity and instability while maximizing the allocative and

---

[10] F. von Hayek, "Spontaneous ('Grown') Order and Organized ('Made') Order," in N. Modlovsky, ed., *Order—With or Without Design?* (London: Centre for Research into Communist Economies, 1989), 101–23, abridged and reprinted in Thompson et al., *Markets, Hierarchies and Networks*, 293–301.

normative benefits of markets. In neoclassical economics, the "new institutionalist" strain associated with Coase and Williamson—transaction-cost economics— stresses the efficiency gains associated with hierarchical (rather than market) firm structure in cases where high levels of asset specificity exist.[11] And in the "new institutional history," the "new institutional sociology," and "neo-institutionalist" or "neo-structuralist" approaches to political science, the emphasis is on the evolution of linkages between economic structures and underlying social structures.[12]

Indeed, many institutionalist social scientists today start from the premise that although the state is not necessarily a superior form of organization per se, states are so deeply entrenched historically, with their national borders, bureaucracies, and belief systems, that markets are still "locked in" to a state-bound international order. This generalized embeddedness has three dimensions. In the first place, the modern nation-state possesses legitimate authority and therefore operates as a hierarchical structure in key situations, such as the enforcement of law and order, property rights, and contracts, or the exercise of Weber's "monopoly of legitimate violence" at home and abroad, thereby internalizing a range of key decision-making procedures. Secondly, the nation-state has a unique cultural underpinning, deriving from a mixture of national distinctiveness (real and/or invented) and ideological hegemony, that subsumes, co-opts, and assimilates groups with otherwise conflicting goals, thereby creating *trust*. Finally, modern states operate at least to some extent in pluralistic fashion to increase the availability of political information and decentralize some decisions in a political marketplace (however limited it may be, as in Schumpeter's famous critique of democracy as a system in which elites merely compete for votes), thereby enabling different groups to have a voice.[13]

Often, however, "embeddedness" is used in a sociologically narrower sense, meaning that for some theorists it must be based upon pre-existing (and organizationally distinct) social networks. These networks are organized according to specifically sociological, political, and/or historical—*rather than* economic—principles, usually deriving from direct or indirect social bonds such as kinship, patriarchy, friendship, habit, geographical contiguity, or bureaucratic, occupational, or professional networks.[14] Furthermore, in other organizational sociology literature, different modes of market regulation or control mechanisms combine and interact, with distinct dimensions forming complex patterns. For example, with regard to firms:

---

[11] R. Coase, "The Nature of the Firm," *Economica* 4 (1937): 386–405; O. E. Williamson, *Markets and Hierarchies: Analysis and Antitrust Implications* (New York: Free Press, 1975); O. E. Williamson, *The Economic Institutions of Capitalism* (New York: Free Press, 1985).

[12] P. A. Hall and R. C. M. Taylor, "Political Science and the Three New Institutionalisms," *Political Studies* 44, no. 4 (1996): 936–57.

[13] J. A. Schumpeter, *Capitalism, Socialism, and Democracy* (London: Unwin, 1943).

[14] See, for example, M. Granovetter, "Economic Action and Social Structure: The Problem of Embeddedness," *American Journal of Sociology* 91, no. 4 (1985): 481–510; M. Granovetter, "Economic Institutions as Social Constructions: A Framework for Analysis," *Acta Sociologica* 35 (1992): 3–11.

The combinations of control mechanisms discussed in this chapter have been characterized as overlapping, embedded, intertwined, juxtaposed, and nested. . . . Much of the complexity results because only occasionally are control mechanisms created on "greenfield" sites. Typically, control mechanisms are grafted on to and leveraged off existing social structures. . . . The most sophisticated mixture of control mechanisms can be seen in the plural form. Here, two distinct control mechanisms are operated simultaneously by the same company. To understand the plural form, . . . the dynamics of whole structures must be examined since the transactional context affects the control that can be brought to bear on individual transactions. . . . matrix structures are a close cousin . . . ; they differ because in matrix structures the mechanisms intersect while in plural forms the mechanisms run in parallel.[15]

What is true of "the dynamics of whole [firm and inter-firm] structures" is even more true of societies and political systems; after all, the state itself is not exclusively a "hierarchical" structure, but rather a "plural" or "matrix" structure characterized by overlapping clusters of differently structured games or transactions.

Therefore the key to understanding the role of markets as structures of governance lies in how differently structured industrial or market sectors—or, indeed, different kinds of activities within firms—develop distinct modes of internal organization, as well as how they interact with each other and with wider social and political structures. In relatively market-oriented (non-specific-asset-based) sectors, that is sectors where assets are more substitutable for each other and consequently where market signals are relatively clear and market prices relatively easy to determine (especially in the presence of the large-numbers condition), market structure may be more diffuse but is no less powerful than in other sectors.[16] Therefore governance structures in these sectors tend to be less formal and more difficult to control through traditional international relations, for example, through intergovernmental regimes, interstate cooperation, or the hegemonic practices of stronger states. Indeed, market-generated transnational norms become self-enforcing on states and are absorbed into state practices through state apparatuses themselves, eager to capture the benefits of the market for their own political or bureaucratic objectives.

The most market-based sector is usually said to be finance. Its impact on both economy and government operates not so much through direct threats of the withdrawal of capital but rather through the decline or slower growth (manifest or threatened) of business investment and/or its redirection to other uses and users, especially in other countries, at the very time when vast swathes of industry are restructuring. The knock-on effects of change in the financial sector are potentially huge, primarily because other sectors are increasingly being reconstituted in vari-

---

[15] J. L. Bradrach and R. G. Eccles, "Price, Authority and Trust," *Annual Review of Sociology* (1989): 97–118, abridged and reprinted in Thompson et al., *Markets, Hierarchies, and Networks*, 290.

[16] For specific and nonspecific assets, see Williamson, *The Economic Institutions of Capitalism*; see also F. M. Scherer, *Industrial Market Structure and Economic Performance* (Chicago: Rand McNally, 1970) for an analysis of market structure in general.

ous ways, requiring a growing and increasingly flexible process of reallocation of financial resources, mainly for investment. These ways include: a shift toward Third Industrial Revolution production processes (post-Fordism); market segmentation, the differentiation of consumption patterns, and the spread of a new consumerist ideology; the convergence of patterns of financial market and corporate governance structures around the stock market or securitization model;[17] and the impact of profound technological innovation and diffusion in many sectors both old and new.[18] States, in turn, are increasingly impelled to enforce market-friendly norms, practices, and outcomes on other sectors and socio-economic interests through a process of pro-market re-regulation (often misidentified as "deregulation").

In this context, both formal and informal private organizations and relationships, which themselves are organized more and more around international competition and transnational linkages, come to set standards and to shape practices (including "best practice" and "benchmarking") which are then transmitted in a feedback process at domestic, transnational and international levels through both private *and* state action operating in mutually reinforcing ways. Therefore states and state actors, rather than being able to sustain genuinely autonomous forms of national capitalism, are increasingly transformed into agents of transnational neoliberalism, albeit with a degree of complex variation in a limited range of sectoral, subnational, national, regional, and international-institutional characteristics with regard to the relative significance of alternative policy approaches—undiluted liberalization and so-called deregulation, on the one hand, *versus* a more social-liberal attempt to pursue "globalization with a human face," on the other.

Furthermore, vestiges of other culturally distinct features of national political-economic models—"state-societal arrangements,"[19] "regulated capitalism,"[20] "competitive corporatism,"[21] "enduring national differences,"[22] et cetera—often act not merely to protect domestic arrangements and resist globalization but also to shape globalization itself and to tailor its imperatives to domestic circumstances. These involve both attempts to spread certain practices entrenched in the domestic model onto the global playing field, as in the case of the United

---

[17] P. G. Cerny, "Embedding Global Financial Markets: Securitization and the Emerging Web of Governance," in K. Ronit and V. Schneider, eds., *Private Organizations in Global Politics* (London: Routledge, 2000), 59–82.

[18] M. Talalay, C. Farrands, and R. Tooze, *Technology, Culture, and Competitiveness: Change and the World Political Economy* (London: Routledge, 1997).

[19] J. A. Hart, *Rival Capitalists: International Competitiveness in the United States, Japan, and Western Europe* (Ithaca: Cornell University Press, 1992).

[20] R. Boyer and D. Drache, eds., *States against Markets: The Limits of Globalization* (London: Routledge, 1996); J. R. Hollingsworth and R. Boyer, eds., *Contemporary Capitalism: The Embeddedness of Institutions* (Cambridge: Cambridge University Press, 1999).

[21] M. Rhodes, "Globalisation, Labour Markets, and Welfare States: A Future of 'Competitive Corporatism'?" in M. Rhodes and Y. Mény, eds., *The Future of European Welfare: A New Social Contract?* (London: Macmillan, 1998), 178–203.

[22] L. W. Pauly and S. Reich, "National Structures and Multinational Corporate Behavior: Enduring Differences in the Age of Globalization," *International Organization* 51, no. 1 (1997): 1–30.

States with its "arm's-length" approach to state-industry relations,[23] and attempts to anchor the globalization process in socially powerful domestic practices, such as Germany's "coordinated market economy"[24] or Malaysia's "Asian values." States and state actors may pursue ostensibly distinct strategies and use different tactics; however, these constitute not so much competing national models as different roads to neoliberal globalization. Domestic politics therefore becomes a principal (if not the principal) terrain of social and political struggle between actors seeking to insulate their constituents from the effects of globalization, on the one hand, and those seeking to capture the benefits of globalization for their political projects by involving both old and new constituencies in a complex process of rearticulating social and political coalitions in new circumstances, on the other.

Toward a Hegemony of Markets?

Whether markets can, however, develop the kind of authority and autonomy required to be seen as fully-fledged governance structures needs to be explored at three levels: the relative decision-making (and implementation) capacity of states and markets; the social legitimacy of transnational markets in a more interdependent world; and the increasing density and embeddedness of those markets themselves in social-structural terms.[25]

In the first place, is the nation-state still the dominant social structure in today's world? Does the state still have the institutional capacity, derived from its mix of control mechanisms—as it did in the First Financial Revolution of the eighteenth and nineteenth centuries and in the Industrial Welfare State phase in the mid-twentieth century—to effectively control (through domestic regulation and/or intergovernmental regimes) transnationally mobile capital? Will this continuing capacity be sufficient for the state to reassert its central role in the authoritative allocation of resources, which has been eroding in recent years because of financial globalization? Or will both international financial intermediaries and their customers in the "real economy" evolve authoritative *self-regulatory* transnational structures, developing effective "private regimes" to challenge supposedly embedded state institutions?

Secondly, does the nation-state still possess sufficient cultural and ideological resources to create (or *re*-create) the kind of *trust* which can permit the short-term goals of market actors to be reconciled in the name of common longer-term goals—

[23] J. Zysman, *Governments, Markets, and Growth: Financial Systems and the Politics of Industrial Change* (Ithaca: Cornell University Press, 1983).

[24] D. Soskice, "Divergent Production Regimes: Coordinated and Uncoordinated Market Economies in the 1980s and 1990s," in H. Kitschelt, P. Lange, G. Marks, and J. D. Stephens, eds., *Continuity and Change in Contemporary Capitalism* (Cambridge: Cambridge University Press, 1999), 101–34.

[25] See Strange, *The Retreat of the State* (Cambridge: Cambridge University Press, 1996); P. Hirst and G. Thompson, *Globalization in Question: The International Economy and the Possibilities of Governance* 2d ed. (Cambridge: Polity, 1999).

especially in making available sufficient finance to pay for the provision of nationally determined public goods? Or will habits of consumerism lead actors, especially bigger institutional investors and multinational corporations, to increasingly act through "exit" rather than "voice"—looking for markets with the lowest transaction costs combined with the highest degree of pro-market regulatory support?[26] Will market actors develop new networks of trust, reinforced by transnational communications technology and cosmopolitan personal relationship structures, which will blur and erode the "them" and "us" distinctions and relationships of friendship and justice which Aristotle saw as the glue of the *politeia*? Or, conversely, will transnational socio-economic networks—"clans"[27] or "global tribes"[28]—develop around the global business community which will penetrate into other economic sectors and into bureaucratic structures (e.g., through transnational and transgovernmental policy networks) to compete with and outflank the nation-state as the dominant structuring mechanism ("plural form" or "matrix structure") of the world economy?

Thirdly, will the continuing expansion of international markets and factor mobility themselves create new conditions of embeddedness at a transnational level? As Bradach and Eccles point out, *recurrent market transactions can themselves create trust*, leading to the construction of institutions only when that "process-based trust" is not disrupted by instability and/or systemic risk.[29] In other words, can an increase in what Durkheim called "dynamic density" lead to a restructuring of the division of labor along transnational lines, creating new forms of "organic solidarity" across borders?[30] In theory, the growth of international capital mobility and transnational network linkages, in the absence of a major international financial crisis that cannot be controlled, may over time serve to further embed transnational markets in a social system of their own, at the crossroads of international, transnational, and domestic politics and economics.

In addition, the development of international markets is effectively oriented toward creating the other of the two most important conditions of market stability posited by Ouchi, that of generating and channeling useful and necessary information to economic and political decision makers:

> . . . in order to mediate transactions efficiently, any organizational form must reduce either the ambiguity of performance evaluation or the goal incongruence between

---

[26] H. Laurence, "Regulatory Competition and the Politics of Financial Market Reform in Britain and Japan," *Governance* 9, no. 3 (1996): 311–41.

[27] Following Durkheim, see W. G. Ouchi, "Markets, Bureaucracies and Clans," *Administrative Science Quarterly* 25 (1980): 129–41, abridged and reprinted in Thompson et. al., *Markets, Hierarchies, and Networks*, 246–55.

[28] J. Kotkin, *Tribes: How Race, Religion, and Identity Determine Success in the New Global Economy* (New York: Random House, 1992).

[29] Bradach and Eccles, "Price, Authority and Trust," 282, citing L. Zucker, "Production of Trust: Institutional Sources of Economic Structure, 1840–1920," *Research in Organizational Behavior* 8 (1986): 53–111.

[30] Ruggie, "Continuity and Transformation in the World Polity."

parties. . . . market relations are efficient when there is little ambiguity over performance, so that the parties can tolerate relatively high levels of opportunism or goal incongruence.[31]

In effect, when markets are characterized by ambiguous information, price signals are likely to be highly inaccurate, and transactions will be highly vulnerable to opportunism, which then must be controlled by hierarchies or networks.[32] However, the more that transnational sectoral markets can expand their activities and penetration within and across different economic activities and geographical areas, the more information they actually provide to a wider range of market actors. If such actors, over time, come to accept those market signals and the information they contain as accurate, then those markets will be seen as more efficient and thus acceptable. In this sense, the very spread of markets themselves can promote a kind of market-based embeddedness, although it is unlikely that this phenomenon would survive for long without the potential for those market actors to develop a kind of non-state hierarchical authority or a more sociological form of supranational or transnational trust as well. This is true not only for financial institutions and major market players, but also for mass consumers. Whereas thirty years ago many were reluctant to give up their cash even to banks, they now are happy to have instant access both globally and locally to 24–hour-a-day cash dispensers and other forms of "electronic cash."[33]

It can be seen from the above that the potential of markets in general to evolve into governance structures at the transnational or global level is a complex issue. This problematic reflects a fundamental ambiguity in the new institutionalist debate, one that needs to be flagged but cannot be resolved here. This ambiguity reflects the fact that different approaches *within* the new institutionalism privilege qualitatively different variables in attempting to explain the direction which "path dependency" takes. On the one hand, the new institutional economics (for which I take Williamson as the exemplar[34]) rests on the assumption that the outcome of the process of development—the type of what he explicitly calls the "form of governance" of the firm—ultimately depends upon economic efficiency criteria as the independent variable. In other words, whether the firm takes a market form or a hierarchical form derives from the fact that distinct kinds of assets require different kinds of production organization: recurrent contracting in the case of non-specific assets (highly marketable, modularized, interchangeable); long-term contracting in the case of specific assets (dedicated to specific purposes, not easily substituted,

[31] Ouchi, "Markets, Bureaucracies and Clans," 251.

[32] Ouchi is specifically referring here to the performance of individual employees in a firm, but the wider implication of his text indicates that "performance" could equally refer to the general ability of the price system to provide sufficient information in the form of market signals for mutually satisfactory transactions to occur without excessive potential for opportunism through going beyond the limits of bounded rationality. (See John Odell's chapter, this volume.)

[33] S. J. Kobrin, "Electronic Cash and the End of National Markets," *Foreign Policy* 107 (1997): 65–77.

[34] Williamson, *Markets and Hierarchies;* Williamson, *The Economic Institutions of Capitalism.*

difficult to price in an illiquid market). In the latter case, a combination of the maximization of technological economies of scale and the internalization of transaction costs may make hierarchical management structures, mergers, and cartels more efficient but also may increase the possibilities for opportunism and monopolistic behavior.

In contrast, sociological and historical forms of new institutionalism see such matters as secondary. Writers in this tradition (Granovetter is the exemplar[35]) argue that in economic terms multiple alternative institutional forms ("multiple equilibria") always exist and that specific historical outcomes are locked in not by any external economic criteria but by the social contacts and common assumptions of the most powerful and/or centrally involved individuals and groups—that is, that the social networks within and through which the outcome is imposed and/or negotiated. If economic criteria are adopted, this is because the actors in such networks believe in the importance of such criteria not because such criteria are inherently superior or more efficient; at the same time, furthermore, most outcomes tend to be suboptimal or merely satisficing rather than maximizing in any purely rational sense.[36]

Most neo-institutionalists, however, do attempt to consider both kinds of variables in some sort of dynamic tension. Hendrik Spruyt, for example, in developing his argument about how the nation-state became locked in as the dominant political-organizational form after the decline of feudalism, makes several linked claims. He argues first that a range of alternative institutional forms that dealt in differing ways with the challenges of feudal decline (the French nation-state, the Hanseatic League, and the Italian city-states) were emerging or already existed. Second, however, the trajectory of change was not predetermined, and indeed each of these alternatives was in some ways politically and economically "suboptimal"; therefore the outcome depended upon the rearticulation of social and political coalitions in response to these challenges, that is, on the outcome of political struggles. Nevertheless, a process of "institutional selection" occurred in which the French state proved to be *relatively* the most "efficient" of a bad lot in key ways in a fluid but demanding political context. The rise to dominance of an institutional form based on the French nation-state—in the context of increasing translocal trade, urbanization, and other well-known socioeconomic developments of the time—created both a workable domestic political arena for endogenous collective action and at the same time enabled rulers to make credible external commitments to other rulers, that is, in the early international system.[37]

Similarly, Thomas P. Hughes, in his magisterial study of the political economy of

[35] Granovetter, "Economic Action and Social Structure"; Granovetter, "Economic Institutions as Social Constructions."

[36] H. Simon, *Administrative Behavior: A Study of Decision-Making Processes in Administrative Organization* (New York: Free Press, 1957), 6; H. Spruyt, *The Sovereign State and Its Competitors: An Analysis of Systems Change* (Princeton: Princeton University Press, 1994), 21, 26.

[37] Spruyt, *The Sovereign State and Its Competitors*; H. Spruyt, "Institutional Selection in International Relations: State Anarchy as Order," *International Organization* 48, no. 4 (1994): 527–57.

the development of electricity grids in Chicago, London, and Berlin in the late nineteenth and early twentieth centuries, shows how the relationship between technological developments, on the one hand, and the role of associations of electrical engineers, on the other, led to different outcomes based on distinct versions of economic rationality—reflecting ambiguities in the development and application of the technology itself at least as much as those in the social, cultural, and political differences between the cities (and countries) involved.[38] Indeed, the fact that such different outcomes could occur reflected the specificity of the assets involved (large-scale, integrated electricity grids), although in later years the transnational diffusion of technology and both industrial and political practices would ultimately lead to a convergence of the three models. Colleen Dunlavy makes analogous points about the early railroad industry in the United States and Prussia.[39] Rational economic choices therefore must not be lost in the midst of social networks in explaining how not only firms but the nation-state and the states system themselves came to be embedded in the first place and how they developed and interacted later on. Rather, the two analytically distinct variables must be seen in a sort of dynamic tension in a path-dependent historical process.

Thus the transformation of markets into governance structures involves not merely the extremely rapid development and expansion of those markets themselves in purely economic terms—in financial markets, for example, through international capital flows, financial innovation, experimentation with a range of new institutional forms (for example, the recent wave of bank mega-mergers in the United States, Europe, and Japan), and the critical contribution of information and communications technology. It involves the development of new transnational and transgovernmental social networks, the emergence of highly significant private institutions for market regulation, and the restructuring of the state around support for market internationalization. Examples of the latter phenomenon include deregulation, central bank independence, "reinventing government" and the New Public Management, and new Type II re-regulation, such as insider trading laws and disclosure requirements. Finally, the transformation involves the rearticulation of domestic socio-political coalitions on both right and left around noninflationary growth and the "embedded financial orthodoxy" of the competition state.

From Different National Roads to Different Sectoral Roads

In this context, any analysis of transnational markets as governance structures must focus away from classical and neoclassical notions of markets as spontaneous orders and integrate a range of other political and institutional dimensions. These dimen-

---

[38] T. P. Hughes, *Networks of Power: Electrification in Western Society, 1880–1930* (Baltimore: Johns Hopkins University Press, 1983).

[39] C. A. Dunlavy, *Politics and Industrialization: Early Railroads in the United States and Prussia* (Princeton: Princeton University Press, 1994).

sions must be seen as interacting in real time and space, locking in structural-institutional features in an historically unique path-dependent fashion—but where changes in *either* social and political structures *or* economic efficiency criteria, or both, can cause those paths to twist, diverge, or converge in new directions and into new forms. The dynamic of that path-dependent process always involves a multilevel dialectic among social networks, political coalitions, evolving technological variables, and economic efficiency criteria.

Sectoral Governance and the Changing Role of the State

Over time, the rapidly increasing dynamic density of cross-border financial transactions, for example, is leading to a restructuring at several levels. This is at one and the same time a restructuring (a) of private sector firms and associations (both within the financial sector and, through the impact of financial market restructuring, in all other sectors), *and* (b) of social networks, *and* (c) of political alliances (domestic, transnational, and transgovernmental) in the face of the global financial challenge. Because of the highly abstract, non-specific asset structure characteristic of the financial sector, the result is not the emergence of distinct, competing, geographically specific forms of governance structure but a convergence of both domestic and international governance structures around a complex neoliberal model.[40]

However, in more asset-specific sectors, different structures may result, especially where they are characterized by location-specific "economies of agglomeration." Such sectors are likely to change more slowly and unevenly, maintaining older patterns for some time.[41] Increasingly, however, instability results. Globalization proceeds at different speeds and down different roads. What is crucial to remember is that those different roads are to a large extent no longer national roads but transnational sectoral (and intra- and inter-sectoral) roads. Economic differentiation engenders the differentiation of transnational governance structures. Therefore, rather than being seen as merely a "spontaneous order," markets need to be analyzed in institutional terms. All markets in the real world actually encompass a complex mixture of market, hierarchy, and network—or, to put it another way, a mutually reinforcing combination of the three underlying bonds of price, authority, and trust.[42] With regard to financial markets, for example, just as nation-states and the states system have constituted the central structured action field for the development of the "modern" international political economy, internationalized financial markets may have the potential to develop not only a high level of

[40] M. Filipovič, "A Global Private Regime for Capital Flows" (paper presented to the annual conference of the British International Studies Association, University of York, 19–21 December 1994); Cerny, "Embedding Global Financial Markets."

[41] Frieden, "Invested Interests"; Kitschelt, "Industrial Governance Structures, Innovation Strategies, and the Case of Japan."

[42] Bradrach and Eccles, "Price, Authority and Trust."

structural autonomy in the international system[43] but also to become a kind of "crossroads structure" in the future—that is, a structured field or institutional matrix within and across which key actors (and their networks) must interact and major social, political, and economic structures overlap.

In this context, the role of the state becomes ambiguous. Some recent scholarship on international finance has sought to resurrect the role of the state in the face of traditional market theories of financial globalization.[44] In some cases, I believe such work mistakes "Type II re-regulation"[45] for general state capacity.[46] In other cases, however, I believe it jumps to hasty conclusions based on mis-specifying state autonomy. Traditionally, key features of the state—its multitasking character and its ability to make side payments to potential opponents—permitted decisions to be made which were both medium-to-long range and redistributive, characteristics which are essential for the provision of public goods and the development of a common sense of the "public interest" to reconcile conflicting goals. Within this context, a situation evolved in which "voice" proved better as a conflict-resolution mechanism than "exit," since exit is not easy or attractive.[47] It would endanger the basic public good of systemic stabilization and integration. However, as Laurence so well argues, international capital mobility (a) makes the requirements of "voice" far more demanding—the larger the market actor and/or the more extensive the market itself, the more that different national financial regulatory systems have to be influenced and conformed to—and (b) makes the "exit" option far more viable and therefore potentially attractive to institutional investors, large financial intermediaries, multinational corporations, and other financial market actors.[48]

What, then, is the role of the national state today, and what are the extent and limits of its autonomy? In *all* markets to some extent, I would argue, the state is in any case less an authoritative actor and more a *facilitator* and *enforcer*. This is the heart of the "competition state." In this context, the state's role is twofold: (a) state actors are integral parts of a wider network of transnational problem-solving, linking transnational actors, domestic actors and state actors negotiating domestic and

[43] D. M. Andrews, "Capital Mobility and State Autonomy: Toward a Structural Theory of International Monetary Relations," *International Studies Quarterly* 38, 2 (1994): 193–218.

[44] D. M. Andrews and T. D. Willett, "Financial Interdependence and the State: International Monetary Relations at Century's End," *International Organization* 51, no. 3 (1997): 479–511; E. N. Helleiner, "Post-Globalization: Is the Financial Liberalization Trend Likely to be Reversed?" in Boyer and Drache, eds., *States against Markets*.

[45] P. G. Cerny, "The Limits of Deregulation: Transnational Interpenetration and Policy Change," *European Journal of Political Research* 19, nos. 2/3 (1991): 173–96.

[46] Compare S. Lütz, "The Revival of the Nation-State? Stock Exchange Regulation in an Era of Internationalized Financial Markets," *MPifG Discussion Paper* 96/9 (Köln: Max-Planck-Institut für Gesellschaftsforschung, 1996), and S. K. Vogel, *Freer Markets, More Rules: Regulatory Reform in Advanced Industrial Countries* (Ithaca: Cornell University Press, 1996) with Laurence, "Regulatory Competition and the Politics of Financial Reform in Britain and Japan."

[47] A. O. Hirschmann, *Exit, Voice, and Loyalty* (Cambridge, Mass.: Harvard University Press, 1970), 83.

[48] Laurence, "Regulatory Competition and the Politics of Financial Reform in Britain and Japan."

intergovernmental responses to transnational changes; and (b) state structures simultaneously constitute a key terrain of political and social conflict over issues which pit globalizing forces against domestic constituencies seeking protection from such forces. The impact of globalization is still highly *indirect* and must be mediated through political agents and state policies. Nevertheless, the overall direction of change is the same everywhere. With regard to financial markets, a combination of the symbolic and fungible character of money itself plus dramatic innovations in communications and information technology have led to huge transnational capital flows and complex patterns of two-way cross-border price sensitivity which dwarf the monitoring and controlling capabilities as well as the public financial resources of states, thereby making preexisting nation-state-based patterns and systems of regulation and intervention less effective.

In pursuing these goals, national financial systems—and the regulatory systems within which they grew up—reflected contrasting historical patterns of economic development; thus they were often structured quite differently from each other, with the primary distinction being between capital-market systems and credit-based systems, particularly in terms of the allocation of funding for industrial development purposes.[49] On the one hand, much of the debate has concerned whether globalization necessarily involves convergence. Such factors as capital mobility, price sensitivity, technological innovation, regulatory arbitrage, and the decompartmentalization of different financial sectors have been seen by neoliberals (and pessimistic Marxists) as part of an inexorable process of marketization and liberalization leading to the convergence of prices (especially interest rates), of corporate structures, of conditions of exit and entry, and of patterns of government intervention. On the other hand, other writers have focused on differing national trajectories of regulatory change. Vogel, for example, asserts that re-regulation takes two forms—"procompetitive re-regulation" and "strategic reinforcement" (of existing patterns of state/economy imbrication)—and that these trajectories closely mirror earlier embedded patterns of national development, with the former still characterizing regulatory change in the United States and the United Kingdom, the latter Japan, France, and Germany.[50]

Three-Level Games

Along with the debate over the fate of national regulatory systems, there are also debates about both international and transnational developments.[51] In this context, I suggest that we are in the presence of *three-level games*. In other words, we do not merely have traditional "two-level games," in which the state is the mediating

---

[49] Zysman, *Governments, Markets and Growth*; F. Renversez, ed., *Les systèmes financiers*, *Les Cahiers Français* 224 (Paris: La Documentation Française, 1986); Vogel, *Freer Markets, More Rules*.

[50] Vogel, *Freer Markets, More Rules*.

[51] See especially R. J. Herring and R. E. Litan, *Financial Regulation in the Global Economy* (Washington, D.C.: Brookings Institution, 1995).

structure between international pressures and "domestic" politics, policymaking and administration. Rather, *in addition to* such two-level games, we are seeing the rapid development of "third-level" games, autonomous transnational processes comprising interactions which flow around, under, and above the state rather than going through it. The development of governance structures in a globalizing economy transcends the distinction between "inside/out" and "outside/in"; instead, such structures develop in a cross-cutting manner, creating not only "transnational" structures but also "cross-cutting affiliations" among agents.[52] The crystallization of third-level game structures can also be seen as constituting a web of relationships which impact the state both *from above* and *from below*, as well as *from within*.

The first and most elaborate debate concerns the national level, as discussed above, where the power of difficult-to-control transnational markets is seen to confront entrenched national economic systems in "first-level games." If governance structures (institutions) do not merely derive from efficiency criteria but are part of a process wherein the existence of "multiple equilibrium points" has a crucial independent impact on the shape of institutions through events, interpersonal networks, and other contingent criteria which are then locked into a path-dependent process, then there is the possibility that national regulatory systems are sufficiently embedded to weather the storm of market transnationalization, regulatory arbitrage, financial orthodoxy, and the like. Governments may be able to create enough "friction" in the market mechanism[53] to contain or reverse the liberalization process and bring other public interest criteria back in. However, even Vogel admits that his exemplar of "strategic reinforcement," Japan, may just be postponing the eventuality of full liberalization, indirectly quoting a former director of the Banking Bureau in the Ministry of Finance to the effect that "MoF officials will start worrying about losing their power once all financial markets are liberalized";[54] indeed, that day may not be far off.

Vogel also argues that national governments are actually *expanding* their power in this context. They are doing this, he argues, in two ways. The first is quite straightforward. As the title of his book (*Freer Markets, More Rules*) implies, re-regulation may be liberalizing, but it is not "deregulating" in the sense of removing rules; rather, it involves the formulation and implementation of complex new rules intended to replace old rules protecting self-regulated, cartel-like behavior with a panoply of *liberalizing and market-promoting* rules—rules aimed at prohibiting market actors from taking anticompetitive actions or engaging in monopolistic behavior. The classic case of such Type II re-regulation in financial markets is the U.K.'s Financial Services Act of 1986, which created a whole new formal struc-

---

[52] See G. Simmel, *Conflict and the Web of Group-Affiliations*, translated by K. H. Wolff and R. Bendix (New York: Free Press, 1955); L. A. Coser, *The Functions of Social Conflict* (London: Routledge and Kegan Paul, 1956).

[53] M. Mayer, *Stealing the Market: How the Giant Brokerage Firms, with Help from the SEC, Stole the Stock Market from Investors* (New York: Basic Books, 1992).

[54] Vogel, *Freer Markets, More Rules*, 195.

ture—indeed, one so cumbersome that despite regular revision it is still regarded as potentially counterproductive[55] and has recently been overlaid by new and even more complex legislation setting up a Financial Services Authority, replacing the previous patchwork of regulatory bodies with a single regulator. Analogous arguments have been advanced about France[56] and Germany.[57]

The second way, much less developed by Vogel, is no less important: that although liberalization may (whether quickly or slowly) reduce *domestic* state power and capacity, it may nevertheless lead simultaneously to an expansion of a country's *international* power and economic clout. Thus Britain's influence in the world may have been increased both in terms of ideas and in terms of competitiveness by engaging so wholeheartedly in the process of procompetitive re-regulation, while Japan's influence, which reached a peak in the 1980s but was undermined by the bursting of the "bubble economy" in 1989, not only has not been restored, but may only be restored by the kind of extensive restructuring promised, but not yet fully delivered, by the Japanese Big Bang program of 1996. Indeed, the various financial crises of the 1990s that occurred in Japan, Mexico, and Southeast Asia only partially slowed, and in some ways accelerated, the process of pro-market re-regulation in ways that have undermined not only the economics of the so-called "developmental states," but also the supposed traditional political values and consensuses upon which their prior rapid development had been thought to rest.

At the other end of the governance spectrum from the fate of national regulatory systems stands the development of relatively formal international cooperation in regulating the sector—"second-level games." Here the picture is more fragmented. Proposals for systematizing international monetary cooperation, for example, have been around for a long time, concerning such issues as targeted exchange rates,[58] but the durability of the system of floating exchange rates, with international monetary relations increasingly embedded in hard-to-control international currency markets makes effective cooperation episodic and often ad hoc.[59] Attempts to develop more systematic cooperation have often just set up different kind of targets— targets for powerful market actors to aim at, as is well known in the case of the European Exchange Rate Mechanism on "Black Wednesday" in September 1992. Attempts to develop international regulatory standards for securities markets have quickly become bogged down in national and inter-sectoral differences of regulatory style as well as content.

International cooperation will continue to be a major aspect of overall policy re-

[55] See Laurence, "Regulatory Competition and the Politics of Financial Market Reform in Britain and Japan."

[56] M. Loriaux, *France after Hegemony: International Change and Financial Reform* (Ithaca: Cornell University Press, 1991).

[57] Lütz, "The Revival of the Nation-State?"

[58] See, for example, J. Williamson and C. R. Henning, "Managing the Monetary System," in P. Kenen, ed., *Managing the World Economy: Fifty Years after Bretton Woods* (Washington, D.C.: Institute for International Economics, 1994), 83–111.

[59] Cohen, "Phoenix Risen."

sponse to globalizing financial markets.[60] Nevertheless, the main process of regulatory change—"creeping liberalization"—has increasingly been accepted at the level of epistemic consensus, without requiring the presence of proactive cooperation to further it. Indeed, such cooperation is not necessary. A combination of regulatory capture and arbitrage means that state agencies compete with each other to open international markets on behalf of their respective clienteles, and "policy transfer" takes place by spontaneous neoliberal emulation rather than by formal cooperation.[61] In such a context, first-level (domestic) games, increasingly dominated by transnational market players, can no longer be said to reinforce the role of the state in a more traditional two-level game structure. Such domestic actors—being linked more and more closely with international markets and being less and less dependent upon state structures and state actors for achieving their policy goals—may well turn increasingly to "exit" rather than "voice," leaving state actors to flounder as they fall over themselves to promote "competitiveness." As domestic actors become more closely locked into transnational markets, they do not focus quite so much on trying to convince domestic politicians and bureaucrats to support their goals; instead they get on with their business, thereby further entrenching transnational structures.

A key issue here for both domestic and international regulators is not just the *amount* of regulation but its substance. At both levels, the *content* of regulation and of what are seen as the proper boundaries of regulatory systems has undergone a major shift in the past couple of decades. The two main non-prudential approaches have involved (a) direct regulations on *entry and exit* to the particular sectors such as the financial system (and to their endogenous compartments) and (b) regulating *prices* (imposing fiat prices rather than market-determined prices). In a world of market liberalization, however, these tools are increasingly being seen as not only unworkable but also illegitimate. Furthermore, regulatory arbitrage—the practice by economic actors of whipsawing one regulatory jurisdiction against another to find the most favorable treatment—does not merely involve competition in laxity or a "race to the bottom." In the matter of prudential regulation, for example, it can involve a "race to the top"—what David Vogel has called the "California effect," in contrast to the "Delaware effect."[62] The role of the U.S. Securities and Exchange Commission, given the powerful position of the United States in international financial markets, has been to defend stronger prudential regulation while calling for

---

[60] E. B. Kapstein, *Governing the Global Economy: International Finance and the State* (Cambridge, Mass.: Harvard University Press, 1994); G. R. D. Underhill, "Keeping Governments Out of Politics: Transnational Securities Markets, Regulatory Co-operation and Political Legitimacy," *Review of International Studies* 21, no. 3 (1995): 251–78; Andrews and Willett, "Financial Interdependence and the State."

[61] M. Evans and J. Davies, "Understanding Policy Transfer: A Multi-level, Multi-disciplinary Perspective," *Public Administration* 77, no. 2 (1999): 361–85.

[62] D. Vogel, *Trading Up: Consumer and Environmental Regulation in a Global Economy* (Cambridge, Mass.: Harvard University Press, 1995); see Lütz, "The Revival of the Nation State?" and Laurence, "Regulatory Competition and the Politics of Financial Market Reform in Britain and Japan."

liberalization through *ex ante* structural regulation. This has added to the inability of the major states to come to international cooperative agreements on the regulation of securities markets, while the U.S. model has nonetheless become the industry standard by default.

So what we have at this point is the continued relative importance of domestic prudential regulation and the patchwork and episodic character of international cooperation. In contrast, in the arena of third-level games, we are not so much in the presence of pure market forces operating on a transnational scale, spontaneously improving the allocative efficiency of markets and reducing transactions costs, so much as we are in the presence of a series of increasingly institutionalized transnational structural developments. We are seeing the emergence not only of "hierarchies within markets" but also of self-organizing networks, that is, governance processes and structures which thrive on globalization and increasingly shape it in complex and uneven ways. The development of such new but still embryonic transnational governance processes and structures represents a shift of the focus of structuration of transnational market regulation away from formal state institutions and state actors per se to a combination of privatized governance and loose, networked public/private interfaces—what David Lake has recently called the *privatization of governance* itself.[63] These are markets, but not as neoliberal economists know them. They are more like networks or even hierarchies—post-modern Foucauldian circuits of power, mini-oligopolies in a world where the economic system is shucking off the constraints of the nation-state *Panoptikon*.[64]

Conclusions

Taken together, these trends represent a fundamental shift in the underlying form of governance—the mix of market, hierarchy, and network. Markets in general are increasingly shaped through an interactive process operating across the international-domestic interface, not merely from outside and inside but also cutting across the categories and linking them in complex ways. Strange spoke of transnational structures as involving "webs of contracts," and indeed it is the changing pattern of these webs of contracts which is becoming increasingly embedded in the governance structures of the internationalized, transnational, globalizing markets of today.[65] This is not the interplay of pure market forces, but a profound reshuffling of organizational sources of power into complex three-level games. In this context, the role of the state is being altered to that of mere prudential supervisor and enforcer—guardian of the safety and soundness of transnationalizing market

[63] D. A. Lake, "Global Governance: A Relational Contracting Approach," in A. Prakash and J. A. Hart, eds., *Globalization and Governance* (London: Routledge, 1999), 31–53.

[64] See H. Goverde, P. G. Cerny, M. Haugaard, and H. H. Lentner, eds., *Power in Contemporary Politics: Theories, Practices, Globalizations* (Thousand Oaks, Ill.: Sage, 2000), especially chapters 2, 3, and 10.

[65] S. Strange, *States and Markets* (London: Pinter, 1988).

mechanisms but not a determinant of the distributional or redistributional impact of their outcomes.

To the extent that state power and traditional forms of market governance through public regulation remain important (and indeed are in some ways expanding in terms of the *overall* weight of state intervention), their focus will increasingly lie in tacking to the markets rather than in trying to control them. Neither inter-state cooperation through the "international financial architecture" nor the quasi-hegemonic instincts of stronger states will suffice. Principal dimensions of state action will include: (a) furthering liberalization through Type II re-regulation, not hindering it by trying to resurrect the Industrial Welfare State of the mid-twentieth century; (b) enforcing market outcomes on losers while providing them with some compensation for purposes of maintaining and/or rearticulating political coalitions; and (c) finding a *modus vivendi* with emerging transnational private interest governments. With regard to market structure, in relatively pure market-oriented (non-specific-asset-based) sectors like finance, governance may be more diffuse but is no less powerful than in other sectors; governance structures in those sectors will tend to be less formal and more difficult to control.

Finally, managing the world's money, as well as other aspects of the international economy, will increasingly involve the evolution of *practices* rather than new hierarchical forms of authority as such. These practices will have to develop incrementally among private-sector and public-sector actors, reflecting first and foremost the self-organization of particular market sectors, as well as the relationship among those sectors and between those sectors and a range of public and quasi-public authorities at different levels. The main role of states and of the intergovernmental regimes they sustain will be to impose sufficient social discipline to maintain, reinforce, and expand—as well as to cushion the impact of—neoliberal market norms, in order to both sustain the confidence of the international "business community" and keep losers sufficiently happy to prevent serious backlashes. Finally, these structural changes will be increasingly embedded in a web of social and economic networks that envelop and colonize the state itself. Managing the world's money is likely to become ever more complex and challenging in the twenty-first century.

INDEX

Acheson, Keith, 68
After Hegemony, 29, 182–183
American Bankers Association, 53–55
Argentina, 3, 69–70, 149, 154, 158, 161, 164, 191
Aristotle, 204
Arrow, Kenneth, 22, 66, 177
Articles of Confederation, 135
asset specificity, 17, 201n16
Australia, 150n10
authority, modes of, 195
autonomy, national, 26–28
Axelrod, Robert, 35, 127

Bagehot, Walter, 165
Baldwin, Robert, 21
Bank for International Settlements, 46–47
    See also central banks
Bank of England, 28, 54, 56
Basle Committee on Banking Supervision, 47
Bauer, R. A., 179–180
Bayoumi, Tamim, 86–87, 97
Becker, Gary, 20
benchmarking, 202
Bensel, R., 139, 143–144
Bernstein, Edward, 44, 50, 52
best practice, 202
Bini-Smaghi, L., 87
BIS. *See* Bank for International Settlements
Blanchard, O. J., 86, 88, 96
Blinder, Alan, 174
Boeri, T., 119
bounded rationality, 17, 168
    as analytical position, 169–172
Bradach, J.L., 204
Bretton Woods:
    Conference, 31, 44–47
    exchange rate regime, 3, 31

explanations for Agreement, 55–58
institutional design, 38–59
institutions, 28, 45; ratification of Agreement, 52–55
    See also International Monetary Fund; World Bank
Bruno, Michael, 161
Buchanan, James, 22
budget-maximization hypothesis, 67, 70
Buiter, Willem, 97
Bundesbank, 93–94
Bush administration, 69–70

The Calculus of Consent, 22
California effect, 213
Canada, 90–91, 96, 101, 148n2, 150n10, 158, 165
capital controls, 57
capital mobility, 4, 91n38, 203
Cardiff process, 121n34, 124
central bank(s):
    and Bretton Woods, 50–51
    cooperation in the 1920s, 45
    development in the United States, 134–139
    independence and inflation, 115–116
    role in Central European stabilization, 48
    role in new international architecture, 47
    See also Bank for International Settlements; Basle Committee on Banking Supervision; Financial Stability Forum
Cerny, Philip, 17
Chant, John, 68
Chicago School, 20–21
Chile, 158
Churchill, Winston, 57
Civil War, as catalyst for U.S. monetary consolidation, 129
Clarke, Stephen, 45

Cornell Studies in Political Economy

A series edited by PETER J. KATZENSTEIN